THE P-38 LIGHTNING AND THE MEN WHO FLEW IT

THE
P-38 LIGHTNING
AND THE MEN WHO FLEW IT

COLONEL WOLFGANG W. E. SAMUEL
USAF (RETIRED)

FOREWORD BY ALFRED STETTNER

UNIVERSITY PRESS OF MISSISSIPPI / JACKSON

The University Press of Mississippi is the scholarly publishing agency of the
Mississippi Institutions of Higher Learning: Alcorn State University,
Delta State University, Jackson State University, Mississippi State University,
Mississippi University for Women, Mississippi Valley State University,
University of Mississippi, and University of Southern Mississippi.

www.upress.state.ms.us

The University Press of Mississippi is a member of
the Association of University Presses.

Publisher: University Press of Mississippi, Jackson, USA
Authorised GPSR Safety Representative: Easy Access System Europe -
Mustamäe tee 50, 10621 Tallinn, Estonia, gpsr.requests@easproject.com

Library of Congress Control Number: 2024047960
Hardback ISBN 978-1-4968-5650-0
Epub single ISBN 978-1-4968-5651-7
Epub institutional ISBN 978-1-4968-5652-4
PDF single ISBN 978-1-4968-5653-1
PDF institutional ISBN 978-1-4968-5654-8

British Library Cataloging-in-Publication Data available

CONTENTS

AN AVIATOR'S GRAVE

I've seen the fields where poppies grow,
Knelt by the crosses, row on row.
I've seen the shell-torn battlefield,
Where men are crushed and forced to yield.

—1ST SERGEANT HARRY R. CHARD

On the following pages I tell the stories of young men climbing into cockpits of airplanes they barely knew how to fly, just for a chance to touch the face of God, as Pilot Officer John Gillespie Magee referred to flying in his classic aviator's poem *High Flight*. In *The P-38 Lightning and the Men Who Flew It* I want to pay tribute to all those who gave their lives so others might live. The hard reality was, that in the early days of flight, it was as dangerous an endeavor as it was spiritually uplifting. All too many idealistic young men perished in training and ordinary flying before ever meeting up with their opponents in mortal combat. Then there were the inevitable combat losses and accidents. So many young men never had a chance to live life, not to mention their dreams. The survivors had to deal with what was. Robin Olds in his book *Fighter Pilot* referred to the high rate of losses of fellow trainees in the P-38 quite casually as "digging holes in the desert." Everyone had to deal with death in their own way.

★★★

Operational losses of bomber and fighter planes in World War II for the 8th, 9th, 12th, 15th, and 1st Tactical Air Force came to a total of 18,369 aircraft, according to the *United States Strategic Bombing Survey* for the war in Europe. Of those aircraft, 9,949 were bombers and 8,420 fighters. These numbers do not include losses suffered due to weather or accident, which were substantial. As a comparison, the

Royal Air Force suffered a total of 22,029 operational aircraft losses over Europe. Personnel killed and missing in action for the US Army Air Forces in Europe came to 79,265 airmen, with the 8th Air Force based in England suffering the highest losses of 44,472 men. The air war over Europe had no victors, only survivors. I address training losses in subsequent chapters of the book.

By chance I met an aviator who sent me a poem written by his great-grandmother, which dealt with the issue of flying and dying, a poem that deeply touched me—and I want to use this opportunity at the beginning of this book to remember those aviators who left life all too early—just to live a dream and touch the face of God.

It was Christmas 2022 when I received an unexpected Christmas card from Captain "Pete" Ashton, an American Airlines pilot, who had flown airplanes since he was ten years old. He wished me a Merry Christmas and a happy new year, adding, "Stephen E. Ambrose was correct, I couldn't put your books down. *German Boy* and *Fassberg*. Fantastic stories. A must read. I bought two more. Can't wait to read them." We corresponded and Pete shared with me the story of his father James E. Ashton (Jim), who attended Purdue University and graduated with a mechanical engineering degree specializing in aeronautics—because they didn't have an aeronautical engineering degree back then. Jim Ashton was hired by the Lockheed Corporation in Burbank, California, and did some work on the A-28 Hudson, and then worked on the P-38 Lightning to help resolve its compressibility issues by replacing their tail sections. After a year or so at Lockheed, in early 1942, Jim and a fellow engineer walked into their bosses office to quit—they wanted to fly in the war. His boss said to them, as told to Pete by his father, "You can't quit. We are short of aeronautical engineers. We need you here at Lockheed." Jim ended up at Gardner Field in Taft, California, learning to fly the BT-13, the same place where Chuck Yeager learned to fly. Jim never saw combat as he had envisioned, but rather ended up ferrying B-17s to combat units needing replacements.

After the war Jim got out of the Army, but he still liked to fly, so he acquired a Bonanza. Pete recalls, "My dad got me into flying when I was a ten-year-old kid. I was born in 1964. He would place his briefcase on the seat so I could see over the airplane hood. I was

Lieutenant Peter Ashton after receiving his pilot wings. (Ashton)

his autopilot when he napped. On one trip flying over the Sierra Mountains to Carson City, Nevada, my dad was napping when the engine quit. I woke him up. He reached down and selected an alternate fuel tank on the Bonanza. The engine roared back to life. I asked him how he knew what to do? 'When an engine quits it most likely ran out of gas,' was his answer. Then he went back to his nap as I flew the plane." Of course Pete wanted to keep on flying as he grew older. He was in Air Force ROTC at Sacramento State when he took his flight physical and was rejected because his eyesight was not a perfect 20/20. At this time Pete already had over 1,500 hours flying time, had his instrument rating and was a multi-engine certified flight instructor. So at age 24, after graduating from San Jose State, he went to fly for Air West, a feeder line, flying the Embraer EMB-110. Round dials, no autopilot, lots of landings, hand flying eight hours a day in all kinds of weather. At age 27 Pete was hired by American Airlines and over the years flew the DC-10, A-300, B-757/767/777.

The Ashtons had a family burial plot. Pete recalls that, when his grandfather died, at the ceremony, he observed his grandmother taking a flower and walking over to an adjacent grave and placing the flower on that grave, an aviator's grave. When his grandmother died his father did the same thing, placing a flower on that aviator's grave. He had no idea why they were doing that. Then one day he found a book of poetry written by his great-grandmother Ella Ashton. Among the collection of poetry he found this poem, which touched my heart, and for the first time Pete understood the meaning of why his grandmother and his father placed a flower on the lone aviator's grave. When Pete's dad died, he followed family tradition and took a flower and put it on the aviator's grave, buried adjacent to their family plot.

AN AVIATOR'S GRAVE

His grave lies next to those of mine, a youth with shining hair;
He gave away his life for love, for so 'tis written there.

Two wings are carved upon the stone, No greater love than this—
And then his name, age twenty-nine, what more his history is

I do not know, sufficient this to read a hero's fame;
A soldier in the ranks for peace, he flew a soldier's plane.

Somewhere he fell. O gallant youth, O avatar from God,
I welcome you a place to sleep beside my sacred sod.

His grave is lone, except for me, forsaken seems the spot;
And so I share the flowers I bring, to show he's not forgot.

—ELLA ASHTON

PREFACE

In the aviation world, as anywhere, I concluded, everything is subject to change.
We must believe this.
—A. SCOTT CROSSFIELD IN *ALWAYS ANOTHER DAWN*

World War II was a brutal struggle for survival. Credit goes to America's industry to turn out the means of war when needed—such as the P-38, P-47, and P-51 fighters and B-17, B-24, and B-29 bombers, Liberty ships, Jeeps, Sherman tanks, and so much more—to overwhelm the Axis powers, principally Germany, Italy, and Japan. For them the war was one of acquisition and ego satisfaction—for their victims it was plain and simply a war of survival. America's productive capability certainly was impressive and a significant factor in the final victory in Europe, and its intellectual curiosity produced the ultimate weapon to assure victory over Japan. But from my personal perspective, the key ingredient for victory over totalitarianism was leadership—both military and political. Uniquely, this kind of leadership in our complex system of government seems to arise only when our nation is at great peril, a time when politicians can put aside their petty quarrels and focus on one goal—national survival. The P-38 Lightning, the fastest operational fighter aircraft of its day, became one of the solutions on the road to victory.

The Lockheed Lightning had its highs in the warm skies over the Pacific and its lows in the cold air over Europe. But no matter what one may think of this airplane, it was unique in many respects, in the tradition of its designer—Clarence "Kelly" Johnson—breaking with the conventional and exploring new paths to solve a problem. With the advent of World War II in September 1939 in Europe, both the British and French air forces were hard pressed with their existing stock of aircraft to challenge the German Me 109. So, in haste, the two countries turned to the United States, where they had heard a new aircraft was being tested that could function in both air-to-ground and air-to-air roles. Orders were hastily placed and the P-38 was redesignated by the British and French as the RP-322B and F, the suffix indicating British or French orders. At this point in time the airplane had undergone very limited testing, but that didn't keep the Royal Air Force from making changes to the aircraft design before even the first test model was delivered to the United Kingdom. The rapid German advance into France resulted in the cancellation of the French order. The RAF soon followed France's lead when in March 1941 President Franklin D. Roosevelt signed the Lend-Lease Act, which authorized the lending of war material to any nation whose defense was considered vital to the security of the United States. That did it for the Brits, and they promptly canceled their order for the RP-322B, with the Lockheed Aircraft Corporation "holding the bag," so to speak. Other than a small order of 13 YP-38s from the Army Air Corps, the RP-322 order was the only significant order for the P-38 the Lockheed Corporation had received so far. After putting much of their own money into the development of the aircraft, suddenly the entire project seemed in jeopardy. Why spend good money, the Brits surely reasoned, when the United States was willing to satisfy their aircraft needs for free? One last thing our British friends did was to name the RP-322—Lightning—even though their modifications to the original P-38 design made the aircraft anything but that. The United States soon was to be a co-belligerent, but at this point in time we were not an active participant in the European war, except as a supplier of war-related needs.

With the attack of the Japanese Imperial Navy on the Pacific Fleet's anchorage at Pearl Harbor, Hawaii, on December 7, 1941, and Germany's and Italy's declaration of war against the United States within days after the Pearl Harbor attack, everything changed. The European regional war now had become a second world war. Aircraft production especially needed to be ramped up quickly, with the P-38 the lead aircraft in terms of development, ahead of the P-47 Thunderbolt and P-51 Mustang. Design work for the P-38 had started in 1937; design of the P-47 and P-51 didn't get started until mid-1940. So the aim was to get the P-38 operational as quickly as possible.

One of three RP-322Bs, modified P-38s, lent to the Royal Air Force for testing with props turning in the same direction and without superchargers—changes that compromised aircraft safety and performance. No wonder the RAF didn't care for the aircraft once they flew it. (John Menzies Collection)

Although in the late 1930s we were not directly involved in the war in Europe, Army Air Forces planners didn't have their heads in the sand and knew that sooner or later this war would become our war as well. So the Army Air Corps wanted aircraft with greater capabilities than the P-40 Warhawk or the P-39 Airacobra had to offer, the principal fighters in the Air Corps inventory at the time. The Army Air Corps was established by an act of Congress in 1926 and merged into the Army Air Forces, AAF, in June 1941. Even though most refer to the Army Air Forces during World War II, the Army Air Corps continued to exist, and was not disestablished along with the AAF until the creation of the United States Air Force as an independent service in September 1947.

P-38 units were formed as quickly as aircraft became available, and training was rushed to get them over to Europe to serve as heavy bomber escorts. That vision soon had to face realities. Not only were the aircrew inadequately trained, but the aircraft, because of its limited testing, revealed some significant liabilities which resulted in heavy losses not only in combat but also in just ordinary flying.

One hundred eighty-six B-17 bombers, never flown in combat, brand new, at Holzkirchen, Bavaria, in 1946. GIs removed the radios and batteries, then placed one-and-a-half-pound TNT charges in each cockpit and blew them up—the fate of much of the American aircraft inventory that made it into Germany. (John Hay)

Pilots made their concerns known. Fixes were installed as quickly as possible and modifications made resulting in a large number of P-38 versions from the original YP-38 test beds to the E, F, G, H, J, and the final L-model, the latter being a very different aircraft from the initial P-38E/F production aircraft.

Although the P-38 could fly at the altitudes flown by our heavies, the B-17 and B-24, from the mid-twenties to over thirty thousand feet, because of P-38 system limitations it was an impractical solution, and our bombers had to fly deep into Germany without adequate fighter protection. The resultant bomber losses at times threatened the concept of daylight bombing. Not able to serve as an effective bomber escort, the P-38 found itself tasked to support the landings in North Africa, and in time all P-38s were transferred to the Pacific, with the exception of one fighter group, which General Spaatz allowed to continue to fly in Europe to the end of the war.

One pilot I interviewed who flew his P-38 until he reached Langensalza, Germany, at the end of hostilities in 1945, told me that his

entire fighter group begged General Spaatz, then the commander
of the United States Strategic Air Forces (Postwar to be renamed
USAFE, United States Air Forces Europe), to allow them to finish
the war in the P-38—he gave in to their pleading, probably against
the wishes of General Jimmy Doolittle, who then commanded the
8th Air Force and was a strong proponent of the P-51. At war's end,
their aircraft never made it home, but were burned and buried on-
site by German POWs, like so many other aircraft.

As for the German perspective of the P-38, Luftwaffe pilots quickly
learned that you did not make head-on attacks against this airplane if
you wanted to see another day. Its four 50-caliber machine guns and
20mm cannon were deadly if given that opportunity. Oberleutnant/
First Lieutenant Franz Stiegler was assigned to Jagdgeschwader 27 in
North Africa, the same Franz Stiegler who later chose not to shoot
down a crippled B-17 bomber over Germany and had his story told
in *A Higher Call* by Adam Makos. Stiegler, with twenty-eight victories in the Me 109, recalls in Jeffrey L. Ethells's excellent book *P-38
Lightning*, "The P-38s could turn inside us with ease and they would
go from level flight to climb almost instantaneously. We lost quite a
few pilots who tried to make an attack and then pull up. The P-38s
were on them at once. They closed so quickly that there was little one
could do except roll quickly and dive down. While the P-38 could
turn inside us, it rolled very slowly through the first 5 or 10 degrees
of bank, and by then we would already be gone. One cardinal rule we
never forgot was: avoid fighting the P-38 head on. That was suicide.
The armament was so heavy and their firepower so murderous, that
no one ever tried that type of attack more than once."

The Germans' favorite tactic was to climb high and dive on their
quarry with the sun behind them—watch out for the *Hun in the Sun*
was as meaningful a saying for Allied airmen as don't attack the P-38
head-on was for German flyers—although a head-on attack because
of the closure speeds of two aircraft was only for the bravest of flyers
anyway. In his autobiography *The First and the Last*, Adolf Galland,
commander of the German fighter force until relieved by Herman
Goering, compared the P-38 to the German Me 110 Zerstoerer, a
twin-engine fighter as well, which didn't do so well in the Battle of
Britain in 1940. It was not really a valid comparison. Heinz "Pritzel"

Baer, a friend of Galland's, with 228 kills to his name, claimed the P-38 was not difficult at all, could be easily outmaneuvered, a sure kill. People like Galland and Baer of course were the best there was in the Luftwaffe, the German air force. The average German fighter pilot by 1944 had his hands full tackling a P-38. According to the *United States Strategic Bombing Survey*, German air force training had been reduced to a level not much beyond learning to take off and land an aircraft. Training hours for German fighter pilots between 1939 and 1942 were, in round numbers, around 250 flying hours. Galland and Baer were a product of that period. By 1944 training hours for German fighter pilots were down to around 100 hours, while the RAF and AAF training hours had risen to nearly 350 hours.

Chuck Yeager, flying a P-51 Mustang, recalls in his book *Yeager*: "On October 12 [1944] leading the group on a bombing escort over Bremen, I scored five victories—the first ace in a day. We were at 28,000 feet and closing fast. Soon I was able to count twenty-two individual specks. I figured they were Me 109s, just sitting up there, waiting for our bombers. We closed to about 1,000 yards, and if their leader saw us, he probably thought we were additional 109s. I came in behind their tail-end Charlie and was about to begin hammering him, when he suddenly broke left and ran into his wing man. They both bailed out. It was almost comic to score two victories without firing a shot. But apparently the big shortage in Germany was not of airplanes, but pilots. I blew up a 109 from six hundred yards—my third victory—when I turned around and saw another angling in behind me. I pulled back on my throttle, came in behind and under him. I opened up that 109 as if it was a can of spam. That made four. A moment later, I waxed a guy's fanny in a steep dive; he went straight into the ground."

Although Yeager thought so, ace in a day was not that unusual. Several other AAF flyers as well as US Navy and US Marine Corps aviators had that distinction, including Gregory "Pappy" Boyington, USMC, and David McCampbell, USN, both being the top scorers for their respective services as well.

In my research for my book *American Raiders*, which dealt with *Operation Lusty* and *Projects Overcast/Paperclip*, the search for Germany's high-end technology and scientists, I met Captain Eric

Pilots of the 474th Fighter Group at Florennes, Belgium, posing in front of one of their P-38 Lightnings. (Lloyd Wenzel)

"Winkle" Brown, a Royal Navy aviator and the counterpart for Great Britain to Colonel Harold Watson, who was the American lead for *Operation Lusty*. As the chief test pilot for Hawker Aircraft, Bill Humble, remarked, "In an era of outstanding test pilots, 'Winkle' was simply the best." It was indeed an honor for me to meet and correspond with this distinguished aviator. He writes in his book *Wings On My Sleeve*:

"In 1944 Lieutenant General Jimmy Doolittle, who had recently taken over command of the 8th USAAF visited the RAE [Royal Aircraft Establishment Farnborough] to ask for a series of hands-on tests on the three USAAF escort fighters, the P-38H Lightning, the P-47C Thunderbolt and the P-51B Mustang. He was worried about the heavy losses suffered by the fighters on high cover over Flying Fortresses. Tests were required into the handling behavior of the aircraft at high speeds up to their tactical [maneuvering] and critical [loss of control] Mach numbers. The test revealed that the Lightning and Thunderbolt fell well short of the tactical Mach numbers of the Me 109 and Fw 190.

"The Me 109 and Fw 190 both had a tactical Mach number of 0.75, so that figure was the name of the combat game at 30,000 feet.

The tests revealed that the Lightning and Thunderbolt fell well short of that figure, with tactical Mach numbers of 0.68 and 0.71 respectively. However, the Mustang with its laminar-flow wing achieved 0.78 tactically, and soon after receiving these results Doolittle asked that his force be supplied with P-51s only. Subsequently, the Merlin engine-powered Mustang proved to be the finest escort fighter in the European war theater."

The fifth Me 109 Yeager downed in a dive most likely exceeded its critical Mach number and the aircraft did not respond to the German pilot's input, flying him straight into the ground. It happened to so many German and Allied flyers, and nearly killed Robin Olds flying a P-38. It had yet to be understood what happened to aircraft controls when flying into that zone of instability around Mach .68 and over.

In the Pacific the air war faced by the Army Air Forces was quite different from the European experience. While combat in Europe was principally over land, in the Pacific it was principally fought over water. If flyers were shot down, their rescue in the Pacific was an iffy thing. The chances of being found and picked up were exceedingly slim. There was no formal rescue organization that trained and focused on rescuing downed aviators. Having two engines flying in this environment was viewed by the pilots as a very positive feature. Also favoring the P-38 in the Pacific theater of war was that the climate was much more benign than in Europe, and the air war was principally fought at somewhat lower altitudes as well. In this environment the P-38's range and heavy gun armament made it a formidable opponent for the Japanese. The crowning achievement for the P-38 was the Yamamoto shoot-down on April 18, 1943, addressed in a later chapter. Although the Japanese had some excellent pilots, the majority were not of the same caliber as those flying for the Luftwaffe up to early 1944. And their principal fighter aircraft lacked self-sealing fuel tanks, a true safety disaster. Once hit, their aircraft tended to go down in a blazing inferno. The Japanese deliberately compromised aircrew safety in their aircraft, and paid dearly during the war for that ill-founded decision. It is here in the Pacific war where the P-38 made its name and produced our highest scoring ace with 40 kills—Richard Bong. As fate would have it, Bong would

Wolfgang, author, next to his EB-66E Destroyer at Spangdahlem Air Base, Germany, in 1970, then assigned to the 52nd Tactical Fighter Wing. Years later his son Charles would as well be assigned to the 52nd Fighter Wing at Spangdahlem, flying the A-10 Warthog. (Author)

survive the war, then perish as an acceptance test pilot in the P-80 Shooting Star, another Kelly Johnson creation.

To be fair to the P-38, in its design Kelly Johnson considered several approaches, and came down on the double-rump approach to carry two engines to reach the speed and climb characteristic called for by the Army Air Corps. In the process Kelly created an aircraft faster than any other at the time, and for the first time had to deal with severe tail buffeting and aerodynamic compressibility, the forces aircraft were subjected to when approaching Mach .68, the speed of sound being Mach 1. In high speed dives, pilots for the first time experienced losing control over their aircraft—and dying.

The P-38 used a liquid-cooled engine, the Allison V-17, at a time when everyone believed air-cooled engines were the ultimate solution. The P-38 was heavier than other fighters, with a tricycle landing gear, and a vicious armament load of four 50s and a 20mm cannon, more deadly than anything carried by fighters of that time. The P-38 looked different—a twin-engine fighter—and was different, and the training provided to young pilots of a powerful new aircraft like the

P-38 was not up to par. So the P-38 was the new guy on the block, as the saying goes, and took the heat for things which in time would become the norm. The reputation it earned in its early days, dealing with compressibility issues, stuck to the airplane like gum to a shoe sole and it was soon retired when the war ended.

I want to thank all the people who gave me a helping hand in this project, recalling how many young men with a dream to reach for the sky gave their lives reaching for the unknown. Chuck Yeager may have been the one who broke the sound barrier, but all too many came before him to pave the way, to acknowledge that there was a barrier and that it could be broken. I especially want to recognize my many friends at the National Air and Space Museum's Udvar Hazy Center in Chantilly, Virginia, who unselfishly helped with their insights and provided essential documentation, pictures and critiques to help make this a worthwhile project. Many thanks to Al Stettner, Tony Kambic, Brian Nicklas, Jack Smith, and Steve Ruff, all docents or staff members at the National Air and Space Museum who took the time to review the manuscript for this book. Others who contributed were Charles Samuel, Rachel Thompson, Tom Jones—the astronaut, not the singer—and Robert Kempel. Special thanks goes to Craig Gill and his team at the University Press of Mississippi, who shepherded so many of my books through the complex publication cycle—thank you Craig! Enjoy the book.

FOREWORD

ALFRED STETTNER

The Pilot was everyone's hero,
He was brave, he was bold, he was grand.
As he stood by his battered old airplane
With his goggles and helmet in hand.
To Be sure, these pilots have earned it,
To fly you have to have guts.
And they blazed their names into the Hall of Fame
On wings with baling wire struts.

—JOHN WOLTER, 483RD BG (H)

The Lockheed P-38 is an iconic aircraft, appropriately lauded over the years by legions of aviation aficionados. Historians routinely highlight its numerous remarkable features: first US fighter to exceed 400 miles per hour; exceptional high-altitude and long-range

capabilities; highly stable and lethal gun platform; and, perhaps most significantly, more victories against Japanese fighters than any other Allied airframe. They praise its unique design, with its twin engines, twin tail booms, and powerful superchargers, and note that it remained in production throughout the entirety of World War II. The P-38 was all this and more. Yet, the Lightning suffered significant development problems, could become a death trap in a dive, suffered debilitating operational issues at altitude, and had the reputation to be highly complicated and a difficult plane to fly.

This somewhat schizophrenic love-hate story of the P-38 Lightning is best told through the words of the people who designed, built, and most particularly, flew them. In this, his eleventh book, Wolfgang Samuel introduces us to these people and enables them to talk directly to the reader, sharing their stories, experiences, emotions, and opinions. Wolf continues his firmly established modus operandi of telling aviation's history through the people who experienced it firsthand. We hear how Kelly Johnson's first major design was a harbinger of the innovation and technical acumen that marked his career. We fly with Benjamin Kelsey, who had the audacity to try and set a transcontinental speed record in the prototype XP-38, which only had forty hours of flight time to date, only to crash on his landing approach. We witness the success and subsequent tragedy of Richard Bong; the competitive drive that eventually defeated Thomas McGuire; the genius that enabled Charles Lindbergh to dramatically enhance fighter operations; the daring that downed Admiral Yamamoto; the nemesis known as Mach Tuck that threatened many pilots; and the exploits of scores of other personalities whose names are less known.

Although the P-38 was designed as a high-altitude, high-speed interceptor and is best remembered for its success as a fighter, it served a variety of other roles. Several hundred had their guns replaced by cameras and conducted highly valuable photo-reconnaissance missions. Others were fitted with bombs or rockets to serve in ground attack roles; leading P-38 bombers were known as "Droop Snoots." Some Lightnings were even configured with medical evacuation pods under their wings where fuel tanks or ordinance were normally placed, certainly a unique ambulance experience for the evacuee.

Wolf tells the stories of the full range of variants through the men who flew them. And since these men's flying experiences was not limited to the Lightning, this book also addresses a wide variety of additional aircraft, from the P-38's colleagues including the P-51, P-47, B-25, B-26, and Mosquito, to its foes such as the Me 109, Fw 190, Me 262, Zero, and many others. The many protagonists we meet who flew these iconic aircraft range from the gregarious and famous, such as Yeager, Hoover, Gabreski, and Doolittle, to the equally successful but relatively reserved Chilstrom, Watson, Schilling, and Zemke. Heroes all.

Wolfgang Samuel's latest book is a wonderful read. By allowing the men who flew the P-38 Lightning to tell their tales in their own words, Samuel brings their incredible experiences to life. It ought to be on the bookshelf of everyone interested in the human aspect of aviation and the air war of World War II.

ABBREVIATIONS

AAA	Antiaircraft artillery
AAF	Army Air Forces
AFB	Air Force Base
Ar	Arado, the aircraft manufacturer of the Arado 234 and others
Aileron	Moveable wing control surface to bank an airplane
Bf	Bayrische Motorenwerke (builder of the Bf 109 and Bf 110), renamed Messerschmitt A.G. in 1938. All subsequent aircraft designs received the Me rather than the Bf prefix. In the text I will use only Me as a designator.
CO	Commanding Officer
DFC	Distinguished Flying Cross
ETO	European Theater of Operations
FEAF	Far East Air Forces
FG	Fighter Group
Flak	German anti-aircraft gun, or generally anti-aircraft fire
Flap	Moveable winglet at inboard trailing edge of a wing to provide increased lift at reduced speed
He	Heinkel, the aircraft manufacturer of the Heinkel 111 and others

Captain Morgan and the crew of the *Memphis Belle*, a B-17F Flying Fortress, the first crew to complete twenty-five combat missions over Europe. The aircraft is currently on exhibit at the National Museum of the United States Air Force in Dayton, Ohio.

HQ	Headquarters
Ju	Junkers, the aircraft manufacturer of the Junkers 52 and others
JCS	Joint Chiefs of Staff
KG	Kampfgeschwader/combat wing
KIA	Killed in Action
LFA	Luftfahrtforschungsanstalt—aircraft research institute
Luftwaffe	German air force
Me	Messerschmitt, the aircraft manufacturer of the Me 109, Me 110, and others
MTO	Mediterranean Theater of Operations
MIT	Massachusetts Institute of Technology
NACA	National Advisory Committee for Aeronautics
POW	Prisoner of War
RAE	Royal Aircraft Establishment (Farnborough)
RAF	Royal Air Force
RLM	Reichsluftfahrtministerium, the Nazi German air staff
ROTC	Reserve Officer Training Corps

8th Air Force Emblem. The 8th Air Force was formed in Savannah, Georgia, on January 19, 1942, called VIIIs Bomber Command, before relocating to the United Kingdom to conduct offensive air operations against Germany. Its heavy bombers were the B-17 and B-24. Its legacy is celebrated at the 8th Air Force Museum, Pooler, Georgia, near Savannah, its place of birth. (Author)

RTU   Replacement Training Unit
Stalag Luft POW camp administered by the German air force—
           Stammlager Luftwaffe—followed by a Roman numeral to
           designate the camp number
Stall   The airspeed at which a wing no longer produces lift
UK   United Kingdom
USAFE   United States Air Forces in Europe
USSTAF   United States Strategic Air Forces in Europe, at war's end
           renamed USAFE

THE P-38 LIGHTNING
AND THE MEN WHO FLEW IT

TEST PILOTS

On the benches in his room were morning vacant spaces
for some that saw the sky turn dark, at noon, with youthful faces.
Too soon, too low, too high, too fast—they hurried on into the past.
The crashes often most were blamed on grievous pilot errors
but on the hill where the coffin was, six pilots were the bearers.
—ARMY AIR FORCES FLIGHT TEST CENTER

War in Europe officially ended on May 8, 1945. As a ten-year-old boy I remember it all too well, a refugee kid fleeing before the pursuing Russian army with a German army unit hell-bent to surrender to the Americans or the British. That April, after surviving Russian tanks, rocket and artillery attacks, strafing by Russian-flown, but American-built, P-39 fighters, we surrendered to the 82nd Airborne Division, near Wismar, in the north of Germany. One of those Airborne soldiers gave me a smile and a stick of chewing gum, something I had never heard of before. To this day I am not a great fan of chewing gum, but the gesture of this American soldier, a man with a gun, was one of the kindest things I had experienced at that time of my life. The soldier's simple act of generosity softened the ugly world I had been forced to become a part of.

The shooting was finally over for nearly everyone. While allied soldiers would soon be going home, my ordeal was just beginning, and would not end until 1951 when I emigrated to the United States, to America, a land that I had heard so much about from my father, the land of unlimited opportunities, as everyone I knew referred to it. In time it would become just that for me, and some of America's World War II airmen would not only become my role models, but fellow flyers and friends as well.

★★★

In July 1945 twenty-two year-old Captain Charles F. Yeager, better known to his friends as Chuck, came home from Europe. He had flown a P-51 Mustang that he had named after his girlfriend—*Glamorous Glennis*—and wondered what he was going to do next. Since finishing training in the P-39 Airacobra in 1943, the same airplanes that earlier in 1945 had so devastatingly strafed my family when fleeing from the Russian army, he had downed an Me 109. Soon after that encouraging event he was shot down himself by a Fw 190 while escorting B-24 bombers at 30,000 feet. Yeager recalls the event in his book *Yeager*: "The airplane began to spin, it happened so fast. There was no time to panic. I knew I was going down; I was barely able to unfasten my safety belt and crawl over the seat before my burning P-51 began to snap roll, heading for the ground. I just fell out of the cockpit when the plane turned upside down—my canopy was shot away." Yeager survived the bail-out, was picked up by the French resistance, the Maquis, crossed the Pyrenees to Spain, and made it back to his squadron in England. He refused to go home, and by the time the war ended he was credited with eleven kills, a double ace. The title Ace is bestowed upon a fighter pilot when shooting down five enemy aircraft in aerial combat. Ground kills do not count, only aerial victories. He no longer was the innocent West Virginia boy who had joined the Army Air Corps in 1943. War changes people.

★★★

General "Hap" Arnold, the commanding general of the Army Air Forces, loved his fighter pilots and made sure that, if doable, they got the assignments they asked for if they would stay in the service. Yeager, like many others, thought being a test pilot was "shit hot," using fighter pilot jargon. Few knew what test piloting involved. They mostly thought it was glamorous flying hot new aircraft, a fighter pilot's dream. The real world was a bit different. Flight testing before, during, and in the early years after World War II was conducted at Wright Field, near Dayton, Ohio, now Wright-Patterson Air Force Base. In his book *Test Flying at old Wright Field*, Colonel Kenneth "Ken" Chilstrom, a test pilot himself and the former chief of Fighter Test at Wright-Field, and later the first commandant of the

The P-51 Mustang was one of the best fighters developed in the Second World War and had the range, with fuel tanks, to escort bombers to their targets throughout Germany. The picture shows Chuck Yeager's P-51 with wing tanks named *Glamorous Glen[nis] II*, after his girlfriend whom he married once he got home in 1945. The picture was presented by General Yeager to Martin Frauenheim, a German aviator, admirer of Yeager and friend of mine. (M. Frauenheim)

Air Force Test Pilot School at Edwards Air Force Base, lists 114 names of military and civilian pilots killed while performing their duties as test pilots. And he cautions the reader that the list is probably incomplete, but was the best information available to him. In those days there were no simulators worthy of the name. If you wanted to wring-out a new aircraft you had to take it up and take it through its paces to find out its strengths and limitations. That is the world Chuck Yeager was getting himself into in 1945.

★★★

Ken Chilstrom, after completing pilot training in 1942 and putting on the brown bars of a second lieutenant, was assigned to the 58th Fighter Group at Bolling Field, Washington, DC, flying P-40 Warhawks. Their mission was to protect the Capital area, from what I don't really know since the Germans didn't have any aircraft with the necessary range to cross the Atlantic. "The 58th had three

squadrons," Ken recalled for me, "my squadron was based at Bolling Field, Washington DC, on the banks of the Potomac River, the
other two were in Baltimore and Philadelphia. Each squadron had
twenty-five pilots and an equal number of aircraft assigned. Since
there was no real aerial threat, we served as a replacement training
unit to make up for the losses suffered by squadrons in combat. In
February 1943 all of my group's pilots took a train to the Curtiss
Airplane factory in Buffalo, New York, and we picked up brand new
P-40N Warhawks."

The P-40 and P-39 were the best fighters around in the late 1930s
and early 1940s, but found themselves outclassed by their opponents in both Europe and Asia. Come war, however, you fight with
what you have on hand and hope that something better is on the
way. "We flew them to Norfolk, Virginia," Ken continued, "where
we embarked on the aircraft carrier USS *Ranger*. None of us had
ever been on an aircraft carrier before, much less flown off one. It
took us ten days to cross the Atlantic, and when we were about 100
miles off the North African coast, all seventy-five of us were told
to strap on our P-40s and get ready to launch for an airfield near
Casablanca, Morocco. I was number 35 when we launched off the
Ranger, somewhere in the middle. They had turned the carrier into
the wind and got her up to maximum speed to get as much wind
across the deck as possible. As I sat there, with the prop turning,
I never saw anyone else fly off. Everyone went off to the left of the
carrier and disappeared. The flight deck was about 75 to 80 feet off
the water. I didn't know if they made it off the carrier or not. We
didn't lose anyone, I later learned, but I didn't know that as I sat
there sweating in my P-40 cockpit wondering what awaited me.
As I launched, and dropped off the side of the carrier, I quickly
discovered, as I got near the water, I picked up additional lift from
the ground effect and I flew on just above the wave tops. The whole
thing was a little disconcerting.

"We got to North Africa just after the disaster at Kasserine Pass,
where the 33rd Fighter Group lost most of its airplanes when Rommel's troops overran their airfield. Since they had experience, they
took our planes, and we waited until our replacements arrived—not
P-40s, but the North American A-36 Apache, the earliest version of

The P-40 Warhawk along with the P-39 Airacobra was one of the best fighters the Air Corps had at the beginning of WW-II. The Warhawk served with the Flying Tigers in China in 1942, and both aircraft, the P-40 and P-39, served in North Africa in 1943. The P-40E shown flew with the Royal Canadian Air Force in the Aleutian Islands and was repainted in the colors of the Flying Tigers. The aircraft hangs in the lobby of the National Air and Space Museum's Udvar Hazy Center in Chantilly, Virginia. (Author)

the P-51 fighter. I strafed myself through North Africa, Sicily and Italy as far as Naples. I was sent home in November 1943 with 80 combat missions to my credit, the Distinguished Flying Cross, and eight Air Medals.

"They tried to send me to the P-40 Replacement Training Unit, RTU, the last thing I wanted to do. I went to see my commanding officer, CO, a major, and told him I wanted to go to Wright Field to be a test pilot. I didn't know anything about being a test pilot, but that's what I wanted to be. My CO checked with Personnel to see if there were any openings at Wright Field. The answer came back—No. I said to the major, 'You let me go to Wright Field and I'll find a job.' To my great surprise he issued orders sending me to Wright Field. Major Chris Petrie, the chief of Fighter Test at the time, he was killed in an aircraft accident on May 7, 1944, told me that he didn't have a job for me in flight test. But, he added, 'I need a maintenance officer. Can you do that?' I lied, 'I am a good maintenance officer, sir.' That's how I got my foot in the door.

The Distinguished Flying Cross is awarded for heroism or extraordinary achievement in aerial flight. The medal was established in 1926 and first awarded in 1927 to Charles Lindbergh. The Air Medal is awarded for heroism or meritorious achievement while participating in aerial flight, established by President Roosevelt in 1942. (Author)

"Being a test pilot exacted a heavy price at times," Chilstrom recalled. "I lost many friends. But for a guy who wanted to fly everything with wings on it, Wright Field was beyond belief. The ramp was always filled to near overflowing with airplanes. I got to fly everything. Among all of the aircraft at Wright Field were two Me 109Gs, two Fw 190s, and a Ju 88 bomber. Two Me 262 jet fighters arrived in the spring of 1945. By the time Colonel Hal Watson, who was responsible for recovering German aircraft in Germany under a program called *Operation Lusty*, brought his airplanes back from Europe, we already had twenty-four German and Japanese aircraft on the ramp, and I got to fly them all. I spent more time testing the Focke-Wulf 190 fighter than any other. Gus Lundquist, one of our best test pilots, told me that the Fw 190D was in the class of our P-51, a pilot's airplane, with an excellent cockpit layout , good visibility, excellent control response, and maneuverability.

"However, the Fw 190 had a flaw which nearly killed me. It was my tenth flight in the aircraft on February 24, 1945, I was doing a functional flight test after some adjustments had been made to the

Colonel Harold Watson, on the right, and Major General Mark Bradley, standing next to a captured Fw 190 at Lager Lechfeld in 1945. (Author)

engine controls. I took her up to 20,000 feet. On final approach I adjusted the tail plane trim switch to relieve some of the forward stick pressure, I was at about 200 feet, when the stick came back and the airplane pitched nose up. I went up several thousand feet before regaining control and discovered that I had a runaway trim control switch that went either full up or full down. I chose the nose-down position which I could manhandle for a landing." A switch malfunction was not necessarily something test pilots recorded or passed on. The problem with that approach was that in the case of the Fw 190 it was a systemic problem in switch design, and Ken's experience wouldn't be the last time an American pilot would have to deal with such a situation. Weeks later, one of Watson's Whizzers pilots, Captain William Haynes, was killed in a low level fly-by when the trim switch malfunctioned and drove him into the ground. Another Watson's Whizzers pilot, Bob Anspach, crashed his Fw 190 on a delivery flight from Newark to Wright Field, but managed to survive. I wonder how many German pilots died for the same reason—a malfunctioning trim switch.

Bob Anspach, one of Watson's Whizzers pilots, was flying this Fw 190 in September 1945 from Newark via Pittsburgh to Freeman Field in Indiana when he experienced runaway trim. He found an open place in Pennsylvania to bring down the recalcitrant Fw 190. The prop spun off when he made contact with the ground. (Robert Anspach)

On the way to becoming Chief of Fighter Flight Test, Chilstrom graduated in the first class in 1945 from the Flight Performance School at Wright Field, which later became the United States Air Force Test Pilot School. In 1949 Ken was appointed commandant of the school, then located at Muroc Army Airfield, renamed Edwards Air Force Base in honor of Ken's friend and fellow test pilot. Glen Edwards was one of Ken's classmates at the Flight Performance School at Wright Field and closest friend. Glen chose to go into Bomber Test and piloted the YB-49 flying wing along with "Danny" Forbes, crashing on a test flight near Muroc, California, in the Mojave Desert on June 5, 1948, killing the pilots and three engineers who were on board the aircraft. Edwards Air Force Base was named after Glen Edwards, and Forbes Air Force Base, where I was stationed for five years with the 55th Strategic Reconnaissance Wing flying RB-47H aircraft, was named after Edwards's copilot, Danny Forbes. Test flying was never routine.

When signing in at Fighter Test at Wright Field, Chuck Yeager soon ran into a fellow fighter pilot—Bob Hoover. Both were assigned

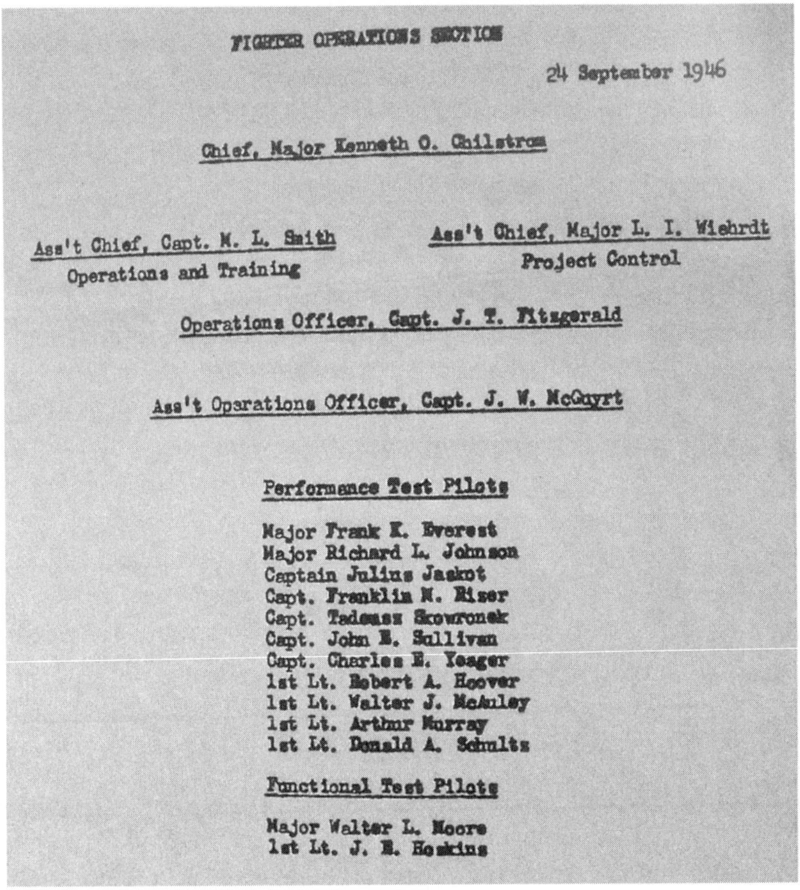

FIGHTER OPERATIONS SECTION

24 September 1946

Chief, Major Kenneth O. Chilstrom

Ass't Chief, Capt. M. L. Smith
Operations and Training

Ass't Chief, Major L. I. Wiehrdt
Project Control

Operations Officer, Capt. J. T. Fitzgerald

Ass't Operations Officer, Capt. J. W. McGuyrt

Performance Test Pilots

Major Frank K. Everest
Major Richard L. Johnson
Captain Julius Jaskot
Capt. Franklin N. Riser
Capt. Tadeusz Skowronek
Capt. John E. Sullivan
Capt. Charles E. Yeager
1st Lt. Robert A. Hoover
1st Lt. Walter J. McAuley
1st Lt. Arthur Murray
1st Lt. Donald A. Schults

Functional Test Pilots

Major Walter L. Moore
1st Lt. J. E. Hoskins

The 1946 roster of the Fighter Test branch headed by then Major Kenneth O. Chilstrom. Ken had succeeded Gabby Gabreski in 1946 as chief of Fighter Test. Among the many pilots who he was in charge of was Richard Bong, our highest scoring WWII ace in the Pacific with 40 victories, Chuck Yeager, John Godfrey, Bob Hoover, Don Gentile, and Walter McAuley. (K. Chilstrom)

to Fighter Test and Chuck and Bob hit it off "right off the bat," so to speak. Before going through the Flight Performance School at Wright Field, Yeager did a lot of functional test flying, checking out airplanes that had gone through maintenance for one reason or another. Hoover, Yeager's newfound friend, was a combat pilot like Yeager. Hoover had been shot down by a Fw 190 on his very first combat mission over the Mediterranean. Hoover's Spitfire engine exploded. "The entire nose of my Spitfire was a ball of flames. I

A Lockheed P-38L Lightning fighter, painted in the colors of the 55th Fighter Group based in England in WWII. The aircraft is on display at the USAF Museum at Wright-Patterson AFB, Ohio. It had a top speed of over 400mph, a ceiling of 40,000 feet and a range of over 1,000 miles. The 55th eventually became a reconnaissance wing, still active, based at Offutt AFB, Omaha, Nebraska, flying RC-135 aircraft. (Museum of the US Air Force)

knew I couldn't save the plane," he wrote in his book *Forever Flying.* "I opened the cockpit, released my shoulder and seat straps, rolled the plane inverted and I was away from the fire." Bob landed in the Mediterranean, some twenty miles off the coast from Nice, France. The vessel which came to pick him up was not what he expected, it was a German corvette, and now he was a prisoner of war, a POW. Bob would spend his time in Stalag Luft I near Barth, Germany, on the Baltic Sea, from February 1944 until April 1945. The camp was filled with famed American flyers such as Hub Zemke, Gus Lundquist, Gabby Gabreski, and others. That April the German guards abandoned the camp on the approach of the Russian army, a camp filled with nine thousand or so Allied airmen who had been shot down over Europe and North Africa. After escaping the camp, Bob and a friend became closely guarded guests of the Russians. When he and his friend managed to get away from the Russians, he wrote in his book, "We had both seen the unbelievable. It was literally an unspeakable horror. We came across an abandoned German fighter base. A few ground crew were still around. Thirty or so Fw 190s sat in revetments. I had some knowledge of the plane because a fellow POW, Gus Lundquist, a Wright Field test pilot, had flown the plane and shared his knowledge with me." Bob Hoover then absconded with a Fw 190, and flew it, gear down, into Holland, hoping he would not be shot down by friendly fighters. He wasn't, although some ar-

Pancho Barnes was a legend at Edwards AFB. If you had not met Pancho Barnes, you were not a test pilot. Colonel Eugene Deatrick, second commander of the Air Force Test Pilot School, in his office at Edwards AFB presenting Ms. Barnes, Pancho, with a model of the A-1E, which Deatrick flew in Vietnam. Deatrick was a close friend of mine, a man I greatly admired. (Deatrick)

dent Dutch farmers nearly pitchforked him. Yeager and Hoover had a lot in common including lots of functional test flying at Wright Field which gave them ample opportunities to "horse around," meaning to do some fun fighter pilot type of flying. So, this day, both Yeager and Hoover were flying around Dayton, neither knowing the other was up in the air.

Writes Yeager in his autobiography *Yeager*, "I took off in the Bell jet, the P-59. It was only my second flight in it, and I really didn't know the systems. Suddenly, a P-38 prop fighter dove in on me. I couldn't believe it! None of the test pilots had ever started a dogfight, but this guy seemed determined to bounce me. I whipped that jet around and pulled up into a vertical climb—not really understanding what in hell I was doing—and I stalled going straight up. I was spinning down, and that damned P-38 was spinning up, both airplanes out of control, and when we went by each other, not ten feet apart, my eyes were like saucers and so were the other pilot's. We both fell out of the sky, regained control down on the deck, engines smoking and wide open. Finally he said, 'Hey, man, we better knock it off before we bust our asses.' I didn't know who he was."

This is how Bob Hoover remembers this encounter. "Even though I was flying a P-38 fighter, I headed straight toward the Bell jet that was circling Wright Field in Dayton, Ohio, spoiling for a dogfight. The pilot in the P-59 may have been startled to see me challenge him, but he never backed away. In the early fall of 1945, the jet fighter and my P-38 battled toe-to-toe. Neither one of us could gain the advantage. As soon as I made a vertical climb, to the stall, to try to get an advantage on the P-59, it was right there staring me in the face. If my memory serves me right, I wasn't the one who called things off. Nevertheless, once we landed, I laid eyes on Chuck Yeager. 'Man, I didn't know the 38 could swap ends like that,' he bellowed while extending his hand."

Wrote Scott Crossfield in his book *Always Another Dawn—The Story of a Rocket Test Pilot*: "Edwards [and Wright Field before that] was not the place to attract non-competitive pilots." All the test pilots I ever knew, from Ken Chilstrom to Bob Hoover to Chuck Yeager to Gene Deatrick to Whitey Feightner and others, fit that mold.

A CHANGING WORLD

The feathering button that didn't work. The gear-down switch with the funny quirk.
Flinders and flames, the names soon forgotten with the blames.
The echoes ring here yet, of engine test cells roaring.
Above drift the skies they touched and tried, alone, aloft, exploring.
The games of chess unfinished still—the rain, the line, the morning chill.
Farewell, once more, my vanished friends.
—ARMY AIR FORCES FLIGHT TEST CENTER

By 1937 it was becoming quite obvious to astute observers that Hitler's Germany was clearly on a road to war. Its fledgling air force, the Luftwaffe, was flexing its muscle in support of Franco's rebellion in Spain, and on April 26, 1937, German bombers of the Condor Legion attacked the Basque town of Guernica. Nearly 2,000 civilians were killed, shocking the world. Guernica provided a prelude of what was to come in the not-too-distant future. In 1921 the Italian General Giulio Douhet had published a hugely influential book entitled *The Command of the Air*. It laid out a strategy of how air power could subjugate an enemy nation by bombing it into submission using a combination of general purpose, phosphorous, and poison gas bombs. Guernica was the first attempt to apply Douhet's principles of aerial warfare, perfected in later years by Bomber Command of the Royal Air Force and the United States 8th and 15th Air Forces against Germany, but without the use of poison gas. Douhet's thinking at the time was in line with others, such as Billy Mitchell in the United States and Hugh Trenchard in Great Britain, who foresaw great possibilities for the future application of air power. Douhet's vision of strategic bombing became the mantra of the United States Air Force, as well, during the Cold War years, with General Curtis LeMay's creation of the Strategic Air Command (SAC). The threat of which, in my humble opinion, eventually helped bring the Soviet

Union to its knees. SAC's weapon of choice no longer was the general purpose or phosphorus bomb, but the much more lethal atomic bomb first used against the Japanese cities of Hiroshima and Nagasaki, bringing World War II to a sudden and final end.

American politicians in 1937 may not have taken note of what had just happened in Spain, and still viewed the United States as being secure against all threats. After all, we were protected by two natural bulwarks, the Atlantic and Pacific Oceans. Our military leadership and the fledgling aviation industry did not hold such sanguine views. In March 1937, the 2nd Bombardment Group at Langley Field, Virginia, commanded by Lieutenant Colonel Carl "Tooey" Spaatz, received its first YB-17A, the prototype of the future B-17 bomber, a four-engine behemoth with multiple machine guns to defend itself against hostile fighters. The B-17 was viewed as a flying fortress, which became its name. The US Army leadership still viewed air power as "flying artillery," and pushed hard for the Air Corps to abandon, in its opinion, the ill advised and expensive effort of a four-engine bomber, favoring the twin-engine B-18, sufficient to serve as a flying piece of artillery. The Air Corps, using every subterfuge available, stuck by its guns; and future fleets of thousands of B-17 bombers would, in the war to come, lay waste the major cities of Germany. Douhet's visions were not realized by the application of massive air power and the destruction of cities. People made do with the reality of the day. What turned the tide against the Germans was when General Spaatz chose for his principal target the weak point in the German economy—oil. Although there for all to see, it took a long time to be recognized. Target selection is everything in war, as we relearned in a war yet to come—Vietnam.

As a ten-year-old in 1945 I lived in Berlin and endured the first 1,000-bomber raid of the 8th Air Force. It was terrifying, as were all of the raids, but especially this one. The bombs came so very close that I just knew I was going to die that day. The nightmares stayed with me for years to come, as they did for everyone else who experienced such raids. Robin Neilands writes about that raid in *The Bomber War: The Allied Air Offensive Against Nazi Germany*, "On February 3, 1945, for example, 1,000 B-17s attacked the marshaling yards in Berlin. Spaatz's biographer, David Mets, records that the bombing

General Carl "Tooey" Spaatz, commander of the US Strategic Air Forces in Europe (USSTAF), being briefed by Colonel Harold Watson at Melun air base near Paris, France, June 27, 1945, where Watson had assembled several Me 262s and Arado 234s for the general to view prior to their shipment to the United States. (Author)

was done visually, accuracy was good, with the bombs hitting the rail yards and administrative center in the city . . . twenty-five thousand Berliners lost their lives [killed and wounded]. Such a casualty rate indicates that this was an area attack. . . . If the accuracy was indeed 'good' [I personally doubt it, since there was no marshaling yard near where I lived at the time] and only precision targets were hit, as this statement claims, German civilian casualties on those US blind-bombing missions in 1944–45 can only be wondered at." In addition to the thousands of people who died in this raid, on a blue sky day, thousands of buildings were turned into rubble—but life went on. Douhet's prediction that people could be bombed into submission was based on the euphoria, in the early days of the twentieth century, that surrounded the airplane, not on facts.

The years 1937 to 1938 had other surprises in store. Frank Whittle tested the first practical jet engine in a laboratory in Cambridge, England. And Hans von Ohain in Germany had already started on a similar effort as early as 1935. The result was the Heinkel 178, the first jet aircraft to fly in 1939 at Germany's test center of Marienfelde. However, politics in Nazi Germany was no different than anywhere else, and the leadership listened to the persuasive arguments of Willie Messerschmitt and postponed entering the jet age until Messerschmitt's Me 262 Schwalbe came along, about a couple of years after the He 178 could have been fielded. In Britain the Gloster Meteor would be their first jet aircraft to fly. Both of these efforts would have a profound future effect on the nature of air power.

In March 1938 the German army marched into Austria without encountering any resistance. Austria became just another province of Germany—the Ostmark. And a year later, in March 1939, Germany had occupied Czechoslovakia as well. The writing was on the wall as to who would come next—Poland. President Franklin D. Roosevelt was leading a nation that had no interest in getting involved in Europe's messy affairs. However, he was a pragmatist and called in his senior leadership to assess the situation and the possible future implications for the United States.

As a result, in 1939, as part of the National Defense Act, which directed military spending for the coming year, Roosevelt called for the Air Corps to expand to 48,000 men, and for industry to get moving and expand its annual production rate to 20,000 aircraft—which seemed an astonishingly large effort at the time. In 1944 the American aircraft industry turned out a total of 96,318 aircraft of all types in a single year. An incredible achievement of American productivity, but in 1939 it seemed that 20,000 aircraft would satisfy our needs, and was viewed as being a superb achievement, if in fact accomplished.

So the American aircraft industry went to work. The B-17 Flying Fortress had been in the works since 1934 and by 1939 the first production aircraft was delivered to the Air Corps. The Bell P-39 also had an early start with an unconventional engine arrangement behind the pilot, rather than in front. Its design work began in 1936, and the aircraft went into full production in late 1940. Many future P-38 flyers would cut their teeth on the P-39. The P-39, among other issues, had a tendency to get into a flat spin, killing many pilots. Bob Hoover, our future Wright Field test pilot, flew the P-39 soon after getting his wings. As an enlisted pilot Hoover, after basic training, reported to the 20th Fighter Group, at Drew Field, near Tampa,

Design work for the Bell P-39 began in June 1936. The first production aircraft was delivered in September 1940. A total of 9,585 P-39s were built, many provided to the Russians, who loved the aircraft, under the Lend-Lease Act. As a refugee I remember being strafed by Russian P-39s. The aircraft shown is a P-39Q in the colors of the 57th Fighter Squadron based on Kodiak and Adak Islands during the Aleutian Campaign. The aircraft is on display at the Museum of the US Air Force, Wright Patterson AFB, Ohio. (Museum of the US Air Force)

Florida. In his book *Forever Flying*, Hoover wrote: "I learned how to fly a fighter plane in a slow landing P-40. Its deficiencies didn't detract from the fun I had flying that plane. But I did hanker to take up the more streamlined P-39 Airacobra. One day I was set to take my Number 46 P-40 up. On the way to the airplane I saw a crew chief working on a P-39 with the same number. "Do you know how to start the engine?" I asked. He did. A few minutes later I was airborne.

"The P-39 had a reputation as a widow maker. There was a song that went, 'Oh, don't give me a P-39. Because the engine is mounted behind. She'll spin, crash and burn. So, don't give me a P-39.' The next verse went, 'Oh, give me a P-38. The props that counter-rotate. She'll not spin, crash and burn. So give me a P-38.' At 10,000 feet, I pulled the nose up steeply, cut the power, and presto, the plane started to tumble. A flat spin followed, and I panicked for an instant trying to get my bearings. I tried conventional recovery protocols, but none of them worked. Instinctively I dropped the landing gear and lowered the flaps to upset the gyroscopic effect. To my amazement, the P-39 went into a conventional nose-down spin. I recovered the airplane with plenty of room to spare." Once Hoover demonstrated the procedure to his squadron commander, it became the accepted recovery method for the P-39.

Design work for the P-38 Lightning started in 1937. The first prototype was flown in 1938, and first production began in 1940. By 1942, 500 aircraft of various models had been delivered. For both the P-47 Thunderbolt, more commonly referred to by its flyers as the *Jug*, and the P-51 Mustang, design work started in 1940 and the first production aircraft of each rolled out of their respective factories, North American for the P-51 and Republic Aviation for the P-47, in 1941. Eventually American industry produced 9,535 P-38s, 15,579 P-47s, and 14,490 P-51s. The three fighters, nearly 40,000 aircraft in total, would provide the backbone of our fighter force in World War II.

In 1937, the Lockheed Aircraft Corporation, which never before had built a fighter aircraft, entered into a design competition for a single-seat fighter against competitors like Douglas, Curtiss, Vultee, North American, Bell, and others more experienced than Lockheed in the fighter business and financially in better shape than Lockheed as well. The interceptor the Air Corps was calling for was to be able to fly at a top speed of 360 miles per hour at altitude and reach 20,000 feet in six minutes. The specifications for the fighter pushed the envelope. The proposal suggested the use of an Allison [General Motors] liquid-cooled engine, the same power plant used in the P-39. The engine boasted turbo superchargers and the design specification strongly suggested a tricycle landing gear, rather than a "tail-dragger" approach used by most aircraft produced up to this point. The tricycle landing gear, a mid-1930s innovation using a nose gear to keep the aircraft straight and level, allowed the pilot to see the runway on entering. Unlike "tail-draggers," using a tail wheel with the nose of the aircraft pointed up, forcing the pilot to taxi obliquely, side to side, looking out the side window of his cockpit to see if he was aligned with the runway. A liquid-cooled engine at that time was viewed with skepticism by flyers as was the tricycle landing gear approach, not to mention a twin-engine fighter, the approach Lockheed was to follow.

The Lockheed design team was led by Hall Hibbard and Clarence "Kelly" Johnson. The challenge facing the team was to meet the required parameters with the proposed power plant. The design that finally evolved was indeed based on a team approach developed by Johnson. First of all "Kelly," a nickname given him in high school that stuck for the rest of his life, insisted on a location outside the factory so his team could work in isolation without having to deal with the usual interruption of the curious. So what do you call a place like that? You have to have a name for it. Quoting Ben Rich in *Skunk Works*, who was a close coworker with Kelly Johnson and took over when Johnson retired, "Around the time Kelly's crew raised their circus tent [there apparently was no factory space available, so he rented a circus tent and set it up near a smelly plastics factory], cartoonist Al Capp introduced Injun Joe and his backwoods-still into his 'L'il Abner' comic strip. Ol' Joe tossed worn shoes and dead skunks into his smoldering vat to make 'Kickapoo joy juice.' Capp named the outdoor still 'the skonk works.' The connection was apparent to those inside Kelly's circus tent forced to suffer the plastic factory's stink. One day one of the engineers showed up for work wearing a civil defense gas mask as a gag, and a design engineer named Irv Culver picked up a ringing phone and announced, 'Skonk Works.' Kelly overheard him and chewed out Irv: Culver, you're fired,' Kelly roared. 'Get your ass out of my tent.' Kelly fired guys all the time without meaning it. Irv Culver showed up for work the next day. Behind his back, all of Kelly's workers began referring to the operation as 'the skonk works' and soon everyone at the main plant was calling it that too. In 1960, Capp's publisher objected to our use of Skonk Works, so we changed it to Skunk Works and registered the name and logo as trademarks." From then on it was known as the supersecret Skunk Works, which along with the P-38 produced the innovative P-80, called the *Shooting Star*, in 180 days, as well as the Cold War F-104 Starfighter, U-2 Dragon Lady, and SR-71 Blackbird.

Well, it was still 1937, and Kelly's team had a job to do. Kelly would turn out to be one of the greatest aircraft designers of his time, on a level with Ernst Heinkel, Willy Messerschmitt, and Kurt Tank in Germany. But in 1937 a reputation had yet to be made or lost. Johnson obtained his degree in aeronautics at the University of Michigan at Ann Arbor, and went to work for the Lockheed Aircraft Corporation. He was an innovative engineer from the beginning and as a

The Bell YP-59 Airacomet first flew in October 1942. It was a great disappointment to General Arnold, who had hoped this would be the aircraft to take on the German Me 262. The limited performance of the P-59 led Arnold to engage Kelly Johnson's design team, which came up with the design and prototype of the P-80 jet in 180 days. Colonel Chilstrom experienced the first crash of an American-built jet, flying a P-59, on February 16, 1945, in Reidsville, NC. Fortunately there was no fire, and he survived. (K. Chilstrom)

team leader for the P-38 development he developed a set of rules to live by for his coworkers and himself. If I take a job, he insisted, I want to have full control across the board including every aspect of the development—technical, financial, and operational. He kept the number of his coworkers to a minimum and personally vetted each of the engineers who were to work on his team. The development of the P-80 jet is a good example of Kelly's mantra: discipline. The Bell Aircraft Corporation was General Arnold's hope for our first jet fighter to face the German Me 262 jet whenever it made its appearance, which it did in July 1944. The XP-59A, the Airacomet, the aircraft Chuck Yeager was to fly against Bob Hoover flying a P-38 in 1946, made its initial flight on October 2, 1942. About 50 P-59s were built, and according to Nathan "Rosie" Rosengarten, a flight test engineer, at Wright Field, "It could hardly be considered a combat airplane—at best it was a good safe airplane, a training vehicle for indoctrinating pilots into the jet age."

Where to turn next for General Arnold was a no-brainer: Kelly Johnson at Lockheed. Johnson's team, after being invited to submit a proposal for a jet fighter in May 1943, submitted their design proposal four weeks later calling for delivery of the first XP-80 in 180 days at

Pilots of the 1st Fighter Group, March Field, California, 1946, in front of one of their brand new P-80 jets. Al Tucker and Robin Olds, both former P-38 pilots, were assigned to the Group. (Al Tucker)

a cost of under $500,000. As promised, according to my dear friend and Wright Field test pilot Colonel Kenneth O. Chilstrom, the first "XP-80 was completed and transported to Muroc Army Air Base on 13 November 1943—less than 150 days after contract go ahead." World War II would end before the P-80 became combat ready. However, in its first combat test over Korea in 1950, the first jet-to-jet fighter engagement with a MiG 15, the MiG lost. Kelly Johnson, an incredibly talented aircraft designer and manager, insisted that once his team submitted a proposal to the US government, they would bring it in on time and on or below budget. He achieved that not only for the P-38 program but also for the P-80, the F-104, and the U-2, an airplane based on his F-104 design but with a greater wingspan and certain significant other changes as well.

Kelly's team proceeded with the design and development of the P-38. It turned out that the conventional approach of building a single-engine fighter did not look too promising with the preselected power plant. So they looked at options, one of which was to build a twin-boomed twin-engine aircraft with the pilot station in the middle, truly thinking "out of the box." It was not a new concept. It had been talked and written about by engineers across the aviation world for some time, not for a fighter but for transports, reconnaissance aircraft, and bombers. A German approach along these lines was the Fw 189, a reconnaissance aircraft that would be widely used on the Russian front in the war yet to come. Other twin-boom aircraft were developed and built during the war, transports in Germany and a night fighter in the United States, the Northrop P-61 Black Widow. But no one had ever built a twin-boom fighter before. So Kelly's team went to work. Kelly Johnson was, if nothing else, a realist. He knew his approach would be viewed with skepticism—after all, who ever heard of a twin-engine fighter?

Kurt Tank, the key designer of Germany's Fw 190, and later the TA 152, in 1936 ran into similar skepticism in Germany. He proposed to the RLM (Reichsluftfahrtministerium) a twin-engine long-range fighter with just a pilot—the Fw 187 Falke. In 1937 the Fw 187 reached a top speed of 326mph using a 1260 horsepower engine. The RLM staff apparently didn't deal in facts any more than people who questioned Kelly Johnson's XP-38 design. They refused to believe that a twin-engine fighter weighing twice as much as their beloved Me 109 could be 40+ mph faster than the Me 109. Three test aircraft were built with the latest model incorporating two Mauser 20mm cannons. The aircraft turned out to be very maneuverable. Yet, Ernst Udet, an experienced WW I fighter pilot with 62 victories and a participant in the 1936 air races in Los Angeles, refused to believe that a twin-engine fighter could turn and roll with the best of them, meaning the Me 109, and the project died. Udet shaped the Luftwaffe and decreed that every bomber had to be capable of dive bombing as well. This resulted in the Heinkel 177 Greif four engine bomber fiasco, and the Me 110 Zerstoerer, a Messerschmitt twin-engine fighter version with a crew of two or three, which during the Battle of Britain would prove to be a total failure as well. The Me 110 redeemed its reputation to a degree later in the war as a night fighter. Udet, who had shaped the Luftwaffe, realized he had made some terrible mistakes and committed suicide in 1942. Skepticism toward a twin-engine fighter—something new, never done before—was endemic not only in the United States but also in Germany and Great Britain. This led to a snail's pace in orders for the P-38 under development, until war came to the rescue.

The Northrop P-61 Black Widow night fighter was a twin-boom aircraft like the P-38, as was the German Gotha 242 cargo glider and the Fw 189 tactical reconnaissance aircraft. In the postwar years the British developed and flew the twin-boom *Vampire* jet. Both the Fairchild C-82 Packet and C-119 Flying Boxcar were twin-boom aircraft. The picture shows a P-61C Black Widow. (Museum of the US Air Force)

The XP-38 turbo-supercharged twin-engine, high-altitude interceptor (initially with a 37mm cannon and two machine guns mounted in the nose, later changed to four 50 caliber machine guns and a 20mm cannon) flew its first flight on January 27, 1939. This was essentially a hand-built aircraft. Lieutenant Benjamin Kelsey, with a master's degree in aeronautics from the Massachusetts Institute of Technology (MIT), assigned to Materiel Command at Wright Field, Dayton, Ohio, had been deeply involved in establishing the parameters for the XP-38. Kelsey followed development of the aircraft at Burbank closely and of course was not to be denied that first flight on January 27, at March Field near Riverside. Not counting some minor issues, all went well. Major General Hap Arnold, then Chief of the Army Air Corps, was very much aware of what Kelsey was doing. Then on February 11, 1939, with Arnold's approval, Kelsey took off from March Field in his 11,500-pound speedster for Wright Field, Ohio, with an intermediate refueling stop in Amarillo, Texas. Once he arrived at Wright Field, General Arnold gave his approval for Kelsey to proceed, possibly setting a cross-country speed record in the process, to Mitchell Field, Long Island, New York. The April

1944 issue of *Skyways* magazine reported on the flight in a detailed article entitled *Evolution of the Lightning*:

"On the morning of February 11, [1939], with Lieutenant Kelsey at the controls, XP-38 streaked eastward. Finding his best level between 18,000 and 20,000 feet, Kelsey reached Amarillo in two hours and forty-eight minutes. There he took on new fuel and in twenty-three minutes was off again. In another two hours and forty-five minutes he slid down on Dayton's Wright Field. Pilot and plane were in good shape, so the decision, after 23-minutes of fueling and conferring with General Arnold and other officers, was to go on. Over Pittsburgh Kelsey reported his cruising speed at 420 mph, to an unbelieving radio operator, estimated time to Mitchell Field 43-minutes. Forty-two minutes later, coming in for a landing at Mitchell Field, wheels and flaps down, Kelsey got caught behind three slow moving trainers." He pulled his power back, when he reapplied power, nothing happened. His carburetors had iced up and there was nothing he could do about it. "Coming in low over a golf course adjacent to the field, she piled into a sand bunker, a heap of twisted scrap metal. Kelsey extricated himself. His body was intact, but his spirit broken. He had crossed the country in seven hours and two minutes of flying time, only 15 minutes behind Howard Hughes' non-stop record, set by a racing plane."

As a result of Kelsey's flight, the Army ordered thirteen YP-38s, follow-on preproduction aircraft incorporating substantial changes from the hand-built prototype. The first of the YP-38s didn't come off the production lines at Burbank until a year later, 1940. The invasion of Poland by Germany in September 1939 led the United Kingdom and France to look for new fighter developments on a par with Germany's Me 109 or better, and they came across the YP-38 being test flown in the United States. Quick decisions were made under the circumstances and the Anglo/French Purchasing Committee placed a combined order for 667 aircraft, referred to as the Model 322. Lockheed was ecstatic about this development, because the only firm Air Corps order they had received so far, after investing several million of their own funds, was for the thirteen YP-38s. So the P-38 went into production in 1940 much sooner than expected, with much testing still to be done. France quickly succumbed to the

This Ju 87 Stuka dive bomber, with missing wheel covers, was flown into Stuttgart, Germany, to surrender on May 7, 1945. The Stuka was a critical element of Rommel's Blitzkrieg. (Roy Brown)

German onslaught using mobile tactics developed by Field Marshall Erwin Rommel, labeled *blitzkrieg* or lightning warfare, consisting of powerful, fast-moving armored formations accompanied by infantry and supported by close air support aircraft, in this case the *Stuka* dive bomber. Air-to-ground radio communications between armor and their Stukas led to a fast and coordinated advance.

The first three P-38 aircraft produced under the French/UK contract, designated 322B for the British and 322F for the French version, were shipped off to England for testing. For reasons of commonality with their P-40 Tomahawks, the 322B/F was to retain the same Allison engines used by P-40s—without turbo superchargers, and propellers turning in the same direction, rather than the counterrotating propellers on the YP-38. The French and British figured on using their aircraft at relatively low flight levels, obviating the need for superchargers that would just present an additional maintenance problem. Anyway, the feeling was that Americans tended to put too many gadgets on their airplanes, so keep it simple: no turbo superchargers. The reason for the props turning in the same direction is more elusive, and hard to figure why you would want to do that. It would complicate aircraft take-off. RAF test pilots who flew the three aircraft shipped to Great Britain were not overly enthusiastic about the performance of this emasculated version of the P-38 and after much back and forth the contract with Lockheed was canceled and the three test aircraft returned to the United States. By that time 143 of these aircraft, called Lightning by the British, had been built.

A significant contributing factor to the British decision to cancel the contract for the 322B may have been President Roosevelt's signing of the Lend-Lease Act in March 1941, which authorized the lending of war material to any nation considered vital to the defense of the United States. So there was no reason for the British to continue with a costly contract of their own, when aircraft could be procured free of charge under the Lend-Lease Act. The RAF would never ask for any P-38s, but focused on the P-51, by now under development as well. With the attack on Pearl Harbor on December 7, 1941, forty of the Model 322s were seized by the government and ended up at Santa Ana Air Base in California being used for advanced pilot training. Here you are talking about flyers with very little experience being put into a first line combat aircraft with both engines rotating their props in the same direction, much more dangerous than flying a P-38 trainer with counter-rotating propellers. Takeoff in the unmodified 322 was made with maximum opposite rudder. Pilot training in World War II was nearly as dangerous as flying combat in Europe. Eventually most of the Lightnings, designated P-322-II, were converted to counter-rotating propellers, but remained without the turbo superchargers that were essential for operation at high altitudes. The turbo supercharger is a compressor driven by hot exhaust gases of an airplane engine feeding rarefied thin air at high altitudes into the carburetor of the engine at ground-level pressure to increase engine efficiency and rate of climb.

There were numerous variants of the basic P-38 production aircraft, each incorporating new capabilities such as rocket pylons and power-boosted ailerons, but variants also reflected essential fixes to problems reported by the pilots. Out of the total of 9,535 aircraft built, the P-38L was the most numerous, with a total build of 3,923 aircraft. The L-version added hard points under the wings allowing it to carry HVARs, High Velocity Aircraft Rockets, drop tanks to extend range and up to 2,000-pound bombs. The Ls were the variants built to support the D-Day landings on June 6, 1944. The F-4A photo reconnaissance version of the P-38 was based on the P-38E/F and carried four cameras. The F-5A/B version carried five cameras and was based on the P-38G/J. The aircraft performed superbly in this role and most of the photographic coverage in the European Theater of Operations was done by F-4/5 Lightnings. The P-38 was the fastest American fighter of that period, flying in excess of 400 miles per hour.

An interesting version of the P-38J was the Droop Snoot, assigned to the 20th Fighter Group. Acting as the lead, other P-38s would fly in close formation with the Droop Snoot, and drop their bombs when the Droop Snoot released its bomb load. Droop Snoot missions were not popular with the P-38 pilots, having to fly in close formation, straight and level. In later years, on bad weather days, this approach was used for F-105 fighters against North Vietnam led by an EB-66 twin-engine electronic warfare aircraft. The F-105 flyers didn't like this mission any more than did the P-38 pilots who had to accompany the Droop Snoot. Anyway, writes Captain Harry C. Butcher, United States Navy, in his book *My Three Years with Eisenhower*, "General Spaatz had one of the new modified P-38 Lightning planes flown in which have been equipped with a bomb sight and a place for a bombardier in the plexiglass nose, which has been extended. In air lingo, the new P-38 is called the '*Droop Snoot*.' Ike inspected one with great interest. The pilot invited him for a ride. He accepted immediately and had about a ten minute ride, twisting and diving, his first ride in a fighter." My hat is off to General Eisenhower to accept this ride in this truly strange-looking aircraft; however, he was a licensed pilot himself, a skill he gained in 1939 while serving as military assistant for General MacArthur in the Philippines.

Eisenhower was farsighted. And one thing you really need to become a good pilot is good eyesight. Well, Ike muddled through and writes Erwin R. Tiongson in the September 2021 *Smithsonian Air and Space Magazine*, "Off he went alone, circled, and landed several times. He was a happy fellow. . . . Even though several biographies note that he earned only a private pilot's license, in fact, the Philippine air force, after reviewing his credentials, awarded him its own pilot rating and wings in 1945."

PLANNING FOR WAR

No graves, no markers in the ground to show or tell their tale.
Yet I still hear them in the wind, their voices never fail.
Blown to bits and pieces, scattered in the skies.
They tell me please do not forget, we live beyond your eyes.
And yes they do, I hear their call, their voices strong and clear.
Each one is burned upon my soul forever year to year.
The debt we owe to all of them, we never can repay.
But listen—cherish peace and love and live them every day.
—AN 8TH AIR FORCE SURVIVOR

As a young child living in Germany, at six years old, I very well remember December 1941. My mother loved to give dinner parties and one evening in mid December, just before Christmas, I was tasked to open the door whenever the bell rang, allowing guests to enter our apartment. I recall an older Luftwaffe officer arriving; he wore a pilot badge on his uniform identifying him as a WWI pilot. I knew all the badges and what they meant. After the guest were seated and dinner was served, I heard the pilot talking. Children in Germany were largely ignored at such semi-formal events, told to be quiet and stay out of sight. I stood by the dining room door listening. And the pilot was saying to a very quiet dinner table that we had just lost the war. Some laughed lightly, nervously, not loudly; everyone was very polite. Then he spoke of the America he knew and had traveled to more than once. An America with giant factories which in time would overwhelm anything Germany did. This totally unnecessary declaration of war against a sleeping giant, as he referred to America, will bring us down. In 1945 I would experience America's wrath as a ten-year-old when living in Berlin.

While the war was raging in Europe and North Africa, although the United States was not yet directly involved in it, plans were being

My mother Hedy, me, and my sister Ingrid in 1941 in front of our apartment house, in Sagan, Germany, not far from the small air base which in the future would hold over 10,000 Allied POWs in an adjacent camp known as Stalag Luft III. (Author)

made in the United States on how to fight a war that everyone on the senior US military staffs knew was coming. On June 20, 1941, the War Department established the Amy Air Forces under Major General Henry "Hap" Arnold. Arnold became the commanding general of the Army Air Forces on March 9, 1942, the only five-star general the air service ever had. The pre-WWII Air Corps officer corps was small enough that most everyone knew each other. Lieutenant Colonel Spaatz at Langley Field of course knew 2nd Lieutenant Harold Watson, one of his B-17 pilots. Spaatz also knew Watson was an engineer by education, and it was no accident that Watson, once war came, was assigned to an aircraft engine plant to assure a smooth flow of engines to aircraft assembly plants. It would have been a waste to put him in the cockpit of a B-17 as Watson wanted. To Hal Watson's surprise, once his time at the Cincinnati engine plant was up, he was sent to Michigan State to get a master's degree in aeronautics, soon to be referred to as aeronautical engineering, the same place where Kelly Johnson got his education. The day came when Watson received the assignment he so desperately wanted— Europe. This assignment was of course no accident either. General Spaatz, like Generals Arnold and Marshall, kept track of their "race horses" and made sure they ended up in the right places when the time came. Spaatz, by now a four-star general who ran the air war in Europe, had his eyes on young Watson since his B-17 bomber days at Langley and wanted him to be the man to lead an effort to find and bring home the German jets and anything else deemed of value. Spaatz only once met with Watson over a cup of coffee at his headquarters in Paris, laying out what he wanted him to do. After that he let Watson do his thing. Watson of course ended up leading Operation Lusty, the code name for the recovery of German Luft-waffe science and technology.

Organizational structure was important as well, and it was a step which in time would lead to an autonomous air service, rather than as a branch of the United States Army. (That step would happen in September 1947, only six years later.) Production of war material, especially aircraft, was already increasing rapidly. What was needed was a plan for how to use the available resources if and when we went to war. That step was formally taken on August 4, 1941, to project the aircraft needed to defeat Germany. The plan was called Air War Plan Directive 1, or AWPD-1. Members of the planning team included Major Haywood "Possum" Hansell Jr., Major Laurence S. Kuter, Lieutenant Colonel Harold L. George, and Lieutenant Colonel Kenneth N. Walker. All would shortly be generals commanding combat units. AWPD-1 was followed by AWPD-42, a closely held production plan for 1943, to attain air supremacy. It was approved by President Roosevelt. Both of these plans were requirement plans, not employment or operational plans.

What was needed was an employment plan for the bomber forces at hand to destroy the German war industry. The target list was adopted from an earlier British plan that listed the following industries in order of priority:

1. German aircraft production
2. Ball bearings
3. Petroleum

The list went down to number 19—anti-tank machinery and anti-aircraft machinery. The initial focus of the upcoming bomber campaign would be the first two categories. In time it changed to category number 3—petroleum, which effectively would bring the German army and air force to their knees. The weakest link in the German wartime industry proved not to be ball bearings, which were obtainable from Sweden, or aircraft production—according to the *United States Strategic Bombing Survey* in 1944 German industry built 39,807 aircraft of all types—but fuel to power their aircraft, tanks, and trucks. As a child I witnessed the effectiveness of that campaign. Trucks were carrying charcoal burners on their backs to power their engines—not a very efficient or reliable source of power. In April 1945 my family was fleeing with a German army unit to reach American lines—a unit of over 100 horse-drawn wagons. Stephen E. Ambrose, who wrote the foreword to my autobiography, *German Boy*, refers to this episode in my life as "reminiscent of Napoleon retreating from Moscow." Even horses were in short supply—farmers were plowing their fields in 1944 with only one horse before the plow, rather than the customary two. The missing horses had been drafted by the army. In spite of massive German efforts to produce the needed fuel synthetically, it wasn't enough.

An interview I conducted for *The War of Our Childhood*, a collection of children's survival stories in WWII, deals with the effectiveness of Allied air attacks against Leuna, one of Germany's largest synthetic refineries. Recalled Wolf Staeglich, "I remember quite well the Allied air attacks against the nearby synthetic petroleum refinery at Leuna. It was a huge complex about twelve kilometers long and two kilometers deep, visible from my home. We experienced twenty-eight major air attacks against the refinery by my count, as well as uncountable minor air attacks and almost daily air raid alarms. The first attack came at night. The entire refinery complex was protected by hundreds of antiaircraft batteries. Not individual guns, but batteries. Each battery consisted of six to eight guns. During these night attacks British pathfinder aircraft preceded the bomber stream and would drop *Christmas trees* over the refinery, target markers, to indicate to the bombers where to drop their bombs. Frequently the *Christmas trees* drifted outside the target area, and most of the bombs missed. When we had a northwesterly wind these parachute borne flare devices drifted over our housing complex with the result that at least half of the bomb load intended for Leuna fell on us, the surrounding fields and forests.

"We civilians had two options. Either we went into the above-ground reinforced concrete bunker, or we went into our own cellars which had provisionally been equipped to serve as air raid shelters. Every night starting at about eight in the evening, my mother listened to the radio where they gave detailed reports on detected enemy aircraft formations, their estimated numbers and heading. From that information she deduced if an air attack was imminent for us. My mother always tried to let me sleep as long as possible. She believed strongly that children needed their sleep to grow up properly. Starting in late 1943 our nights were nearly always interrupted by the threat of air attack. From then on I don't think there was a night when I slept all the way through, waking at least once to the sound of sirens, antiaircraft guns, the drone of heavy bombers, or the rippling boom-boom of exploding bombs.

"Every night my mother had to make the decision if we should stay in the house or go to the bunker. It was a life-or-death decision. Since she tried to give me the opportunity to sleep as long as possible, the decision most frequently was to stay in our house and to go down into our less-secure shelter. My father, Felix, was a division chief at Leuna and responsible for repairs to the refinery complex after each air attack. He was seldom home. I recall him talking about the monumental repair task that he faced after a major raid. Within twenty-four hours after a raid they were operating again. That was his job, keeping the gasoline flowing. I often thought it was magic how my father did it, because I had seen the fires burning in the refinery and found it nearly impossible to believe that he could restore its operation within such a short period of time. But he did it. How did he do it? He had large numbers of Russian prisoners of war at his disposal who often had to risk their lives to work the magic to get the severely damaged refinery back into operation.

"Then the Americans began their daylight raids. When their huge bomber formations passed overhead everything on the ground vibrated—the glass in our windows, the vase on the table, the furniture in the room, the house. It was difficult to hear anything other than the drone of the hundreds of bomber engines overhead. One Sunday I ran up to the rail embankment behind our house after the all-clear was given. Below me I could see Leuna. Flames were shooting fifty meters into the air. It wasn't a good feeling I had watching the inferno, because I knew my father was right in the middle of it. After three or four hours the fires were out, and by the following day gasoline was again flowing into the storage tanks. It was an incredible achievement.

"By early 1945 the air raids by high flying bombers and *Tiefflieger* became more and more frequent and occurred at all hours of the day and night. I saw what happened to Allied air crews when they were shot down. Farmers often reacted brutally toward downed airmen. One day I saw an aircrew abandon its bomber, six or eight parachutes. They came down not far from us in the fields. I saw farmers heading toward their landing sites with pitchforks, or anything usable as a weapon they had been able to lay their hands on. At the last moment German military police arrived and kept the irate farmers at bay with their submachine guns. Often there was no military police to save the unlucky flyers. War, I came to understand, awakens feelings in people which are at times uncontrollable."

★★★

The United States Strategic Bombing Survey (European War) shows the debilitating effect of American bombing on the German aviation gasoline supply. While in January 1944 production capacity was considered at 100 percent, that capacity declined to a catastrophic 29 percent by November 1944 and to nearly zero percent by March 1945.

The nascent American aircraft industry in 1940 consisted of twelve major companies and many smaller plants, including Douglas, Boe-

What remained of Germany when the war came to its final end. (Author)

ing, North American, Lockheed, Curtiss, Martin, Grumman, Chance Vought, Bell, and so on. Their combined output in 1939 of all types was 2,141 aircraft. The German invasion of Poland in late 1939, and the subsequent declaration of war by France and England, was a game changer and industry managers responded accordingly. Military production plans such as AWPD-1 provided the necessary guidance and led to the rapid expansion of design and production efforts to satisfy military needs, which led to an output of 96,318 aircraft in 1944.

While American wartime production ramped up to meet the needs of the combatant forces and our Allies, the men who had made up the Air Corps in the lean years of the 1930s suddenly found themselves rapidly elevated to higher positions of responsibility and leading America's war against its rapacious enemies. An extraordinary event happened in September 1939, that fateful month when Hitler's armies invaded Poland. The event looked ordinary enough, but would shape the future war in many ways. General George C. Marshall was sworn in as Chief of Staff of the United States Army—an extraordinary leader who arrived just at the right time, like Churchill did for the British in 1940. Marshall succeeded General

Malin Craig, who had succeeded General Douglas MacArthur, who had assumed a post in the Philippines to establish an army and get the country ready for independence, slated for 1946. Major Dwight D. Eisenhower served under MacArthur from 1935 until 1939. MacArthur was not an easy man to work for, and for Eisenhower to hold this position for four years said a lot about the man, his ability to cope and to deal with controversy and egos.

Marshall saw two immediate problems once he took office; one was training of the existing forces and the other was leadership. He realized that equipment does not an army make, and he suffered the same problem President Lincoln had faced at the beginning of the civil war—aging colonels and generals not up to the task. So, soon after taking over Army command, writes Forrest C. Pogue in *George C. Marshall, Ordeal and Hope 1939–1942*, "It was Marshall's belief that one could best judge the preparation of men for battle by testing them in prearranged maneuvers. Most civilians failed to agree. They saw them as confused and expensive affairs. . . . The General talked with one senator who objected to the money that was being spent on maneuvers. The Senator was particularly upset because the troops had made numerous mistakes, and he asked why maneuvers were being held with so many errors. The Chief of Staff replied, 'My God, senator, that's the reason I do it. I want the mistake down in Louisiana, not over in Europe, and the only way to do this thing is to try it out, and if it doesn't work, find out what we need to make it work.'"

Maneuvers of the scope held in 1939 had never been done before. But 1939 was only a rehearsal for the maneuver to follow in September 1941, held in Texas and Louisiana. "An armored corps was committed in the most extensive use of tanks ever seen in the United States," writes Pogue, "parachute troops were used in exercises for the first time; and more than 1,000 planes saw action. . . . General Marshall's attention was focused on the brilliant planning of the Third Army Chief of Staff, resourceful Colonel Dwight D. Eisenhower, and the slashing attacks of the 2nd Armored Division Commander, Major General George S. Patton. . . . For his outstanding performance in the maneuvers the colonel was to be promoted to brigadier general before the end of September."

Marshall was rumored to have carried a Little Black Book in which he recorded the names of officers who had made a positive impression on him. Historians disagree if there really was such a book; however, in one way or another, General Marshall kept track of his "race horses." Among them in 1941 was rumored to be, according to Pogue, "Bradley, Patton, Eichelberger, Hodges, Collins and Eisenhower." On the Air Corps side, "Spaatz, Vandenberg, Kuter" and others. "I tried to give Arnold all the power I could," said General Marshall in 1957. "I tried to make him as nearly as I could Chief of Staff of the Air without any restraint although he was very subordinate. . . . My main difficulties came from the fact that he had a very immature staff," not immature in years, but experience. "Antique staff officers or passe airmen—passe flyers, I guess—because they were not trained." Arnold relied on the men he respected and had worked with for years, such as Eaker and Spaatz. In spite of much opposition on the congressional side, both Marshall and Arnold got what they wanted—to have younger, experienced men in charge of the combat arms. So with great diligence General Marshall had solved both of his major problems—adequate combat training for his troops and putting the right people in charge, like young Patton and Eisenhower. They were men who could fight a war if it came.

War came soon enough. With the United States forced into war on December 7, 1941, Marshall's faith in Arnold paid off in spades. The 8th Air Force was activated in Savannah, Georgia, on January 28, 1942, and by that June the 8th headquarters bedded down in a leafy London suburb by the name of Bushy Park. In 1955, as an airman, I would serve in the same barracks in Bushy Park once occupied by the 8th Air Force and Eisenhower's staff. The flow of American air power to England had begun. On February 23, Major General Eaker took command of the 8th Bomber Command, part of the 8th Air Force, and on December 1, 1942, he assumed command of the 8th Air Force with General Spaatz's departure for the Mediterranean, where he took command of the Allied Air Forces, American and British, the 12th and 15th Air Force. Within months after Pearl Harbor the United States was deeply involved in the war no one wanted. Initially, the brunt of the air war in North Africa was borne by P-40s and Spitfires. They were soon augmented by three fighter groups—-the 1st,

14th, and 82nd—flying P-38 Lightnings. The 1st and 14th groups had barely settled down at their home stations in England, still getting up to speed in their new aircraft, and off they went to the sun and sand of North Africa. North Africa was an excellent environment for the P-38 to hold its own. The temperatures were mild compared to central Europe, the humidity low and counter-air and air-to-ground operations were what this airplane seemed to be made for, not high-altitude bomber escort.

On April 18, 1942, a lieutenant colonel by the name of James H. Doolittle would lead sixteen B-25 bombers, launched from the aircraft carrier *Hornet*, to bomb Tokyo and other war production centers in Japan. The Empire of the Rising Sun was put on notice of things to come. Only four months after the attack on Pearl Harbor, Doolittle's Raiders entered their names into the history books. Doolittle was not one of the chosen boys, did not attend "the Point"; he sort of entered the stage on his own terms. Flying was his thing. Not just boring holes in the sky, but pioneering instrument flying—never done before. When the chance came to take the war to Japan with sixteen B-25 bombers, Jimmy said he would do it. And he did—pulling our nation out of depression and delivering hope, hope which would lead to ultimate victory. Only eleven months after Pearl Harbor, American and British troops landed in North Africa to take on the vaunted Afrika Korps. It is important to understand how quickly, we as a nation, responded and put the aggressors on the defensive. Advanced planning and good leadership had everything to do with it.

One man who was to play a key role in the air war over Europe was not in Marshall's Little Black Book, nor was he a West Point graduate. Instead he came from Nome, Alaska, and graduated in 1922 from the University of California, at Berkeley, with a Bachelor of Arts. In between graduating from high school and obtaining his college degree in 1922, World War I broke out, and James Harold Doolittle, better known as Jimmy, became a pilot and served in several Aero Squadrons here in the United States. On July 1, 1920, at age twenty-four, he was commissioned a first lieutenant in the regular army. Flying had become young Doolittle's obsession. The Army Air Corps sent him to various schools, culminating with a

The USS *Hornet* in April 1942 ready to pass under the Golden Gate Bridge in San Francisco, with sixteen B-25 Mitchell bombers on its deck. (Pritzker Military Library)

doctorate in aeronautical engineering from the Massachusetts Institute of Technology in 1925. Not one to sit on his laurels, Jimmy
pioneered "blind flying," instrument flying, and in recognition was
awarded the prestigious Harmon trophy. Come January 1942, Jimmy
was assigned to Army Air Forces Headquarters in Washington, DC.
General Arnold recognized talent when he saw it and tasked the
newly promoted Lieutenant Colonel to come up with a plan to carry
the air war to Japan. Doolittle did that and once he presented his
plan, Arnold approved it, as well as Lieutenant Colonel Doolittle's
request to lead sixteen B-25s against targets in Japan.

Doolittle survived the raid against Japan, a huge morale booster
for the United States, was promoted to brigadier general a day after
the attack, skipping the rank of colonel, and was then assigned to
the European Theater of Operations, where he commanded first
the 12th Air Force in North Africa, then took command of the 15th
Air Force, and finally in January 1944, now a lieutenant (three star)
general, he became the commander of the 8th Air Force, relieving
General Ira C. Eaker. By this time Tooey Spaatz had moved from the
Mediterranean back to England, been promoted to three-star level,
and appointed in November 1943 as commander of the United States
Strategic Air Forces, USSTAF, in Europe—the future USAFE, that I
served in, after serving in a war many years in the future, Vietnam.

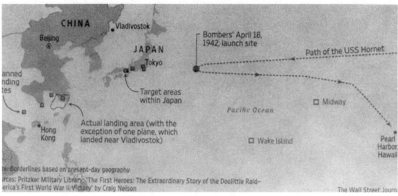

The *Hornet's* route, launch site, and targets. (Source as shown on picture)

Spaatz would change targeting, away from hardware to petroleum; Doolittle, as 8th Air Force commander, would change fighter tactics and by doing so destroy what remained of the once mighty Luftwaffe.

Doolittle's raid on Tokyo on April 18, 1942, took place as the Battle of the Coral Sea had begun. President Roosevelt was kept informed by General Marshall. On May 12, 1942, Marshall wrote a memorandum to General Arnold with the following instructions: "Have one of your people draft what you think should be the citation for a Medal of Honor for Doolittle. It should be ready at the time of his return, having had prior approval by the President. It will be necessary to keep this citation secret for a long time. However, the fact of the award of the Medal of Honor should be made public the day it becomes known that Doolittle is in town. I wish to arrange the affair so that he is kept under cover until received by the President and decorated." On May 19, 1942, President Roosevelt presented the medal to Doolittle in a surprise ceremony.

Although today we view Doolittle's daring raid as a shift in momentum in the war in the Pacific, at the time there was the usual amount of criticism. A Philadelphia manufacturer by the name of William Harm wrote to General Marshall on October 23, 1942, about the "shock a group of his peers had had upon hearing a respected speaker at a luncheon vigorously criticize the government for lying about the results of Doolittle's raid, which the speaker asserted was one of the war's greatest strategic mistakes and an ineffective,

President Franklin D. Roosevelt awarding the Medal of Honor to newly promoted Brigadier General James "Jimmy" H. Doolittle. Left to right: General Hap Arnold, Josephine "Joe" Doolittle, Jimmy Doolittle, and General George Marshall. (From the Jonna Doolittle Hoppes Collection)

politically motivated gesture." General Marshall responded thus on November 4, 1942:

> Dear Mr. Harm: I have read your letter concerning the criticism you have heard of the strategy of the Tokyo raid. I cannot agree with the view that the raid was a strategic mistake or that it was ineffective. As a matter of fact the information received by the War Department indicates that the raid was successful far beyond our most optimistic hopes. It did damage out of all proportion to the number of planes employed, created a diversion at an important moment and gave us most valuable technical information and experience. The public

confusion comes out of the fact that no one talking about the matter knows the details. In order to protect our own people and to keep the Japanese in a disturbed state requiring activity and protection on their part, it was important that we did not make public the actual details of how the raid was mounted and the fact that the planes could not immediately be operated again from China against Japan. Further, we were not going to tell the Japanese to go and look in one of their controlled areas in China to find a crew of our men who, if not already apprehended, were undoubtedly trying to work their way into Chinese-controlled territory.

Confidentially, the fact of the matter was that the planes arrived in China in the middle of the night in a very heavy storm, instead of in the morning and we hoped in fair weather. This was due to the fact that they had to take off much farther at sea than was intended and this in turn was due to the fact that the Naval escort had been sighted by the Japanese. With the primitive set-up of the Chinese fields, the darkness, and the storm, it was not possible to land the planes. Now if we never attempted anything because we might have bad weather, we might have enemy interference, we might have any of the this or thats that are the difficulties of any military operation, we would do nothing anywhere and would quickly be destroyed.

Again the trouble is that we have only reached a position in this war, on the part of most of the people, of abstract debate where they are insisting on information for their satisfaction which imperils the lives of young American soldiers and sailors and would inevitably lead to the failure of our operations. In time, as the fighting becomes heavier, people will realize that we cannot have general publicity on our side and complete secrecy on the enemy's side and hope to succeed or to protect the lives of our young men.

Faithfully yours, G. C. Marshall.

The impact of the Doolittle raid both on the Japanese and at home was not necessarily perceived the same way by everyone, but it was not lost on our senior leadership, both military and civilian.

GOING TO WAR

Mach 1 is the speed at which sound travels through the air. On an average day at sea level, the speed of sound, or Mach 1.0, is about 760 miles an hour. At higher, colder altitudes on the same day, it is less. For example, at 35,000 feet it might be only 660 miles an hour.

—A. SCOTT CROSSFIELD

War is frequently described in impersonal statistics such as numbers, dates, and associated events. Actually, war is very personal to everyone involved, from the pilot flying an aircraft to those below, often civilians. As a child of ten I lived in Berlin and remember the terror that air raids induced in me sitting in a basement waiting to die. I had no personal animosity against those dropping the bombs, after all I knew none of them and knew nothing about why all this was happening. I just knew one day I was going to die. I would sit next to my mom and close my eyes. She thought I was going to sleep. Actually, I was escaping into another world. My favorite books were about American Indians, books written by Karl May and James Fenimore Cooper. I loved *The Last of the Mohicans,* and while the raid was going on, that's where I went—to be with them, with the Mohicans. When the raid was over, my mother would tap me on the shoulder and say, "Wake up, Wolfgang. Time to go upstairs." She never knew how I managed to keep my sanity.

Some years later I interviewed Hans Herzmann who lived in Remagen as a child. He shared with me the experience of one day in 1945 that changed his life. "On March 2, 1945, my grandparents' house was destroyed by a single bomb," he told me. "The bomb crashed through the roof of the house and exploded in the cellar. Nine people were in the adjacent air raid shelter. Three survived. My mother died that day, as well as her sister and the two twins, Christa and Rolf, who were not quite two years old yet, as well as

An 8th Photo Reconnaissance Squadron, the Eight Ballers, F-5E taking off from a field in the Philippines. The 8th Squadron flew for the 5th Air Force in the Pacific. (Barney Dobbs)

my grandmother and my father's sister. I was only seven then. At the time of the attack I was very close to my grandparents' house helping in the construction of an air raid shelter. I didn't like going into a cellar. I was deeply afraid of being buried alive. I saw the aircraft that dropped the bomb. It was an American double-rump P-38 Lightning. The P-38 was being pursued by two German fighters, and I could imagine that the American pilot released the bomb as an emergency measure to escape his pursuers." I have no idea if the P-38 pilot managed to escape, nor did the pilot know anything about the damage his bomb had done. Such is war—very personal, but impersonal at the same time.

In addition to the P-38 fighter versions, two photo reconnaissance types were built, the F-4 and F-5. Fighters still carried the P designation for Pursuit, a World War I term, and reconnaissance aircraft had the prefix F, for Photo. While the P-38 fighter version had its issues in Europe, the photo reconnaissance versions, no matter where employed, were highly successful aircraft, and one of my close friends, Barney Dobbs, flew them in the Pacific. His story is in a later chapter.

Robert F. Dorr, a prolific writer and fellow book-signer at the National Air and Space Museum's Udvar Hazy Center in Chantilly, Virginia, died on June 12, 2016, aged seventy-six. Bob had an informed opinion on anything having to do with airplanes, so it is no surprise that he took a close look at the P-38. Like most of us, he loved the airplane—but it had its issues and a relatively steep learning curve for its would-be flyers. Bob Dorr wrote a seminal article on the P-38 just before he died, which was not published/aired on the *History Net* until the following year. In tribute to him I will use his commentary to address the P-38's issues, and there were many. The P-38 had its heyday in the Pacific, and did all right in North Africa, but over the continent, in Bob's words, "it flunked."

Lloyd Wenzel and Robin Olds, both Lightning pilots in Europe, were not quite as harsh as Bob Dorr in their assessment of the P-38, yet they agreed with him—the P-38 was not an easy plane to fly. Lloyd Wenzel ended up flying in the 474th Fighter Group. It was the only group to move with its P-38s to the continent, and to keep its airplanes until war's end. Other fighter groups converted either to the P-47 or the P-51, and their P-38s were shipped to the Pacific. Recalled Wenzel for me when I interviewed him: "I first flew the PT-17, a Boeing biplane, then the BT-13, known as the Vibrator for all the noises it made. Next came the AT-9, a twin-engine high perfor-mance aircraft, and then the RP-322. The RP-322 was a twin-engine P-38 ordered by the British before the start of Lend-Lease in early 1941. I got about ten hours in that airplane. After I was awarded my pilot wings I was assigned to a P-38 RTU in California. I found the airplane to be a high-performance beast and if you didn't pay attention it would kill you quicker than the Germans could." Wrote Robin Olds in his book *Fighter Pilot*, he had just racked up two kills in the P-38, shooting down two Fw 190s at low level: "I loved the P-38, but I got those kills in spite of the airplane, not because of it." Wenzel's and Olds's experiences sort of summarized how pilots felt about the airplane—ambivalent. One thing everyone loved about the P-38 was its firepower—a 20mm cannon and four 50 caliber machine guns—fired straight ahead, no convergence zone, as for wing-mounted guns. It gave the aircraft a greater reach than that of other fighters with wing-mounted guns.

"Struggling to keep the air campaign over Europe alive," wrote Bob Dorr in his assessment of the P-38 as a bomber escort, "and in the

TO HONOR THOSE WHO SERVED WITH

55TH FIGHTER GROUP

NUTHAMPSTEAD · WORMINGFORD
1943 – 1945

FIRST LONG RANGE FIGHTERS IN EUROPE

FIRST FIGHTER GROUP OVER BERLIN

TWO DISTINGUISHED UNIT CITATIONS

Plaque honoring the 55th Fighter Group located at the 8th Air Force Museum in Pooler, Georgia. (Author)

face of disastrous bomber losses, the U.S. Army Air Corps rushed two P-38 combat groups to England, the 20th and the 55th. On October 15, 1943, the 55th Fighter Group became the first to conduct operations." They soon mixed it up with Me 109s and Fw 190s and scored their first victories. However, one of the pilots said, the Luftwaffe was facing us head on and we were not winning. "The P-38 performed usefully but suffered from a number of problems. Its Allison engines consistently threw rods, swallowed valves and fouled plugs, while their inter-coolers often ruptured under sustained high boost, and turbo-charger regulators froze, sometimes causing catastrophic failures. The P-38's General Electric turbo-superchargers sometimes got stuck in over-boosted or under-boosted mode. This occurred mainly when the fighter was flown in the freezing cold at altitudes approaching 30,000 feet," the altitude where the bombers flew, and to fly effective escort the fighters had to be up there with them.

Colonel Hal Watson, who in 1945 led the team that recovered German jet aircraft as the war was coming to its end, recalls his experience flying the P-38, and the issues he faced as someone who had never even seen a P-38 before. Watson graduated from Rensselaer Polytechnic Institute in Troy, New York, with a BS in electrical engineering. He went to work for Pratt & Whitney Aircraft Corporation, then decided to join the Army Air Corps, Pratt & Whitney's major customer.

Watson went through pilot training with guys like Hubert "Hub" Zemke and Philip Cochran. Zemke in the war to come would lead the 56th Fighter Group, the Wolf Pack, flying the P-47 and the P-38 as well, as commander of a down-and-out fighter group, the 479th, and spent the final days of the war in Stalag Luft I at Barth, Germany, alongside Bob Hoover and Gabby Gabreski, who had preceded him. Philip Cochran would organize the 1st Air Commando Group in 1943 and lead it into Burma against the Japanese. Many of Watson's classmates would rise to fame and general officer rank, including Watson, in a war that would define their generation. Hal Watson went through pilot training at Randolph Field in San Antonio, Texas. At Randolph, Watson's flight commander was a lieutenant by the name of Curtis E. LeMay, who in time would rise to four-star rank and command and build America's strategic air forces during the Cold War years. Reporting to LeMay, Hal Watson said, "Now look, I'm not in here for the long haul. I'll serve out my time, but I have a job waiting for me at Pratt & Whitney."

"It won't do you any good, Watson," LeMay replied caustically.

"What do you mean, it won't do me any good? I serve my time. I ought to be able to get out when my time is up."

"Do you know what's going on in Europe right now?" LeMay asked. "If you get out, we'll have to call you right back." Watson didn't realize it at the time, but he was in for the long haul.

After pilot training Hal was assigned to Langley Field, where the bombers were stationed at the time, and his commander was a lieutenant colonel by the name of Carl "Tooey" Spaatz, a World War I fighter pilot, and one of the crew that flew the *Question Mark* in 1929, a Fokker trimotor, to demonstrate aerial refueling. Ira C. Eaker and Elwood R. Quesada were on the *Question Mark* as well. Spaatz was a West Pointer and a close friend of Hap Arnold. The Air Corps was a small adjunct of the United States Army, and nearly everybody knew each other, so future assignments frequently were based on these personal relationships. Hal and his fellow officers enjoyed the

Graduation picture of Watson's pilot training class before a P-12 fighter. Watson standing, 2nd from right, second row from top; Hub Zemke, standing, second row from bottom, 3rd from left; Phil Cochran, sitting, bottom row, 3rd from right. (Ruth Watson)

off-duty hospitality of Ruth and Carl Spaatz, when on weekends Ruth had them over for coffee and cake to meet some young ladies. Ruth was affectionately called "Mama Ruth" by the young lieutenants.

★★★

In 1939 Watson was assigned to the Power Plant Laboratory at Wright Field, the flight test center of the Army Air Corps. He quickly became friends with a flight scheduler getting him to fly newly ar-rived airplanes delivered by civilian contractors. "As a pilot you were expected to be able to fly anything and everything with a propeller at the front," Hal noted. He recalled being sent to the West Coast in March 1942 to pick up a P-38E Lightning fighter for testing at Wright Field. The E model was the first combat-ready variant with self-sealing fuel tanks armed with a 20mm cannon and four .50 caliber machine guns. Two hundred ten P-38Es were built and were the first to see combat in 1942 in the Aleutians. Once Watson got to the Lockheed plant at Long Beach, he asked who was going to check him out in the airplane. He had never even set eyes on a P-38 until he arrived at Lockheed. People looked at him skeptically and told him to go home if he didn't know how to fly the plane. Hal then ask a sergeant for help in getting into the aircraft; then he figured out how to take off and fly it. He landed in Tucson and El Paso to refuel. As he approached Dallas, one of the P-38's engines quit. He made a single-engine landing in this twin-boom aircraft, a type in which he had less than ten hours total flying time, all acquired on the current trip. His landing was, according to Hal Watson, uneventful. Meaning, that it wasn't pretty, but he didn't crash. He changed the fouled spark plugs in both engines and took off for Memphis, where he remained overnight. He flew on to Wright Field the following day. Watson was not only a superb pilot, but when it came to aircraft engines he knew them like the back of his hand and felt he could fix any problem. Fouled spark plugs, which could quickly turn a routine flight into a problem, was only one of the P-38's problems at the time.

A November 13, 1943, mission flown by the 8th Air Force against targets in the Bremen/Kiel area was "One Unlucky Day" for the newly arrived P-38s, according to Bob Dorr. It was a bad day for both the bombers and the accompanying P-38H fighters of the 55th Fighter Group based at Nuthampstead. The H-model the 55th was flying was an upgraded F/G model. All of the models of the P-38 reflected some improvements, often minor, which, if there had been enough time would have gone through flight test at Wright Field. However, this was wartime, and aircraft were shipped to fighter groups as they became available, and improvements were made on the production line resulting in another variant. Of 268 B-17 and B-24 bombers dispatched that day, 141 reached the target area. The majority of the non-effective bombers turned back because of weather. Of the total force of bombers launched sixteen were lost—two B-17s collided during assembly, one caught fire on climb out, two B-17s collided en route, and two B-24s collided during the bomb run. The remainder were lost to enemy action. The 55th Fighter Group launched forty-five aircraft, the longest escort mission flown to date by fighters of the 8th Air Force, according to the *Combat Chronology of the Army Air Forces in World War II*. Seven out of forty-five P-38s failed to return to base.

Writes Bob Dorr about this ill-fated raid, "At 26,000 feet over Germany, pilots shivered in bitterly cold cockpits, flying conditions were unusually bad. The 55th was heavily engaged near the target as they strove to defend the bombers." Seven P-38s were shot down by enemy fighters and another seven suffered battle damage, two of which were damaged severely enough to have them written off after landing. Dorr quotes 2nd Lt. Jim Kunkle: "The critical problem with us was we didn't have much heat in the cockpit. On high altitude missions it was very cold. And we didn't have the engine in front of us to help keep us warm. Bomber guys had those heated blue union suits that they wore but we tried heated clothing and it didn't work for us." The only source of heat in the cockpit was warm air ducted from the engines, and it was of little help. By the time the air reached the cockpit it had lost its heat. Lightning pilots suffered terribly. "Their hands and feet became numb with cold, and in some instances frost-bitten; not infrequently a pilot was so weakened by conditions that he had to be assisted out of the cockpit upon return."

A 20th Fighter Group Issue Summary of the P-38 states, "The aircraft lacked an effective heater and pilots returning from missions often had to be helped from the cockpit as they were so cold. The 20th Fighter Group commanding officer, Lieutenant Colonel Mark Hubbard, sent a strongly worded letter up the chain in March 1943 bitterly criticizing the P-38 as being unsuitable for the task it was being asked to carry out. Colonel Hubbard was shot down and taken POW days after sending this letter. The 20th Fighter Group struggled on slowly finding fixes to each issue as it appeared. However, when the group was able to operate at lower levels and against ground targets the aircraft came into its own. With its heavy armament the aircraft proved ideal for attacking ground targets."

Major General William Kepner, the commanding general of VIIIth Fighter Command, wondered why the P-38 wasn't producing the results everyone expected. Wrote Colonel Harold J. Rau of the 20th Fighter Group: "After flying the P-38 for a little over one hundred hours on combat missions it is my belief that the airplane, as it stands now, is too complicated for the 'average' pilot. I want to put strong emphasis on the word 'average,' taking full consideration just how little combat training our pilots have before going on operational status." Rau wrote that he was being asked to put kids fresh from flight school into P-38 cockpits and it wasn't working. Rau asked his boss to imagine "a pilot fresh out of flying school with about a total of twenty-five hours in a P-38, starting out on a combat mission." Rau's young pilot was on "auto lean and running on external tanks. His gun heater is off to relieve the load on the generator, which frequently gives out. His gun sight is off to save burning out the bulb. His combat switch may or may not be on. So, flying along in this condition," wrote Rau, "the kid suddenly gets bounced by German fighters. Now he wonders what to do next.

"He must turn, he must increase power and get rid of those external fuel tanks, and get on his main fuel tank. So, he reaches down and turns two stiff, difficult gas switches to main, turns on his drop tank switches, presses his release button, puts the mixture to auto rich, increases his RPM and manifold pressure, turns on his gun heater switch, turns on his combat switch—and he is ready to fight." Says Bob Dorr, "To future generations this would be called multi-tasking, and it was not what you wanted to be doing when Luftwaffe fighters were pouring down on you."

★★★

During advisory visits to his fighter group, Lockheed and Allison Aviation representatives asked for suggestions. Rau wrote that their number-one request was a unit power control, incorporating an automatic manifold pressure regulator, which would control power, RPM, and mixture by use of a single lever. Adds Bob Dorr, "He may not have known that P-51 pilots could perform all these functions with one hand, never possible in the P-38, even in later versions. Ergonomics was another issue, switches and levers being located in awkward positions. That was not a small thing given the need to wear gloves in the Lightning's frigid cockpit.

"Critics and champions of the P-38 alike," writes Dorr, "often failed to remark on the obvious—that it was a multi-engine aircraft while most fighters were single engine. A P-38 pilot usually got his training in two ways. The first was twin-engine advanced training in the Curtiss AT-9. After six hours of this the student received ten hours of AT-6 or AT-9 gunnery training." Another former P-38 pilot stated that "near the end of training in the AT-9, the usual practice was to give a student pilot a piggyback ride in a P-38 with a second seat, and then check him out in the RP-322. The P-38 did not have a two-seater version, but by removing the radio console behind the pilot's seat it was possible to squeeze in a second person."

Richard Kirkland, a young second lieutenant, found himself flying a P-38 Lightning in the Pacific, and soon was to discover the strengths and weaknesses of his airplane while coping with Japanese Zeros. He was assigned to the 49th Fighter Group based at a rudimentary air base at Dobudura, New Guinea. Here he was, a second lieutenant, outranked by every one of his fellow flyers who had lots of combat experience flying the P-38, which he of course hadn't. Writes Kirkland in *Tales of a War Pilot*: "I felt somewhat intimidated by first lieutenants who were experienced combat pilots. Two of my tent mates, with several victories to their credit, had both been shot down by Zeros on a single mission. I flew in the same squadron with the top American fighter ace, Major Richard I. Bong. He was modest and quiet outside the cockpit, but in the air he was fearless, aggressive and deadly. It was a shock for me flying combat missions with a famous aviator such as Charles A. Lindbergh, who was already a living legend." It was in many ways an unsettling environment for a young fighter pilot who still had to prove himself.

Continues Kirkland: "The Lockheed P-38 was one of the great fighters of World War II: it was fast, and had deadly firepower. But the cockpit was small and would not accommodate a pilot much taller than five feet nine, and I was six feet tall. I had wanted to fly the P-38 so badly that during the cadet physical exam I had managed to shrink down when they measured height. I paid for that little deception in spades. Then came the day when I finally tangled with a Zero. As we got near our target area, our squadron leader gave the signal to clear guns. That meant fire a short burst to make sure they worked, tighten up the formation, and sharpen the watch for enemy aircraft. I just completed the procedure when radio silence was broken with: Bogeys! Bogeys at 3 o'clock high. And an instant later: Drop tanks now. On the longer missions we always carried external fuel tanks, which we dropped off if we got into a fight.

"I saw my element leader's external tanks drop off, spewing fuel as they tumbled away. I quickly flipped the arming switches on mine and punched the salvo button. About a half second later, a stream of tracers arched across our flight path from a V of three Zeros that came screaming down through our formation. I followed my element leader into a steep left bank, just as both my engines quit. I had forgotten to switch the fuel selector from drop position to internal tanks. Although both Allison engines roared back to life quickly after I switched the fuel valve, one did a little sooner than the other, which caused an unequal surge of power—and now, among other things, I found myself flying upside down. I was agonizingly aware that my clumsy mistake caused me to break formation. I suddenly realized there was a Zero directly in front and slightly below me. There he was, with those huge red balls plainly visible on the top of his wings.

"I rammed the throttles to full power and dove after him. Within seconds his silhouette filled my gun sight, and I jammed down hard on both the 20-mm cannon and the .50 caliber machine gun firing buttons. My nostrils stung from the acrid smoke that always sifted into the P-38 cockpit, since the gun compartment was just forward in the pilot's gondola. I saw my tracers falling behind the Zero, so I pulled back on the yoke to gain some lead. But about that time I guess he saw me, because suddenly he reversed his direction into an incredibly tight left bank. I couldn't believe any aircraft could turn that quickly. I slammed into a left bank and pulled back on the yoke to stay with him, but all I succeeded in doing was pulling a solid black curtain down over my eyes. I shook my head violently, trying to fight off the blackout, as we had been taught in training. Then I remembered my element leader's caution: 'Don't try to turn with a Zero, whatever you do.' I slammed the yoke forward, which, in turn, slammed my head against the top of the canopy. Now I saw stars in my blackout. Anyway, with the G-forces relieved, my sight began to return.

"I glanced around, but the Zero was gone. I seemed to be all alone over Wewak, New Guinea. Until I realized that those red things flying by my canopy were 20–mm cannon shells made in Japan. I looked back, and sure enough, there he was. My element leader's words rang in my head: 'If you get one on your tail, dive away quickly, you can out dive a Zero.' I saw pieces of my airplane spewing off into space. I managed to put my rapidly deteriorating aircraft into a power dive

The War in Europe and North Africa. Source: Reporting WWII

at full throttle. And I discovered that it was true, the P-38 could out dive a Zero. But there was a complication, which I remembered when I saw the needle on my airspeed indicator spin past the number six, and the aircraft began to shake. 'The pilot should monitor airspeed closely in a power dive to prevent compressibility,' the folks at Lockheed had written in the flight manual.

"I jerked the throttles off and tried to pull back on the yoke. I might as well have been pulling on the Empire State Building, the yoke wouldn't budge. Then I remembered another little scrap of timely information: 'In compressibility use the trim tab.' The P-38 hadn't been designed to break the sound barrier, so when it approached

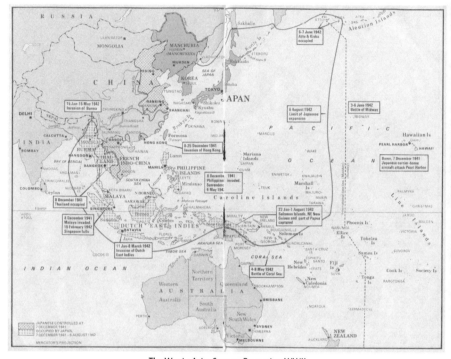

The War in Asia. Source: Reporting WWII

that speed, it went berserk. We called it compressibility. I guess that pulled me out of the dive, because the next thing I knew I was wandering around the skies over Wewak trying to find somebody to fly with. Then, loud and clear over the radio came, 'Kirkland, where the hell are you? Is that you trailing smoke from your left engine?' I glanced at my left engine. Yes, it was trailing smoke alright, a lot of smoke. Yes, sir, that's me. 'Well, you better shut it down and get your ass back in formation.'

"A lot of World War II pilots thought the twin-engine fighter was no match in combat for a single-engine fighter, because of less maneuverability. And to some degree that was true. But then no American fighter could out-turn the Zero anyway, so the P-38 lost nothing, and it was superior in other ways. For example, that day when I shut down my smoking engine, feathered the prop and got back in formation—I'd like to see a single engine fighter do that." Lieutenant Richard Kirkland, in one mission, experienced most of the pros and cons of the P-38. But his final comment revealed how the P-38 flyers felt about their aircraft flying over a huge ocean with little land to land on or bail out over.

The P-38, Dorr rightly observes, played an important role in every theater of war, but came into its own in the Pacific. There they fought in a warmer climate and at lower altitudes, and while some of their Japanese adversaries were seasoned pilots, few were as skilled as the typical Luftwaffe fighter pilot of December 1943.

MACH TUCK AND THE
GRAVEYARD DIVE

The speed of sound, or Mach 1, is named after Ernst Mach, a physicist who in 1887 photographed an object moving faster than the speed of sound. The first manned flight to equal or exceed the speed of sound was made by Chuck Yeager on October 14, 1947, flying the X-1 at Mach 1.06. Mach tuck—an uncommanded and possibly violent, nose down pitching motion at high subsonic speeds, possibly resulting in an unrecoverable graveyard dive.

—CAMBRIDGE AEROSPACE DICTIONARY

The Kelly Johnson–designed twin-tailed P-38 was powered by two Allison supercharged twelve cylinder V-1710 engines with an initial gross weight of 13,500 pounds, twice as heavy as most single-engine fighters of the time. Later versions such as the P-38L, of which 3,923 were built, came in with a gross weight of up to 18,000 pounds, depending on its mission. The aircraft could achieve a maximum level speed of 425 mph at an altitude of around 25,000 feet. It was the fastest operational airplane of its time, and in a dive it could quickly reach Critical Mach, loss of control, also called *Mach tuck.* As the pilot got his aircraft into a region near its critical Mach number, anywhere from Mach .68 to Mach .70, the control surfaces, flaps, ailerons, elevators, would no longer respond to his inputs, the aircraft would begin to shake violently, and he would find himself in an unrecoverable *graveyard dive.* This happened not only to the P-38 but to every fast mover from the Me 109 to the Fw 190 to the Me 262 to the P-51—if they got beyond that critical red line speed for their respective aircraft, usually in a dive when trying to evade a pursuing aircraft, they were "goners."

According to Robert Kempel, a senior aerospace engineer at Edwards Air Force Base, the U.S. Air Force Flight Test Center, it was virtually impossible to achieve a free-stream Mach number for propeller-driven or early turbojet aircraft. Loss of airplane trim, controllability, and structural failure was the usual outcome when flying beyond the aircraft's red line or critical Mach number. The highest verified Mach number achieved by a conventionally powered aircraft was 0.91 flown by a Spitfire at the Royal Air Force experimental facility at Farnborough, England. In that case the aircraft lost its propeller and portions of the engine cowling. The pilot was able to land the aircraft with the flight records. The Spitfire's Mach number was then lowered to 0.89, an amazing number for a piston-driven aircraft.

A German Me 262 pilot, *Faehnrich*/Cadet Hans Guido Mutke, for years claimed that he flew through the sound barrier in a high speed dive to assist a fellow flyer who was under attack by an American P-51. In the dive his engines flamed out and the aircraft suffered severe buffeting until he slowed down and was able to restart his engines. Mutke managed to land at Lager Lechfeld where he was undergoing jet training, but the aircraft was severely damaged. Mutke, throughout his life, maintained that he had flown through the sound barrier although there never was any proof that he did so. He did fly into that zone of high speed compressibility when approaching Mach 1.

It was not uncommon for pilots to believe they had flown through the sound barrier, although they never did. Colonel Harold "Hal" Austin, a personal friend, recalled when flying the RB-45C reconnaissance jet, "The day I took it up to 49,500 feet, when I pulled the power back, I was in a stall, or right between buffet and stall. It took me thirty minutes to get back to 40,000 feet. There was no way to slow that aircraft down. [The RB-45C did not have speed brakes.] We also pushed it through Mach 1 more than once. Our Wing, the 91st Strategic Reconnaissance Wing at Barksdale Air Force Base, Louisiana, lost eight airplanes in the first year of RB-45 operations. One of the first we lost, we think the guy went through the Mach with it—rough as hell going through, rougher coming back out. The one that crashed had the tail come off. He was southeast of Barksdale at 43,000 feet when it happened. That's the altitude where I pushed mine through, the only time I ever pushed it through the Mach. We lost other aircraft going through the Mach before anyone survived to tell us what happened. An aeronautical engineer finally explained to us that the rigid wing passed to the tail section the vibrations encountered going through the Mach. Unfortunately, the airplane wasn't designed to handle such stress. It was basically a World War II airplane powered by jet engines."

Although Hal Austin, a highly decorated reconnaissance pilot, believed he had gone through the Mach—he never did. It just felt like he did. Robert Kempel, a NASA flight research engineer at Edwards AFB wrote me after reading Colonel Austin's story in my book *I Always Wanted to Fly*. "I think Hal's comments were excellent. These are the first-hand accounts I really cherish! Hal wasn't alone in thinking he exceeded the sound barrier. I wasn't there when the first jets were knocking on the sonic wall. I appreciate hearing the pilot's accounts. Real history. The empennage of the B-45 may have been susceptible to tail flutter. This can be and has been a catastrophic event on many airplanes. I suspect that many 1930s race planes suffered this same fate. Sometimes airliners have a normal shock wave standing on their wing. If the sun angle is just right this shock wave is visible. Airliners continue to have swept wings so they can have a high critical Mach number, they want to fly fast and not use too much gas. The critical Mach number is the speed at which the Mach effects can or may be felt by buffet. At the critical Mach number the drag rises abruptly, so airliners fly just below it."

However, there is one airplane that beat the odds, the XF-88B, a weird looking aircraft with a turbo-prop engine in the nose and two J-34 jet engines with afterburners. John M. "Fitz" Fitzpatrick, an Edwards test pilot, was flying it at the McDonnell factory in St. Louis, Missouri, to determine its performance before flying the aircraft to Langley AFB where it was to undergo testing under the supervision of NACA, which was responsible for propeller development flights. So up he went. "I overflew the field slightly during the level flight acceleration, so as to aim at the field I rolled over and did a split-S. About the time I pulled through the vertical, a lot of things began to happen at once. The altimeter jumped, overheat lights came on for both engines and a fire light came on for the turboprop. I retarded both jets to idle, shut down the prop, extended the speed brakes and pulled out as hard as I could. As I came level at about 25,000 feet the propeller went to the feather position and acted like a canard, really wagging the aircraft. Even before I landed the tower operator informed me that I had definitely gone supersonic. Later the Mc-Donnell people said that they had over 3,000 claims submitted for damage caused by the sonic boom. All of which proves that you can really get supersonic behind a propeller."

The sound barrier with its associated turbulence and drag proved to be an enigma to all, pilots and engineers, until test data found in May 1945 at the German test center at Voelkenrode near Braunschweig, Germany, revealed how to get through it. I cover that aspect in a later chapter of this book.

In an excellent book by Warren M. Bodie entitled *The Lockheed P-38 Lightning: It Goes Like Hell*, he addresses the P-38's most significant problem—compressibility. He writes, "Back in 1937 Clarence 'Kelly' Johnson's report, endorsed by his immediate supervisor, Hal Hibbard, had been directed at Air Corps officials to warn that 'as airplane speeds and operating altitudes increase, consideration must be given to the effects of compressibility.' Army Air Corps engineering data of that era completely ignored compressibility effects, even after it was known that propellers were affected by compressibility. . . . The problem became very serious at 500 mph true air speed (TAS) and over." So it was recognized by the P-38 design team as a future issue to be dealt with. It came sooner than expected.

On November 4, 1941, Ralph Virden, one of Lockheed's best test pilots took up a YP-38 to run through a prescribed test routine including high speed dives. This was one of the thirteen test aircraft ordered by the Air Corps. "It was reported that the airplane was traveling in excess of 500 mph over the small town of Glendale," according to Robert Kempel, and "an eyewitness reported the airplane was in a 'screaming' dive when it broke apart and crashed into a private residence. Pilot Ralph Virden was killed. Kelly Johnson knew that the P-38 was capable of penetrating unknown aerodynamic realms at high speeds at altitude where theory was unknown—even the most knowledgeable aerodynamic scientists were baffled and called it *compressibility tuck* at a high Mach number." In a high speed dive, exceeding the aircraft's red line, the critical Mach number, the aircraft's tail section would shake violently and the nose would tuck under, ergo *Mach Tuck.* Once caught in such a dive, your "goose was cooked." You just became another unexplained statistic. To provide some form of method to slow the airplane's speed, according to Bob Kempel, Kelly Johnson's fix was to retrofit operational P-38s with underwing pilot operated dive flaps. These pilot-controlled flaps could be deployed to slow the airplane to a lower speed until the airplane became controllable again.

Jim Ashton was an aeronautical engineer, got his education at Purdue University, and worked for Lockheed on P-38s trying to fix the tail sections on Eddie Rickenbacker's 94th Fighter Squadron airplanes, known as the Hat in the Ring squadron. Ashton wrote a brief report, provided to me by his son Peter Ashton, dated March 1942, Long Beach, California. "I was a field engineer for Lockheed," Jim wrote, "assisting in the maintenance and supervising engineering modifications on P-38s of the 94th. We were losing P-38s in training and operations unexplainably. They were going into dives and not pulling out. All P-38s in the world were suddenly grounded; at least the ones in Long Beach were. Lockheed sent me kits to check and reset the up elevator limits on the controls. It included drawings to set the travel and castellated nuts and cap screws that could be safety wired. I was provided six men and a tracked vehicle with a generator for light and electricity, tools, and air compressor. We never stopped or slept until we had modified all the planes. While I was there Eddie Rickenbacker came for a visit, and I was there at the formal military formation honoring him."

Not only was the 94th Fighter Squadron experiencing unexplainable crashes as early as 1942, but by the time the 20th Fighter Group deployed to England the problem hadn't been resolved. One fatal crash and two close calls made everyone uneasy about flying this airplane. The 20th Fighter Group was one of the first P-38 groups to arrive in England, along with the 55th Fighter Group. These mysterious crashes spooked the 20th flyers and everyone else who was flying the P-38. Lockheed decided to send its very experienced test pilot, Tony LeVier, to RAF Kings Cliff where the 20th group was based, to calm down the situation. The P-38 was beginning to acquire a reputation, and it wasn't all good. By this time Lockheed's Kelly Johnson had developed new dive flaps for the Lightning, and the airplane LeVier took to England was so equipped; however, the planes the 20th and 55th were flying were not.

To quote a P-38 Association Museum release, "In the early days of the P-38, LeVier received an emergency summons to get to England. Too many pilots were crashing in P-38s in emergency situations due to a lack of training on the new aircraft. Apparently the counter-rotating props, and the necessity to fly with one prop feathered was an adjustment for which the pilots had been ill-prepared. LeVier didn't blame the pilots, but the training. He proceeded to explain the pros and cons of the 38 and demonstrated various maneuvers, such as recovering from a dive and taking control with one engine feathered. The pilots of the 20th were not overly impressed with his lecture. LeVier proceeded to take up his P-38, equipped with new dive flaps. At 25,000 feet LeVier dove straight down, and the pilots rushed out to see what they thought would be a crash. LeVier easily pulled out without any problems, and for extra emphasis, he performed several low level one-engine rolls. The P-38s in the ETO, European Theater of Operations, were not equipped with this flap, but he was attempting to showcase the new features which would be arriving soon. The pilots were shown that they would be able to pursue a German fighter diving out of trouble."

Unfortunately a C-54 carrying dive-flap modification kits was misidentified by a British fighter pilot as a German Focke Wulf 200 Condor weather reconnaissance aircraft, and unceremoniously shot down. Nothing is easy in war. So the P-38s deployed in the ETO and later in North Africa had to wait a little longer to get this safety fix for their airplanes. P-38s arrived in Europe in mid-1942 and soon found themselves sent to North Africa in support of Operation Torch, the code name for the landing of American and British forces in North Africa.

The P-38 Lightning was the first combat aircraft to reveal the dangers of high speed flight when approaching what was referred to as the sound barrier. Hal Watson was sent by the Air Corps to the University of Michigan at Ann Arbor to get his master's degree in aeronautical engineering, the same place Kelly Johnson went to earn his degree in aeronautics. Watson's thesis was entitled *Why Man Will Never Break the Sound Barrier.* No one had any idea how that was going to come about. However, airplanes were getting faster and faster and began to tangle with what jargon referred to as compressibility tuck due to increasing Mach number and loss of control. Robert W. Kempel pointed out to me examples of this phenomenon as experienced by Germany's jet and research aircraft.

On October 2, 1941, Heini Dittmar was test flying an Me 163 Komet. Per his flight plan he was to exceed the "magical" 1,000 km/hr (621 mph) indicated airspeed in his Me 163 V1, the first prototype. He described his experience in the German periodical *Flug Review*, of November 1999: "When I approached the measured distance, the speedometer indicated 910, then 950, 970, and finally 980 kilometers per hour. This time the engine did not cut out on me. When I looked at the instruments again, I had gone over the 1,000 kilometer mark, but the airspeed indicator was unstable, the elevator started to vibrate and at the same time the aircraft plummeted out of the sky, gathering speed. I could not do anything. I immediately turned off the engine and was certain that the end was near, when I suddenly felt the steering responding and managed to get the Me 163 out of her nose dive relatively easily. Nothing else happened. The so-called Mach phenomena, compressibility, which I was the first pilot to ever experience, was nothing else than the knocking at the sound barrier with an aircraft which had not been designed to break through the barrier."

Adam Makos, in his book *A Higher Call*, tells the story of Franz Stigler, no longer flying an Me 109 but an Me 262 jet with JV 44, based at Munich-Riem airport. JV 44 was a jet squadron formed by Adolf Galland after he was fired as Germany's fighter boss by Hermann Goering. On April 5, 1945, the war is nearly over, Franz was flying White 3 and experienced and survived the effects of Mach tuck and the graveyard dive. The full story starts on page 303 of *A Higher Call* and covers four pages and is worth your read. Here is an abbreviated excerpt when Franz knew he was in trouble: "White 3 raced faster and faster toward a layer of clouds at twenty-thousand feet. Franz's eyes watered. His airspeed indicator wound past the 600 mph mark. The jet's red line was painted on the dial at the 625 mph mark. When the needle reached that point, the jet's controls would freeze and the craft could potentially break apart. He tried to

An Me 163B Komet on display at Freeman Field, Indiana, a sub-base in 1945 to Wright Field in Ohio. Many of the aircraft returned from Germany were displayed at Freeman Field at an open house. Wright Field was so crowded with aircraft, it just couldn't accommodate many of the German aircraft brought back by Colonel Watson and his crew. An FE catalogue number was assigned to all German captures. This particular aircraft is now on display at the National Air and Space Museum's Udvar Hazy Center in Chantilly, Virginia. (Fred McIntosh)

pull up, but the flight stick was frozen, locked by an 'evil spell.' The speedometer needle quivered at the 625 mph mark. He had flown past the plane's limits. He had forgotten a rule of the 262, to never dive in a jet so fast it needed no help from gravity. Now *White 3* was frozen in a death dive. Franz struggled to pull the control stick, but it felt as unbending as an iron bar. Pinned to his seat, Franz knew he could not bail out. He felt himself grow cold as the thought struck him—*I just killed myself.*

Franz did eventually regain control of his aircraft, as he got into denser air, leveling out, and pulling up in front of an astonished group of farm workers, setting their hay on fire with his jet exhaust as he climbed back to safety. That was a close call. I am not an aeronautical engineer but according to my friend Bob Kempel, when Franz went through the critical Mach, compressibility set in and of course resulted in a loss of control. The tailplane's trailing edge elevator was frozen in place and could not be moved by the pilot due to the local

An Arado 234 reconnaissance bomber of KG 76 at Grove airfield, Denmark. (Roy Brown)

high Mach number, the jargon was *Shock-stall*. Once the 262's speed and Mach number were reduced, the pilot's control was returned to normal and recovery was then effected. Franz lived through an ordeal and survived to tell about it. Mach 1, or the speed of sound, varies and decreases with altitude and lower temperature.

The other German jet to become operational in 1944 was the Arado 234B reconnaissance aircraft, also capable of serving in the capacity of a bomber. Wrote Captain Eric "Winkle" Brown, "When I first saw my first Arado at the Danish airfield of Grove I was immediately impressed by its aesthetically attractive contours. This airplane looked right and in my experience this was always a good omen with regard to flying qualities. With its slender shoulder-mounted wing, slim underslung engine nacelles and smooth fuselage profile, it exemplified careful aerodynamic design." By October 1944, KG 76 had fifty-seven Arados operational, yet its pilots were still learning to understand the aircraft. Most transitioned straight from their previous assignments in Ju 88s, or the dated Ju 87 Stuka dive-bomber, into the Arado 234B. The sound barrier, now familiar to every aviation buff since chuck Yeager broke it in October 1947, was a totally unknown phenomenon to the flyers of KG 76, who manned a new jet which in a dive could quickly find itself entering a zone of high compressibility where drag suddenly increased exponentially and lift faltered. Many a Me 109 or Mosquito pilot, diving to escape a pursuing foe, had paid the price as his aircraft began to disintegrate in a downward dive while entering the region of high drag and low lift when approaching Mach 1. Pressure and consequently drag built up on the edge of a straight wing as it approached Mach 1, quickly destabilizing the aircraft and frequently causing structural failure. Germany's engineers, operating the most advanced wind tunnels in the world at Penemuende, later moved to Kochel in Bavaria, knew all about the effects of high-speed flight on an aircraft at speeds just below, at, and beyond Mach 1, but evidently none of these learned men thought or had the opportunity to pass this information on to the combat flyers of KG 76. Writes J. Richard Smith and Eddie J. Creek in their book *Arado 234 Blitz*: "Sergeant Ludwig Rieffel was practicing a gliding attack when he experienced a reversal of the controls approaching Mach 1. He bailed out successfully but the shock of the parachute opening at that speed ripped three of its six sections from top to bottom. A freshly plowed field prevented him from being seriously injured. This happened later to Oberleutnant [first lieutenant] Heinke. He was unable to escape from the aircraft which crashed into the ground in a vertical dive on March 7, 1945." The German flyers still had much to learn about their new aircraft and the dangers faced by a high-speed straight-wing aircraft when entering that zone of high compressibility.

In the transonic speed range of Mach .8, sonic flow can exist over an airplane's surface and will form shock waves that will adversely interact with control surfaces like freezing the trailing edge elevator for example. Recovery can only be accomplished by decreasing speed and reducing altitude. Franz Stigler's so called death dive had been repeated many times by WWII pilots in higher-performance aircraft such as the P-38 Lightning. The problem was resolved by the research done by Dr. Adolf Busemann, one of the German scientists brought to the United States by Colonel Donald Putt under Project Paperclip, and Chuck Yeager with the development of the X-1. Writes Bob Kempel in his paper *Mach Tuck and the Graveyard Dive*, "Captain Charles E. Yeager was the program test pilot and his first flight was on 6 August 1947, an unpowered glide for familiar-

The X-1A flown by Chuck Yeager to Mach 1.06 on October 14, 1947, is now on display at the Smithsonian Udvar Hazy Center in Chantilly, Virginia. The picture shows the X-1 displayed at the Washington location prior to the museum's renovation in 2022–23, when the X-1 was transferred to Udvar Hazy near Dulles IAP. (Author)

ization followed by two more unpowered flights with landings on the vast Rogers Dry Lake. The first powered flight was flown on 29 August to a Mach number of 0.85 or very close to the X-1's critical Mach number. The Critical Mach number is where the air flow over the wing first becomes supersonic and the drag begins to rise, as Dr Busemann had proven in his wind tunnel tests in 1945. Subsequent flights, numbers 2 to 8, were flown by step-by-step increases of Mach numbers into the transonic speed range investigating the trim changes of the suspected degrading of elevator effectiveness up to Mach 0.997.

Continues Robert Kempel in his paper, "From these flights and Mach numbers it was determined that the trailing edge elevator effectiveness became drastically reduced and the entire tailplane would be required to provide the pilot's primary pitch control." For the P-38, that so critical control was achieved by adding a toggle-switch atop the pilot's yoke which allowed small increments of tailplane adjustments in the appropriate speed conditions—to preclude a *Mach Tuck* situation.

As for the X-1, it was shaped like a 50 caliber bullet to provide little resistance to airflow. On flight number 9, on October 14, 1947, Yeager reached a Mach number of 1.06 at 43,000 feet, a truly historic achievement. The highest Mach number the X-1 achieved in all subsequent flights was 1.45 at 40,130 feet on March 26, 1948. Notes Robert Kempel in his *Mach Tuck* paper, "Runaway trim situations were usually catastrophic and as a counter future high-performance fighters adopted the use of the entire tailplane for pitch control and trim."

HUB ZEMKE

P-47 THUNDERBOLT/P-38 LIGHTNING/P-51 MUSTANG

One of the German pilots we had shot down was among the Luftwaffe's most promising fighter leaders, Major Wilhelm Galland, an ace with 55 victories to his credit. His brother was the famous General Adolf Galland, Hitler's General of Fighters.

—HUBERT ZEMKE IN ZEMKE'S WOLF PACK

Colonel Hubert A. Zemke, better known as "Hub," commanded the 56th Fighter Group flying their P-47s out of RAF Boxted in England. Among his pilots were Gabby Gabreski and Dave Schilling. The Wolf Pack was a "hot outfit," as the saying goes. Their job was mostly air to ground, lots of exposure to anti-aircraft fire. Recalls Zemke in his book *Zemke's Wolf Pack: The Story of Hub Zemke and the 56th Fighter Group in the Skies over Europe*: "Another returnee I was pleased to see was Dave Schilling, who had lost none of his zest for living and fighting. My old Flying Executive took his first mission out on the 19th [July 1944], the day Egan was killed. The perils of airfield strafing were once more underlined boldly next day. Gabby went down. It was hard to take; that grinning face had seemed almost a permanent part of the Wolf Pack. But the good news was that the chances were that Gabby was alive. While strafing Bassenheim airfield near Coblenz, he had flown too low in avoiding a welter of tracer and his prop struck a small rise on the far side of the airfield. He bellied in and ran. Francis Gabreski, the greatest American ace from the war in Europe, did survive to fight again in another air war, Korea." Gabby had 31 kills against the Luftwaffe, and added 6½ more in the Korean war. For the time being anyway he would spend his time in Stalag Luft I, on the Baltic Sea, a German POW camp for

On January 7, 1951, Gabby Gabreski, then the commander of the 51st Fighter Interceptor Group in Korea, is shown after pinning the Air Medal on Lieutenant Frank Robison. Frank had the unique distinction of getting credit for shooting down two MiG 15s flown by Russian pilots—without ever firing a shot. The MiGs got into Robison's jet wash, already near a high speed stall, snap-rolled twice, then went into a flat spin. "Just as I started to pull the trigger, the pilot ejected. I put the pipper on the other MiG, and that pilot ejected." Frank got credit for both. (Frank Robison)

downed flyers run by the Luftwaffe. Hub Zemke was to join Gabby in the near future.

Zemke continues, "Three of the 8th Air Forces Fighter Command's four P-38 Lightning groups had converted to the P-51 Mustang during July and I learned there was a good chance of acquiring one of their cast-off *Droop Snoots*. My request was granted by 'Ajax' and with the memory of our successful use of this type of aircraft in May, I had high hopes we could do similar good work. The *Droop Snoot* was painted up in our colors and the services of a bombardier, Lieutenant Arthur Scroggins, acquired. On the late afternoon of 25 July we put it to work.

"Earlier that day, while returning from a dive bombing mission, I had noticed four Ju 88s being pushed under some trees at Montdidier airfield, north of Paris. Reaching Boxted, I ordered the *Droop Snoot* made ready with a 500 pound bomb under each wing. Tying in with the next P-47 mission, which Schilling was leading, Scroggins tagged along behind until just north of Abbeville where I broke away to seek Montdidier. There was no difficulty in locating my objective and the *Droop Snoot* was lined up at 12,000 feet for a one minute run. At the same instant the count-down reached zero and Scroggins released our bombs, there were four violent explosions and the aircraft fell into a right-hand spiral. Looking out I saw that the propeller, spinner and part of the right engine had disappeared. With concerted effort the *Droop Snoot* was righted and headed north to escape the flak. On the way home, an ever enlarging oil slick appeared along the cowling of the good engine. This concentrated the mind wonderfully. I suspected that we had taken a piece of flak in the oil tank—which proved to be the case. After landing, the brakes failed and we hurtled off the end of the runway into a field. It would be no exaggeration to say that pilot and bombardier were very relieved when they finally climbed out of that kite. This was to be the one and only mission with our own *Droop Snoot*. We did not have the facilities to repair it, nor the experienced ground crew to conduct maintenance. On top of that I was now convinced that flying straight and level at 12,000 feet with a close formation in trail tended toward the suicidal. So we decided to persevere with dive bombing and strafing and saw plenty of it during the next few days as the ground forces finally broke free of the Normandy bridgehead and swept across France.

"The volume of light flak and small arms fire we encountered seemed to grow with each passing day. To survive you learned to keep high enough for it not to reach you or low enough so they didn't see you coming in time to draw an accurate bead. More often it was the latter. Several times Thunderbolts came back to Boxted with damage caused by trees. Fred McIntosh must have flown through a forest judging by the branches embedded in both wings. After jumping down from my plane one day I noticed slashes in the fuselage and found a considerable length of telephone wire wound round my prop. But we couldn't escape all the fire and more than once I heard the clunk clunk of shell splinters or bullets smashing into my P-47.

"Our attrition was nothing compared to the hammering the Luftwaffe had taken. Despite the large number of his planes shot down and shot up, plus the bombing of his aircraft factories, Jerry still seemed to have plenty of fighters. What he couldn't replace was the

A Republic P-47D flown by Roy Brown, one of Watson's Whizzers pilots. Roy named the aircraft Pick, after his girlfriend and wife-to-be, whose last name was Pickering. (Roy Brown)

experienced flyers who fell in battle. Since the early spring we had noticed a general deterioration in the quality of the fighter pilots we met and this became more pronounced as the weeks went by. A great many showed poor airmanship, pathetic gunnery and lack of tactics, all indicative of insufficient training, which proved to be the case. The P-51 groups, with their range and endurance, had some spectacular turkey shoots at this time, intercepting huge enemy formations where the majority of the pilots seemed to blindly follow the formation leader and make only clumsy attempts to avoid the attack. This was in marked contrast to the high caliber of the average German fighter pilot when we had arrived on the scene the previous summer.

"There were now ten P-51 groups in VIIIth Fighter Command and the plan was to convert others before the end of the year with the 56th last in line. We figured that the way things were going the war would be over by then. I expected that we would move to the continent which would put us nearer to our area of operations. General Spaatz, however, decided that this would only impose unnecessary logistic problems and that his strategic air force could fulfill all its duties quite satisfactorily from permanent bases in the UK. And so the lot of the four P-47 groups was mostly bombing and strafing, for which we were better suited than the more flak vulnerable P-51s.

Occasionally we were given a Type 16 sweep where we would be directed to enemy aircraft by radar control, but this was rarely fruitful."

Zemke was called into his commander's office in August 1944. General "Butch" Griswold commanded the 8th Fighter Command. The Wolf Pack and the 479th Fighter Group, a P-38 outfit, were part of his command. "'We lost Kyle Riddle yesterday and I need another commander for the 479th,'" Griswold told Zemke when they met. "'As you know it's the youngest group in the command and they don't have anyone with the necessary experience to take over. You've had Dave Schilling a long time. It's time he had a command of his own. I'd like him to take the 479th.' There was a brief silence at my end; it was a surprise. I guess I thought Dave was sacrosanct. But he certainly deserved a command of his own and was more than able to handle it. 'Okay, General. I'll talk to Schilling and call you back. He's off base now and I may not be able to come back until morning. Griswold hung up the phone." When Schilling reported to Zemke, he said to him, "'I've got a group for you.' Dave's face sparkled. 'The 479th,' I continued. 'Riddle went down.' There was an abrupt change of attitude: 'Hell no, not P-38s.' I told him they were about to transition to P-51s but his disquiet at the prospect of commanding the 479th was expressed in a few choice four letter words. This was the response I had anticipated. 'Okay, Dave, I'll tell you what we'll do. You take the 56th and I'll go to the 479th.' He was incredulous. Twice it seemed command of the Wolf Pack was his, only to have it snatched away, and now here was Zemke handing it to him on a plate. Sure he would take over.

"I called Ajax and spoke to Griswold, 'Dave prefers to stay with the 56th at Boxted, but I would be delighted to go to the 479th at Wattisham.' Griswold didn't even query it. 'Fine. How soon can you get over there?' 'This afternoon,' I replied. And that was that.

"Wattisham lay about twelve miles due north of Boxted, but it appeared to entail twice that distance to reach along the narrow winding roads in this part of England. The base, of similar vintage to Horsham St. Faith, was built just before the war for the RAF and fitted out with centrally heated brick built barracks. Bombed during the Battle of Britain, one of the hangars was still without a roof. I was already familiar with Wattisham as a large air depot had been

This gleaming P-38 is part of the Red Bull collection based at Salzburg airport, Austria, and is maintained in perfect flying condition, however, without the aircraft's original armament. The P-38s Zemke and his boys in the 479th Fighter Group were flying could only dream of such caring maintenance. (Martin Frauenheim)

constructed on the south side of the field which handled all the major fighter overhauls for VIIIth Fighter Command. The 479th Fighter Group occupied the northern side with the original hangars and the old camp. I didn't know a great deal about the 479th other than it was the last fighter outfit to join the 8th Air Force, that it flew P-38 Lightnings and had taken some pretty heavy losses.

"A careful look at the 479th operational record revealed the group had arrived in England in May 1944 and set a record going operational in eleven days, although I suspected it might have been hustled so as to have some missions under its belt by D-Day. In two and a half months the group had shot down ten enemy aircraft while losing some 35 of its own pilots killed or missing. True, most of the combat losses had been to ground fire during strafing raids. Even so, they appeared excessively high and I suspected a weakness in technique and general leadership.

"A contributing factor to these high losses," according to Zemke, "was the type of aircraft. The Lockheed P-38 Lightning was heralded as a wonder fighter when it first appeared in 1939, faster than anything else in the sky, very maneuverable and with good firepower. It transpired that the design had some inherent weaknesses that were never fully overcome. The most serious was tail buffeting in high speed dives which led to restrictions that were a handicap in combat. Due to the peculiarities of the design aerodynamics, at very high speeds air flow over the cockpit and wing center section became turbulent and hammered round the tailplane linking the two fuselage booms. Lockheed and the Air Force tried in vain to cure this: they never succeeded as far as I know.

"A large plane for a fighter, the P-38 could turn as well as most single engine interceptors at low altitudes and it had good speed. In the Pacific our people developed a successful technique of employing it against Japanese fighters with great success. It was popular there by virtue of its range being superior to other American pursuits available during the early war years and, with plenty of over-water flying, two engines were a comfort. The same should have applied to Europe but the operational circumstances and climate conditions were different. Here the P-38 was a big flop, although the Air Force would never admit it as they believed their own propaganda.

"The Allison engines were the main trouble. At low and medium altitudes they were fine, at high altitude they were hopeless. The design just couldn't take the combination of extreme cold and high humidity that characterized flight over Europe, especially in winter. Engine failure had been rife during the winter of 1943–1944 when the P-38s really began to see action. The position had improved, but they still were not 100 per cent. There was a standing joke that the P-38 was designed with two engines so you could come back on one. A P-38 mechanic's life was not easy, the type demanded a hefty maintenance load.

"There were several good points about the type. Without doubt it was an excellent gun platform. All five guns—four 50s and a 20mm cannon—were in the nose compartment ahead of the pilot. This made the estimation of range much less critical as, unlike the P-47 and P-51 with their wing mounted guns, the fire didn't converge. Although I had a little time in P-38s I needed to become really familiar with the type before leading a mission. So one of my first priorities was to get in some flying hours so that the operation of flaps, gear and other controls became near automatic. I didn't anticipate having to fly many missions with P-38s because the 479th was about to convert to P-51s. I began by setting up a number of lectures and discussions on tactics in order to better appraise the pilots and operations personnel. Nearly all the officers were strangers to me, most being youngsters not long out of flying school. I was surprised to find that one tall, broad-shouldered ball of energy was Robin Olds, who I think I had last seen in the pool at Langley when he was a young teenager and his dad commanded the 2nd Bomb Group. Robin got himself mixed up with a flock of Focke-Wulfs a couple of days after I arrived at Wattisham, and claimed two."

Zemke led his first mission, all three squadrons, on August 18, escorting B-24s against a German airfield in France. "We took off from Wattisham mid-afternoon," recalls Zemke. "A pleasant day with some clouds scattered around the sky. Our 50 P-38s made rendezvous with the B-24s at the coast near Bayeux, went south of Paris and then headed to eastern France. As planned, two squadrons of the 479th—the 434th and the 436th—took up positions on either flank of the bomber formations while I led the other squadron, the 435th, to scout ahead. On reaching a point near St Dizier, I took the freelance squadron well ahead to sweep across the target area with the specific intention of scouting what was on the airfield. As we went by I was pleased to see the field was well stocked with twin-engined planes.

"The bombers had an unobstructed run on the target and their aim was good. No flak was seen, and after hearing from others in my squadron that they had seen none, I called the rest of the group down to start a traffic pattern for strafing. On a rough estimation there were a good 70 aircraft dispersed around the field, most of which appeared to have escaped damage during the bombing. The majority were Heinkel 111 bombers and by the time we had finished just about every one was on fire. Wave after wave of P-38s swept over the field for around 25 minutes until the pall of smoke from the burning aircraft was so large and dense that to continue would have put our people at risk through collision. One of our number who didn't make it had been seen to crash into the town of Nancy. There were only a few reports of shooting from the ground but perhaps he caught some of this.

"Climbing out of my aircraft back at Wattisham I was confronted with P-38s skimming along only a few feet above the grass, doing

The Heinkel 111 was a Battle of Britain bomber and by 1944 was extremely vulnerable to American fighters such as the P-38, P-47, and P-51. It was mostly used on the Eastern Front, where vintage aircraft such as the He 111 still had a chance of survival. (Fred McIntosh)

victory rolls and generally buzzing the place. No doubt I was going to be labeled a sourpuss for stamping on this show of exuberance, but to me it was unnecessary and dangerous. Names of the offenders were obtained from the tower, and they were later summoned to my office and fined a half month's pay. On August 25, one of the squadrons on an escort mission near the Baltic coast, ran into a gaggle of Me 109s, apparently from an operational training unit, and shot down five. Robin Olds claimed three of these to become the 479th first ace. A one-time All-American football star, Olds proved to be a talented fellow with a great sense of humor which he employed in drawing cartoons that caused much amusement in the Officer's Club.

"On the same mission I experienced one of the P-38's known problems. We had just arrived over the B-24s we were to support when a small gaggle of Me 109s was seen below. Pressing the R/T button and giving my flight the order to follow me, an abrupt roll into a dive was made and as the speed built up the throttles retarded so as not to exceed the given dive limitations for the aircraft. To my astonishment both engines cut out. Thrusting the throttles open brought them to life again only to produce engine over-speeding. As I wrestled with the power settings the revolutions on one and then the other engine fluctuated wildly. All considerations of engaging

A 487th Bomb Group B-24 on its bomb run over Wiener Neustadt, Austria, in May 1944.

the enemy in combat was given up as attempts were made to master the bucking Lightning. It took a great deal of sky and a much lower warmer altitude to effect stability. What had happened was that the oil in the hydraulically controlled turbo-supercharger regulators had jellyfied in the low temperatures. A not uncommon happening with P-38s in high altitude operations. I wasn't the only member of my group to fly home streaming blue smoke that day—the air was blue inside my cockpit too.

"Around the beginning of September we finally began to receive brand new P-51Ds. I took one of these gleaming Spam cans—as they were irreverently dubbed—as my personal machine and gave it the markings 9B-Z. The 479th first mission with the Mustang was on 13 September but thereafter the supply dried up again and the group was forced to fly several operations with a mixed force of P-38s and P-51s. With the staging of the airborne operations to secure bridges in Holland and thus provide the Allied armies with a passage over the Rhine river into Germany, our P-38s were used to patrol over the landing sites, where the unmistakable shape of the Lightning ensured friendly identification to the trigger-happy Allied gunners below."

The Group received enough P-51s to equip one squadron, flying a mix of Mustangs and Lightnings. Success finally came for both the

Below—a 15th Air Force B-24 crew. Left to right: Henry Wilson (Nav), John Lightbody (CP), Marion Mixson (P), Howard Kadow (B). In addition there were six gunners/radio operators. In later years Colonel Mixson was my wing commander when I flew in the 55th SRW. (Marion Mixson)

Mustangs and the Lightnings on a sweep over the Rhine. The group destroyed twenty-nine enemy aircraft for the loss of one P-38. Robin Olds became the leading ace in the 479th Group and more than twenty years later earned fame in the air fighting over Southeast Asia. He attributes much of his success to Zemke's influence. On October 30, 1944, Zemke strapped on his P-51 to escort some B-24s deep into Germany. It was to be his last flight before being transferred to a desk job. His aircraft hit severe turbulence, went into a spin, stabilized but kept heading for the ground. He pulled back on the stick, then he recalls a resounding crash, a punishing blow, his helmet, goggles, oxygen mask ripped off his face. It was time to bail out, which he did, to join his fellow flyer Gabby Gabreski at Stalag Luft I. No matter how good you are as a fighter pilot, if you fly combat long enough something unexpected will get you—and Hub Zemke was one of the best. It wasn't the enemy this time—but the weather.

Zemke landed somewhere between Hannover and the small county seat of Celle in northern Germany. Celle had a small fighter base just outside of the town, and in 1948, only three years after the end of WWII, this airfield became one of the Berlin Airlift bases,

used to fly coal into Berlin. At that time I, a thirteen-year-old teenager, lived in a refugee camp not far from Celle, adjacent to Fassberg
airfield, which became the second Berlin Airlift base from which
coal was flown to the city of Berlin. Once apprehended, Zemke was
taken to Celle airfield and then, after interrogation, to Oberursel,
near Frankfurt. There he was interrogated by Hans Scharff, a well
known and very professional German interrogator. Zemke ended up
in Stalag Luft 1 near Barth on the Baltic Sea. Hub was as talented an
organizer as he was a fighter pilot. Before you knew it, he was meeting with the German camp commander and organized the 5,000
American and British POWs into something resembling a fighter
group, appointing barracks commanders, and such. What helped
immensely was Zemke's German heritage and his ability to speak
German. He was the senior American officer in the camp, and the
American complement was the largest, so it was logical for him to
assume the mantle of leadership. All the men held at Stalag Luft I
were flying officers, except for some enlisted personnel who served
as cooks and filled other positions requiring manual labor which
officers, according to the Geneva Convention, were not required to
do. The setup was similar to Stalag Luft III, at Sagan, where I grew
up as a youngster, not far from the camp. At night I could see the
subdued lights of the camp, but I was too young to know what I
was looking at. As the war came to its bitter end, Stalag Luft III held
over 10,000 Allied airmen, while Stalag Luft I's numbers grew to
around 9,000. A stark testimonial to how bloody the air war over
Germany had become.

In his book, *Zemke's Stalag: The Final Days of World War II*, Zemke
mentions that Francis S. Gabreski—twenty-eight WW II victories—
and Robert S. Johnson—twenty-seven WWII victories—were held at
the camp. No mention was made of some other prominent American
prisoners, such as Gus Lundquist, a Wright Field test pilot, and Bob
Hoover. Hoover had learned from Lundquist the cockpit layout of
German fighters, including the Focke-Wulf 190, which were flying
combat missions against the Russians from an airfield adjacent to
Stalag Luft I. As the Russian army approached, the German guards
became uneasy and Zemke negotiated with the camp's commander
for the German guards to leave before the arrival of the Russians. So,

in fact, for a few days, Zemke commanded Stalag Luft I, and waited for the arrival of the Russian army.

Bob Hoover couldn't wait. He saw an opportunity, escaped from the camp, and made it to the nearby German airfield. This is the way Bob Hoover described this episode to me when I interviewed him: "I found an Fw 190 that looked to be in fairly good shape. It had a few holes in the wings and tail, but otherwise wasn't damaged and appeared airworthy." Best of all the plane had full fuel tanks. Using a small .25 caliber pistol obtained from a French woman, he convinced a German ground crew man to start the aircraft, and off he went. "The Fw 190 performed well, and I headed west, knowing if any American or British fighter saw me, they'd blast me out of the sky. I flew just below an overcast at 4,000 feet, allowing me to escape into the clouds should I come up against some of our fighters. I followed the coastline to the Zuider Zee in Holland, then chose an open field for my landing. I ground looped the plane. I didn't know how to pull up the gear, so I flew to Holland with the gear down. I climbed out of the Fw 190 and tried to figure out what to do next. A group of Dutch farmers with pitchforks came running toward me. Since I landed in a German plane, they thought I was an enemy deserter. Despite their strong reservations, they escorted me into a small town where they turned me over to the British." Hoover was then turned over to a nearby American unit and he was a free man again, soon to return to the United States, to do what? Of course, to become a test pilot at Wright Field.

Once the Russian army arrived, Zemke negotiated with the Russians with the result that they left the camp alone. It helped again that he was able to speak broken Russian which he learned when he helped deliver P-40s from England to the Soviet Union in 1940. In time an armada of B-17 bombers arrived to return the British and American former POWs to England. I describe that event in some detail in Al Tucker's story. Hub made it back to the United States and home to Montana. After an interim assignment in Florida, in 1949, he was assigned as commander of the 36th Fighter Group at Fuerstenfeldbruck air base, near Munich, flying P-80 Shooting Stars. He remained in Germany until 1954, by which time the 36th Fighter Wing had been transferred to Bitburg Air Base in the Eifel

Wolfgang standing under a C-54 transport in 1949 during the Berlin Airlift at Fassberg Air Base, near Celle, where Hub Zemke was interrogated in 1944 after bailing out of his P-51 Mustang. (Author)

mountains west of Frankfurt. I found it interesting that in January 1951, when I immigrated to the United States, I received my medical clearance at the Fuerstenfeldbruck Air Base hospital. My stepfather was assigned there with the 36th Fighter Bomber Wing commanded by Colonel Zemke. Years later, after my combat tour in Vietnam, I did my flying with the 36th Tactical Fighter Wing out of Bitburg and nearby Spangdahlem air bases. It seemed that I was following in Hub's footsteps from Celle to Fuerstenfeldbruck to Bitburg.

Colonel Hubert Zemke retired at age fifty-two after thirty years of service in the Army Air Corps and the United States Air Force. As fighter pilots go, he was one of the very best—and a survivor, but not a fan of the P-38.

CHARLIE SCHREFFLER

P-38 LIGHTNING/F-5I MUSTANG

This story goes on, it has no end.
You lose a ship and you lose a friend.
Maybe some day you won't come back.
And they chalk you up to fighters and flak.
—EDWARD A. GREENLAW

On November 8, 1942, Operation Torch was launched and British and American troops landed near Casablanca, Oran, and Algiers under the command of General Dwight D. Eisenhower. American servicemen for the first time would meet up with their German and Italian adversaries. A setback came in February 1943 at Kasserine Pass and resulted in the loss of aircraft when the Afrika Korps overran some Allied airfields. Additional P-40s were flown in. And P-38s, within weeks after their arrival in the United Kingdom, were moved to North Africa. Writes Jimmy Doolittle in his book *I Could Never Be So Lucky Again*: "The victory over Tunisia we had hoped we could achieve was not possible in December 1942. Heavy rains had kept us on the ground and stalled the advance of our ground troops. The day after the Casablanca conference ended, I sent a confidential memo to my commanders." [At this time Doolittle was commanding the 12th Air Force.]

Reads Doolittle's memo: "You and I know that the 12th Air Force was faced with tremendous problems when it arrived in North Africa. Expected equipment did not arrive, was incomplete, or wouldn't work. Officers and men alike lacked training and experience in the type of warfare with which we were faced. We arrived in the rainy season, and the mud made airports impossible and living conditions unpleasant. . . . We have had losses too, but the enemy has paid a price of more than two to one for every airplane we have lost." At this time Doolittle was a great fan of the P-38 and in numerous passages in his book he praises the aircraft and its performance, as did General Spaatz, who at this time commanded the 15th Air Force. Writes Doolittle, "Tooey wrote—of all our fighter aircraft, the P-38 deserves special mention. As reports indicate, P-38s have been shot down but the enemy refuses to attack unless he has superior numbers and altitude advantage. In spite of these unbalanced encounters, the P-38 has accounted for 127 German aircraft of all kinds while losing only 74 to enemy aircraft [as of February 5, 1943]. This ratio might well be higher except that escort missions necessarily limit freedom of action.

"As escort for bombers, P-38s have contributed largely to successful bombing by actively denying enemy attacks on bombers (especially over the target), by boosting the morale of bomber crews and by furnishing cover for straggling crippled bombers. On January 12 a section of 12 P-38s successfully defended a badly damaged B-17 from persistent enemy fighter attacks while returning from Tripoli more than two hours overdue. As a low altitude ground support aircraft, the P-38 has established itself as a dual purpose weapon. The ship has high speed for surprise and the necessary heavy fire power. Its distinctive appearance assists the pilot materially in that he may operate at very low altitude without hesitation or fear of friendly ground fire, thereby permitting more complete concentration on the job at hand."

One of those 12th Air Force P-38 drivers referred to by Tooey Spaatz was a young man by the name of Charles E. Schreffler. Said Charlie Schreffler when I interviewed him, "I'll never forget December 10, 1941, three days after the Japanese attacked Pearl Harbor. My friends and I, in patriotic fervor, went to the army recruiting office in Fort Wayne, Indiana, and signed up for the Army Air Corps. I was born in 1921 in Coshocton, Ohio. When I was still very young, my parents had moved to Indiana. I always wanted to fly, ever since the barnstormers came by when I was seven and gave me a five-minute ride. I passed my physical and became an aviation cadet. I went

The Boeing-built PT-13D Kaydet designed by Stearman Aircraft was a popular trainer with a maximum speed of 135mph and an air cooled radial Lycoming engine, the instructor pilot sitting behind the student. Communication obviously mostly was by prearranged signals. No radio. The picture below is of the more advanced Vultee BT-13 "Vibrator" trainer. Its windows rattled. (Author)

through preflight and primary training in the PT-13 Kaydet and the Vultee BT-13 Valiant 'Vibrator.' The BT had flaps and a sophisticated set of instruments, none of which the PT had. In advanced training I got to fly the fighter-like AT-6 Texan at Luke Field, Arizona.

"I graduated in December 1942, and that same day was put on a train to transition into the P-38 fighter at Glendale, California. In March 1943 I crossed the country by train, processed through Fort Dix in New Jersey, and embarked on a ship which joined a large convoy across the Atlantic, bound for Oran, Algeria. From there I shipped to a dusty base outside Casablanca for P-38 refresher training. Finally, I got to fly my first combat mission. It was against a small harbor in Sardinia. I had never dropped a bomb before and felt a little foolish not knowing how to aim my bomb or even when I was to drop it. I watched my flight leader closely and did exactly what he did. When he released his bomb, I let go of mine. I don't know where the bomb went or if it hit anything other than water.

"On my next mission over Sicily, we ran into some German Me 109s. In the ensuing melee one of our own aircraft shot up my leader, and we both returned to base. Up until then everything seemed sort of unreal, even comical at times. After all, I was a fighter pilot, not a bomber pilot, and I didn't expect our own planes to fire on us. But then everything in combat is confusing. My perception of war changed drastically on my next mission, a long-range sweep by over 100 P-38s against German and Italian air bases around Foggia on the Italian mainland. I finally got to use my guns. We came in from the Adriatic side, flying at 50 feet to avoid detection. We totally surprised the enemy and destroyed more than 100 of their aircraft on the ground."

Colin D. Heaton did an extensive interview with Johannes Steinhoff, shortly before Steinhoff died in February 1994. "Macky" Steinhoff was one of Germany's highest-scoring fighter pilots, scoring 176 victories. He, like so many German fighter pilots, earned the scorn of Germany's leadership, and he joined Adolf Galland when Galland formed JV 44 (Jagt Verband 44), a rebel fighter squadron, flying Me 262 jets. Steinhoff was badly burned in an Me 262 take-off accident. He survived the war and served in the postwar Luftwaffe as chief of staff. Writes Heaton, "Steinhoff served in combat from the first days of the war through April 1945. He flew more than 900 missions and engaged in aerial combat in over 200 sorties, operating from the Western and Eastern fronts, as well as in the Mediterranean theater. Victor over 176 opponents, Steinhoff was himself shot down a dozen times and wounded once. Yet he always emerged from his crippled and destroyed aircraft in high spirits. He opted to ride his aircraft down on nearly every occasion, never trusting parachutes. . . . Pilots such as Steinhoff, Hannes Trautloft, Adolf Galland and many others fought not only Allied aviators but also their own corrupt leadership, which was willing to sacrifice Germany's best and bravest to further personal and political agendas. In both arenas, they fought a war of survival. 'Please describe your humorous encounter with a Lockheed P-38 pilot named Widen in Italy in 1944,' Colin Heaton asked Steinhoff. 'This is a good story,' Steinhoff replied. 'I was test flying an Me 109 with my aide near our base at Foggia. This was before I had been exiled from Germany, during my first tour as Kommodor of JG 77 (Jagd Geschwader 77). Well, we were attacked at low level by a flight of P-38 Lightnings, about 100 American fighters in all, but the two of us figured, why not attack? We turned into them, and I flew through their formation going in the opposite direction, getting good strikes on a couple of them. I poured a good burst into this P-38 and the pilot rolled over, and I saw him bail out. I had this on gun camera also. Well, he was picked up and made a POW, and I invited him to my tent for a drink and dinner, as well as spend the night. We drank some of the local wine. . . . and drank and drank. I thought to myself, what am I going to do with this guy? Well, it was long after midnight, so I lay down in my tent and stretched my legs so I could reach his head. He woke up and said, 'Don't worry. I won't run away, you have my word as an officer and a gentleman. Besides, you got me too drunk.' We slept, and he kept his word, and I never placed a guard on him.

"So, you subdued your opponent with alcohol?"

"Yes, that's right, and it worked very well. He was a very likeable man, and I was very pleased to have the victory, but as I told him, I was even more pleased to see him uninjured and safe."

"Of all the Allied fighters you encountered, which was the most difficult to handle with a good pilot at the controls?"

"The Lightning. It was fast, low profiled and a fantastic fighter, and a real danger when it was above you. It was only vulnerable if you were behind it, a little below and closing fast, or turning into it, but on the attack it was a tremendous aircraft. One shot me down from long

An Me 109 replica on display at the 8th Air Force Museum in Pooler, Georgia. (Author)

range in 1944." In a more detailed assessment in Jeffrey Ethells's *P-38 Lightning*, Steinhoff is quoted as saying: "I had encountered the long-range P-38 Lightning fighter during the last few days of the North African campaign. Our opinion of this twin-boomed, twin engine aircraft was divided. Our old Messerschmitts were still, perhaps, a little faster. But pilots who had fought them said that the Lightnings were capable of appreciably tighter turns and that they would be on your tail before you knew what was happening. The machine guns mounted in the nose supposedly produced a concentration of fire from which there was no escape."

"Soon after that mission," Charlie Schreffler continued, "I learned about fear and how to fly through it. It was August 30, 1943. We were escorting a group of B-26 Marauders up the Italian boot when we were jumped by 75 to 80 Me 109s and Fw 190s. We got all the B-26s into the target and out without losing one, but we lost eleven of our own. I lost an engine in the melee. In the confusion of the air battle, a German Me 109 suddenly came into my sights, and I fired instinctively. The 109 burst into flames and exploded. I added one more probable enemy fighter destroyed that day before returning to my base." For this extraordinary performance on that mission, First Lieutenant Charles E. Schreffler was awarded the Distinguished Flying Cross. Read the official orders awarding Charlie his first DFC:

Headquarters Twelfth Air Force
APO #650

13 October 1943

Charles E. Schreffler, O-734000, First Lieutenant, Anderson,
Indiana. For extraordinary achievement while participating in
aerial flight in the North African, Sicilian and Italian Theaters
of Operations as a pilot of a P-38 aircraft. On 30 August 1943,
while escorting a B-26 bombardment group over Lago di Patria,
Italy, Lt. Schreffler's flight of 4 P-38s was attacked by thirty Me
109s. Observing a lagging comrade in grave danger he unhesi-
tatingly led his flight in an aggressive assault on the threatening
enemy aircraft, destroying one Me 109 and probably destroying
another. Lt Schreffler so expertly maneuvered his small flight,
despite one engine being disabled by hostile fire, that the flight
safely rejoined his squadron. His outstanding ability as a flight
leader and combat pilot has reflected great credit upon himself
and the armed forces of the United States.

By command of Major General Doolittle

Although Charlie Schreffler's tour of duty with the 12th Air Force
had come to an end by June 6, the day of the D-Day landings in Normandy, the P-38s of Charlie's former command made their presence
known over Ploesti, escorting vulnerable B-24s and B-17s. Ploesti,
Rumania, was Germany's major oil production center and heavily
defended by AAA and Me 109s and Fw 190s. The initial forays of
the P-38s into this environment were bloody "learning experiences."
The Germans made extensive use of smokescreens and on June 24,
P-38s carrying 1,000-pound bombs made a low level attack on the
refinery complex. They were intercepted by German fighters before
they got to the refineries, losing twenty-six of their own. Lesson
learned, and a place for the Droop Snoot. Writes James Dugan in
Ploesti, "He sat high over the target, inspecting Ploesti for holes
in the smoke screen," then led the attacking P-38s to their targets.

Accompanied by P-51s the P-38s took their revenge and "not long after that the Luftwaffe was a negligible factor."

On November 7, 1944, according to the *Army Air Forces Combat Chronology*, the P-38s were back in strength, 124 of them, strafing troop concentrations and railroads at Podgorica, Montenegro; Raska, Prijepolje, Nis, and Novi Pazar, Serbia; Visegrad, Hungary, and other places near Ploesti. Things happen in war. The P-38s mistook a Russian column for Germans and in he process killed Lieutenant General Gregory Kotov. In the resultant melee two P-38s were shot down as well as two Russian Yak-9 fighters. Another Yak was shot down by Russian AAA fire. The incident became known as the Nis Incident, causing a diplomatic uproar. Friendly fire incidents happened all too often on both sides.

"By September 1943 I had racked up fifty combat missions over Italy and was returned home to Bradley Field, near Hartford, Connecticut," Charlie Schreffler continued his story. "There I stayed until April 1945 as a P-47 Thunderbolt instructor pilot. I wanted to stay, but was discharged that October along with thousands of other pilots. I returned to Fort Wayne, Indiana, to my old job as a draftsman. I stayed in the Air Force reserve, and to my great surprise, in 1947, I was offered a regular Air Force commission. I accepted immediately and was assigned to Andrews Air Force Base, near Washington, DC, as a maintenance officer. In July 1948 I transferred to the 18th Fighter Group at Clark Air Base in the Philippines. World War II should have been my only war. I was wrong. Within days of the North Korean invasion of the South, I was involved in another equally brutal war. The 18th Fighter Bomber Group was quickly thrown into battle to stem the surging tide of the North Korean People's Army.

"Our household goods were picked up as scheduled. That evening my wife mentioned a curious thing to me. The household goods people had contacted her and asked if she wanted to change the destination of our shipment. When she asked them why she would want to do that, they told her that her husband wouldn't be accompanying her. 'Is that true?' she asked me. That's how I found out about the invasion of South Korea by the North. My wife took the ship home to San Francisco, while I left for Johnson Air Base, near Tokyo, Japan, to pick up an F-51. By the time her ship docked in San Francisco harbor, some of the returning wives learned that their husbands had died in South Korea, in a war of which they knew nothing."

The F-51 was not ideal for its intended mission of ground support, but it was rugged enough to operate from crude airfields, carried a lethal weapons load, and was still available in large enough numbers. The "indestructible" P-47, which did such a great job in Europe supporting ground troops, unfortunately was no longer available in adequate numbers. Like many other World War II aircraft such as the P-38, it had been turned to scrap or been given to needy allies. The F-51 would have to do, and the decision was made to swap the 18th Fighter Group's P-80s for F-51 Mustangs. All 18th Group pilots were F-51 qualified. Many of them had extensive World War II experience. The Group had three squadrons—the 12th, the 44th, and the 67th. The pilots of the 12th squadron, augmented by flyers from the other two squadrons, were the first to convert. They were flown to Johnson Air Base where they picked up thirty reconditioned F-51s that had been in storage. The Dallas Provisional Squadron, as they were to be called, flew their Mustangs to Ashiya in southern Japan, then moved on to a dirt airstrip, K-2, near Taegu, South Korea, flying their first combat missions on July 14, 1950. The war had started on June 25, just a bit over two weeks earlier.

In the meantime, 145 F-51s assigned to the Air National Guard were rounded up and loaded on the aircraft carrier USS *Boxer*, which left the port of Alameda on July 15 with its load of Mustangs and seventy pilots. After a maximum speed voyage, the *Boxer* arrived in Japan on July 22. Pilots of the 67th Fighter Bomber Squadron from Clark picked up a batch of the newly arrived Mustangs and became part of the 51st Fighter Group (Provisional), joining the advance party of the Dallas Squadron at K-2 to carry the war to the enemy. By August 4th the name-game ended when the two squadrons regained their original designations as the 12th and 67th Fighter Bomber Squadrons of the 18th Fighter Bomber Group. They fought under this designation for the remainder of the war and accumulated an outstanding combat record. The 12th Squadron "Blue Noses," the former Dallas Squadron, became known as the Flying Tigers of Korea, after South Korean President Syngman Rhee commented on their gallantry and compared them to the Flying Tigers

Charlie Schreffler standing on the wing of his F-51 "Little Audrey," across from his maintenance people, at K-10, Chinhae, Korea, 1950. (Charlie Schreffler)

of World War II fame. Their aircraft soon sported shark's teeth. The Red Noses belonged to the 67th Squadron, and Charlie Schreffler flew a red nose out of K-2 in July 1950.

"I remember leading a flight of two Mustangs," Charlie recalled during his interview, "on a road reconnaissance mission in the area of Hamhung, North Korea. As we turned south to return to base, the visibility began to deteriorate and our position was not completely clear to me. As we crossed over a coastline, all hell broke loose. We had flown over Wonsan harbor, which was loaded with North Korean ships. They let us know we were not welcome. From Taegu the 18th moved first to K-9, Pusan East; then to K-23, Pyongyang East; then to K-13, Suwon near Seoul; and finally to Chinhae, K-10, which became our main operating base—dirt, rocks and tents defined the base. But we didn't lose our sense of humor, and we called Chinhae 'Dogpatch' and 'Lower Slobovia.' Al Capp, the guy who drew the Li'l Abner comic strip, somehow got wind of us and took us under his wing. He designed a patch for us. I still have mine. The patch shows Li'l Abner riding a F-51 Mustang firing its guns, with the inscription "Dogpatchers." That's how we got our name Dogpatchers.

"Major Louis J. 'Lou' Sebille was my squadron commander. On a routine close-air-support mission on 5 August [1950], one of Lou's 500 pound bombs didn't release. He tried to shake the bomb loose on his second firing pass, but by then the enemy had his range, and he took several hits. Again the bomb didn't release. Lou should have returned to Chinhae, had the bomb removed and the holes patched. Instead, he chose to continue his attack. On his next firing pass, getting hit all the way in, he never pulled out and flew directly into the enemy vehicles and exploded. For that action Lou received the Medal of Honor. I can't vouch for the exact number of firing passes Lou made, but the squadron's reaction on hearing of his loss was one of great sorrow. Lou was a fine pilot!

"My bunch, the 67th Squadron, launched its first mission in June 1950 from Ashiya, Japan. By the first week in August we were operating from K-2, at Taegu, within the Pusan defensive perimeter. It was a dusty, rock strewn field with quick access to the bomb line, constantly moving south. One problem we soon discovered was differentiating between friend and foe. We were moving so fast and close to the ground it was difficult to determine who was who. The GIs were supposed to display colors of the day; they didn't always do so. Mistakes were made and sometimes there were the unavoidable friendly fire losses." But there wasn't a GI whose heart didn't jump for joy when he heard the high-pitched whine of an F-51 engine bearing down on the enemy at thirty feet above the ground. The F-51's killing power became legendary. With six-wing mounted .50 caliber machine guns, three in each wing, and a load of nearly 1,900 rounds of ammunition, the 'Stang' could put on a very impressive firepower display. Napalm was the weapon most feared by the North Korean infantry, and their rockets were the most dreaded by the North Korean tanks. The two 18th Group squadrons quickly established a tank-killing unit of ready-to-go, rocket armed aircraft. Whenever a call came in that enemy tanks had been sighted, this unit went after them. When the Pusan perimeter really got tight, pilots flew as many as five or six missions a day. Almost immediately after take-off, they found themselves over enemy lines. For a pilot to fly 100 missions in two months wasn't difficult—if he lived that long. Losses were high operating so close to the ground, where every enemy weapon could reach them. There was an aggregate loss of 351 F-51s in more than 60,000 combat missions. Nearly 50,000 of those missions were flown by the pilots of the 18th Wing, including a South African F-51

K-9 Pusan. Charlie Schreffler's P-51, 18th Fighter Bomber Wing, armed and ready to roll to kill North Korean tanks. (Charlie Schreffler)

equipped squadron—the Flying, Fighting Cheetahs—which were under the control of and flew with the 18th Wing. The 18th F-51s, along with the twin-engine B-26 Invaders of the 3rd and 452nd Bomb Wings, helped break the back of the initial North Korean invasion force and gave the US Army the time needed to reconstitute itself.

Charlie Schreffler's second war in one lifetime was more intense than anything he had experienced in fifty combat missions flying the P-38 in Europe. The Korean War was fought largely by the men who had fought in World War II, using the weapons of that war.

JIMMY DOOLITTLE

8TH AIR FORCE COMMANDER, B-25

When a Navy pilot sighted a small vessel only 12,000 yards away, Halsey ordered the Nashville to sink it. It was decision time. Halsey quickly flashed a message to the Hornet. LAUNCH PLANES TO COLONEL DOLITTLE AND GALLANT COMMAND GOOD LUCK AND GOD BLESS YOU.

—JIMMY DOOLITTLE IN HIS AUTOBIOGRAPHY *I COULD NEVER BE SO LUCKY AGAIN*

On September 3, 1943, an Italian general, representing Marshal Pietro Badoglio, signed a secret agreement with the Allies to surrender all their forces on September 8, which they did as agreed to. Writes Jimmy Doolittle in his book, on September 6, "Nearly 150 of the 12th Air Force's P-38s flew the first mass, long-range, low-level strafing mission of the war, against several airdromes around Foggia." Charlie Schreffler was involved in this mission. "Photos from the area showed that the Germans had gathered 230 planes there, which would pose a serious threat to the forthcoming landings by our forces. The P-38s destroyed or damaged 143 of them, while losing only two.

"The day the Italians put down their arms, I wrote to Brigadier General Hoyt Vandenberg, my former chief of staff, who had been transferred to Washington to become deputy chief of staff to Hap Arnold: 'Every day brings its air battle, and while we are more than breaking even, the Hun has the advantage of initiative, fighting over his own territory, and the inherent advantages in a short-range fighter over a long-range fighter. Our losses will increase until the Hun is knocked out. Our crying need now is for escort fighters. I appreciate Eaker's need for escort fighters [commander of the 8th

Air Force at the time], but I feel that our need is equally great. We will soon require escort fighters with the same range as our heavy bombers, so we might just as well start facing that difficult prospect. Meanwhile, B-24s of the 9th Air Force struck oil refineries at Ploesti, and a substantial part of Ploesti's refining capability was destroyed. However, 54 B-24s and 532 men were lost. U.S. forces operating from the United Kingdom lost 120 bombers and hundreds of crewmen. During one week Eaker's 8th Air Force lost 148 planes and had to cancel further deep raids into Germany. He pleaded for long-range escort fighters—P-51s with auxiliary drop tanks—which were then on the production lines."

In November 1943 the decision was made to split the 12th Air Force, Doolittle's command, into separate tactical and strategic elements. To that end the tactical fighters and bombers, like the P-38s and B-25s, would remain in the 12th Air Force, and the B-17s and B-24s would become part of the newly created 15th Air Force. The change of command took place on November 1. General John C. Cannon would take Doolittle's place as 12th Air Force commander, and Doolittle became the commander of the newly created 15th Air Force, with its headquarters in Foggia, in the south of Italy, where the heavy bombers would be located. Moving a headquarters and staff of over 200 officers and men was of course a challenge and dragged on for a number of days, weeks. They were not really settled down yet, writes General Doolittle, when "On the night of December 2, about 30 Luftwaffe bombers dropped parachute mines and bombs on the city and harbor [of Bari]. They hit two ammunition ships in the Bari harbor. The resulting explosions caused fires in adjacent ships, and the whole harbor was set ablaze. The explosions blew out windows in our new quarters. When we assessed the damage the next day, 17 ships had been destroyed by fire and 1,000 men had been killed or injured."

Bari, on the Adriatic Sea, was attacked on December 2, 1943, by Ju 88 bombers dropping chaff to blind Allied radar, and achieving total surprise. Not 17, but 29 ships were sunk, more were damaged, putting the harbor out of business for three weeks. Among the ships sunk in the harbor was the Liberty ship *John Harvey* carrying a cargo of mustard gas bombs, just in case the Germans were to use chemical

The Ju 88, in Rumanian colors, was one of Germany's most effective combat aircraft. As a child in 1948, living in a refugee camp near Fassberg airfield, I often played pilot sitting in my favorite abandoned Ju 88 until it was cut up for scrap. At age 13 I was unable to reach the rudder pedals, greatly frustrating me. (Museum of the US Air Force)

warfare. In addition to the loss of 1,000, in round numbers, military and merchant marine personnel, nearly that many civilians perished as well. Bari was a disaster.

On November 22, 1943, another strategy meeting was held in Cairo, between Prime Minister Churchill and President Roosevelt. Eisenhower, Spaatz, Norstad, and others were present as well. One result of this particular meeting was an agreement that General Eisenhower would assume the position of supreme commander effective January 1, 1944. Spaatz was to move back to England to take over as commander of the United States Strategic Air Forces, which included the 8th as well as the 15th Air Forces. After the Cairo conference, Roosevelt and Churchill continued on to Teheran, Iran, to meet with Stalin. They again reconvened in Cairo on their return trip to confer with the president of Turkey. Subsequent to that meeting, on December 7, Roosevelt met with his senior commanders at La Marsa, Tunisia, where his son Elliott was serving as the commander of the 90th Reconnaissance Group. Recalls Jimmy Doolittle: "On December 9, Hap Arnold flew to Foggia where he met with Tooey, Cannon, and me to discuss what the conference discussions meant to us. As a result Tooey returned to Washington and recommended

La Marsa, Tunisia, December 7, 1943: Lt. Colonel James Setchell (P38/F5 pilot, his story is in a later chapter) is sitting at the far end of the table. To President Roosevelt's right sits General Dwight D. "Ike" Eisenhower. On the president's left sits Lt. General Carl "Tooey" Spaatz, then the commander of the 12th Air Force and the Northwest African Air Forces (NAAF). Major General Bedell Smith, Eisenhower's chief of staff, is sitting next to General Spaatz. Major General Lauris Norstadt sits next to General Smith. Colonel Roosevelt sits across from his father, and to his left, in civilian clothes, sits the ever-present Harry Hopkins, President Roosevelt's trusted advisor. (Bill Setchell)

General Eisenhower, Ike, speaking to President Roosevelt and senior Army Air Corps commanders at the December 7, 1943, La Marsa conference. (Bill Setchell)

that Ira Eaker be transferred to the Mediterranean to be commander in chief of the Mediterranean Allied Air Forces; I was to take his place as head of the 8th Air Force. Major General Nathan F. Twining would replace me as head of the 15th Air Force."

Replacing Eaker was in effect a firing, although in official terms much softer words were used. Hap Arnold had pushed for the longest time for Eaker to come up with a 1,000-bomber raid, like the British had done more than once. But flying at night in a bomber stream was quite a different thing from flying in broad daylight in a huge formation. The huge bomber formations of the 8th Air Force were assumed to provide the bombers a modicum of self-protection against German fighters. Losses were incurred in the process of assembly, not to mention to the German flak and fighters. Eaker was the one who at the Casablanca conference in January 1943 had successfully argued his case for daylight bombing to Churchill, but he was never able to corral 1,000+ bombers, and there were good reasons for it. The lack of escort fighters resulted in significant losses and replacement aircraft and crews never arrived in sufficient numbers to make up for it. Then of course there was the diversion of bombers and fighters from England in support of Operation Torch, the landings in North Africa, in November 1942. I interviewed Colonel Robert M. Slane, who flew B-17s in the Eighth Air Force who demonstrates in one of his flights that Eaker was indeed scraping the bottom of the barrel, yet he never had enough to come up with that magic number of 1,000.

"I was assigned to the 401st Bombardment Squadron," Slane recalled, "of the 91st Bomb Group at Bassingborne. On October 14, 1943, our target was Schweinfurt. I had my regular navigator back, no substitute this time. My flight position would be 'tail-end Charlie' in our group, and the group leader was my roommate, Captain Harry Lay—this was to be Harry's last mission, his 30th birthday. Our aircraft was from another squadron—the 323rd. A distraught crew chief informed me, 'There has to be a mistake. This is an old aircraft, used only for training.' While we were talking the bombs arrived and were being loaded." Slane and crew went down, one of 60 bombers lost that day. Harry Lay didn't make it either. Put bluntly, whatever the reasons for Eaker's reassignment, Eisenhower had lost faith in

B-17s of the 381st Bomb Group, Ridgewell, England, with P-51 escort, heading for flak country. (Author)

him, and Spaatz, as commander of USSTAF, after consulting with Arnold, was the bearer of the bad news. Jimmy Doolittle took over.

"By the time I arrived in England," Doolittle recalls, "150-gallon tanks were available and we were able to hang two of them on a P-47, so they had a tactical radius of 425 miles. The Lockheed P-38 Lightning and the North American P-51 Mustang had greater range than the P-47s; they began to arrive in the theater in November 1943. These were given even more range with the addition of drop tanks, so that eventually the escorts could fly a very welcome 850 miles from their bases. This steadily increased range of the escort fighters was an inheritance from which I benefitted as commander of the 8th; their genesis began long before I took over. It was my job to use this increased capability to best advantage.

"The mission of the escorts was unequivocal at that time: protect the bombers and not leave them. This policy concerned me because fighter aircraft are designed to go after enemy fighters. Fighter pilots are usually pugnacious individuals by nature and are trained to be aggressive in the air. Their machines are specifically designed for offensive action. I thought our fighter forces should intercept the enemy fighters before they reached the bombers. The 'Don't leave the bombers' escort philosophy came to a halt when I visited Major

General William E. 'Bill' Kepner's 8th Fighter Command. On the wall in his office was a sign:

THE FIRST DUTY OF THE EIGHTH AIR FORCE
FIGHTERS IS TO BRING THE BOMBERS BACK ALIVE.

"I took one look at the sign and asked Bill, 'who dreamed that up?' 'The sign was here when I arrived,' Bill Kepner replied. That statement is no longer in effect, I told him, take that sign down. Put up another one that says:

THE FIRST DUTY OF THE EIGHTH AIR FORCE
FIGHTERS IS TO DESTROY GERMAN FIGHTERS

"'You mean you're authorizing me to take the offensive?' he asked. I am directing you to, I said. Tears came to Bill's eyes. He had been urging Ira and Tooey for months to give him permission to go after the enemy fighters and had been turned down repeatedly. I knew how he felt. As we shook hands and I turned to leave, I looked at that sign again. Bill, take that damn thing down, I said as I went out the door. I heard him tear it off the wall."

This was a key decision Jimmy Doolittle made, and it would lead in a short time to the demise of the German fighter force, leaving the AAA as the principal weapon the Germans had left to inflict losses. It is interesting to note that the Luftwaffe during the Battle of Britain had their fighters go looking for Hurricanes and Spitfires before they could reach the bombers. The bomber crews complained to Hermann Goering, the chief of the German air force, that they never saw any German fighters, not knowing that their fighters were keeping the British fighters away from them. The policy was reversed without consulting Ernst Udet, the then chief of the fighter force, nor such German fighter aces as Werner Moelders or Adolf Galland. With that decision, in effect, the German fighters had just lost the initiative, and bomber losses rose accordingly. The 8th and 15th followed the same approach of keeping the escort fighters close to the bombers, until Doolittle took over the 8th Air Force.

Jimmy Doolittle in a Curtiss R3C won the 1925 Schneider Cup race which was reserved for seaplanes only. He, an army pilot, on the Chesapeake Bay, bested his navy competitors. Picture portrays Jimmy behind his aircraft. The picture is dedicated to his friend and fellow aviator Bob Hoover, "To Bob Hoover. Pilot extraordinary and friend exemplary. Sincerely, J. H. Doolittle." (Bob Hoover)

JIM SETCHELL

MOSQUITO/F-4/5 LIGHTNING

Come and join the Air Corps it's a grand branch so they say,
You never do no work at all just fly around all day.
—AUTHOR UNKNOWN

Good information is the key to success not only in business but especially in the military. But when General Doolittle arrived in North Africa, reconnaissance aircraft were hard to come by. Recalls Doolittle, "One of the capabilities we needed badly in the early days in North Africa was photo reconnaissance, so we could assess the results of our attacks and determine future targets. The first photo mission flown was made by Lieutenant Colonel James Anderson in a modified B-17. A unit of camera-equipped British Spitfires had been transferred from England to help us, but their airfield at Maison-Blanche was bombed day and night by the Luftwaffe after the Allied landings. Within a few days the Spitfires were only piles of wreckage.

"Anderson's flight of November 19, 1942, was one to remember. He headed for the Kasserine Pass where the Germans were massing their forces. He stayed above the flak level until he reached the pass, then dove the Fortress down to about 6,000 feet to photograph the activity below. . . . When he returned, we had his film developed quickly. Since we had no photo interpreters assigned, the two of us analyzed the pictures ourselves and saw what targets had to be hit as soon as possible. They were. One of those responsible for getting us excellent photos during this campaign was Elliott Roosevelt, son of the president. He was not a pilot but flew on many missions as an

observer. I wrote to Joe (the name he went by) that I had the pleasure
of decorating him 'to get even with his old man for decorating me.'

Dec 7, 1943
North Africa

Dear Hag,

This is a very important letter as it is being carried on the private
airplane of the President of the United States on his return trip
from the famous conference in the Middle East with Churchill
and Stalin [Cairo and Teheran]. For the first time I can tell you
that president Roosevelt personally inspected my Group at our
Airport and also very closely looked over The Spook. Tonight
the few officers that live with Elliott R[oosevelt] are having the
honor of supper with the President. I think it is something swell
to attend this supper and I look forward to having pictures to
show you covering the evening. There will be several other high
Government officials on hand tonight so your Old Man will
really be mingling with the "big shots."

Love to Bill and the Folks,
Jim

This letter was hurriedly written by then Lieutenant Colonel James
"Jim" Setchell to his young wife, Dorothy, in Ennis, Texas, near Dallas, her hometown, where she lived with their one-year-old son,
Bill, awaiting her husband's return from war. Jim at the time was
the commander of the 3rd Photographic Group of the 90th Photographic Wing commanded by President Roosevelt's son Colonel Elliott Roosevelt. Elliott and Jim shared a tent at the La Marsa airstrip
in Tunisia. When Elliott learned of his father's plans to stop over
at La Marsa, he invited his tentmate Jim to join him, the President
and his generals, for supper. Before leaving for the war in Europe
Jim and Dorothy had decided on code names for each other to be
used in their correspondence. He became Hero, Dorothy would be
referred to as Hag, and young Bill Setchell, just a newborn, became

The De Havilland Mosquito photo reconnaissance version flown by Lieutenant Colonel Jim Setchell in North Africa. It was a popular aircraft of its day flown in various versions as a bomber, fighter, and reconnaissance aircraft. Its frame was constructed mostly of wood. (Bill Setchell)

Spook. A curious collection of names, but it worked for the Setchells. The aircraft Jim Setchell flew at the time was a De Havilland F-8 Mosquito which he named *The Spook*, after his young son. *The Spook* would not survive the war; Jim would—but just barely.

James Frederick Setchell was born on August 9, 1913, in Chicago, Illinois, not far from the present-day O'Hare International Airport, which didn't come about until the early 1940s. Jim was one of four children, a typical American family trying to make ends meet in difficult economic times. Like so many youngsters of his generation, Jim was inspired by all the hoopla that surrounded the airplane between the wars. Barnstormers flying surplus army biplanes, and performing daring stunts, inspired young and old at county fairs or wherever there was a level landing field with people willing to pay five dollars for "the ride of their lives." The hero status accorded men like Charles A. Lindbergh, the conqueror of the Atlantic Ocean, flying *The Spirit of St. Louis* in one daring swoop from Garden City Airport, Long Island, to Le Bourget Field in Paris, France, on May 20 to 21, 1927, was the equivalent of that given to the Mercury astronauts taking the world into space with John Glenn's first orbit around the world on February 20, 1962. The overused word "awesome" was indeed appropriate in both cases. President Calvin Coolidge awarded Lindbergh the Distinguished Flying Cross, which had been authorized by Congress only the year before—another indication of how flying influenced even the politicians of the day to do something that would show how inspired they were as a group by "those magnificent men in their flying machines." Well, young Setchell knew what he wanted to do when he grew up—fly airplanes.

In 1938 Jim entered the Army Air Corps, receiving his pilot wings in 1939 at Kelly Field, San Antonio, Texas. War was on the horizon and the buildup had begun. He was sent to the photographic school at Lowry Field, Colorado, and subsequently assigned as commander of Headquarters Squadron of the First Photo-Mapping Group at Bolling Field, Washington, DC. He quickly assumed the position of Group Operations Officer until transferring to Peterson Field in Colorado Springs, in the same position but this time as operations officer of an F-4/5 combat replacement training unit. The F-4 and F-5 were the photographic reconnaissance versions of the P-38 fighter. The F-4 was the photo version of the P-38E/F, and the F-5 used the P-38G/J airframe. Peterson Field was named after Lieutenant Edward J. Peterson, who died from injuries received in a Lockheed F-4 Lightning crash on August 8, 1942. Peterson was the operations officer of the 14th Photographic Reconnaissance Squadron, a position filled by only the best among his fellow flyers.

It is interesting to note how fate brings people together. When Captain Setchell assumed the position of operations officer at Peterson Field, Barney Dobbs and his friend Al Blum, whose stories will follow in a later chapter, were there as well, getting their training in the F-5 before deploying to the Pacific. Jim Setchell was slated to head in the opposite direction—to North Africa and Europe. While they were at Peterson Field, a curious thing happened to Jim and his young bride Dorothy. They married in January 1942 just before Jim was transferred to Colorado Springs. As a junior captain, Jim was assigned many additional duties, as I presume is still customary in the Air Force of today; at least it was in the days when I served. One of his additional duties was as unit mortuary officer. He never gave it much thought, just another job title behind his name. But then one day one of his planes went down in the mountains west of Colorado Springs, and off he went in his own car to the accident site. The pilot of the unlucky F-5 had died in the crash, and not giving it a second thought, the accident investigation team put the pilot's body in the trunk of Jim's car for return to Peterson Field. On the way back Jim stopped by his home to change his uniform. Dorothy thought it was an opportune time to make a quick run to the grocery store—they only had one car—not knowing what was in the car's trunk. Fortunately she put the groceries in the back seat. Jim was frantic when he looked outside and saw the car was gone. Dorothy soon returned and Jim quickly drove off to deliver his unusual cargo. I have no idea if Jim ever told Dorothy what was in the trunk of their car. Those were simpler times and things were done a little differently from how they are done today.

In mid-1943, Jim had by now been promoted to major, the long-expected orders arrived for him to go to war. He and his navigator, Captain Jerome Alexander, went off to Toronto, Canada, and picked up a brand-new F-8 Mosquito photo reconnaissance aircraft. They flew it to Wright Field in Dayton, Ohio, for some modifications, then set off for La Marsa, Tunisia, where they had been assigned to the 3rd Photo Reconnaissance Group. Jim named the aircraft *The Spook*, with the name prominently painted on the nose of the aircraft. The route to their final destination was long and taxing for both man and machine. The particular route that Setchell and Alexander were to fly across the Atlantic was referred to as the North Atlantic Ferry Route, one of four such routes developed just a year earlier to allow the routine transfer of aircraft from the United States to the ETO. The North Atlantic route, coincidentally, was surveyed and established in early 1941 by then Captain Elliott Roosevelt, President Roosevelt's son, who by that time had achieved the rank of colonel and was to be Setchell's and Alexander's wing commander at La Marsa. They took off from Wright Field on September 24, arriving in Goose Bay, Labrador, the same day. Here Setchell and Alexander were stuck waiting for the weather over the North Atlantic to clear sufficiently to allow them to proceed to Blui 1, a newly constructed emergency airfield in Greenland. On September 30 they were still stuck at Goose Bay, so they took *The Spook* up for a forty-five-minute test flight. They encountered no problems with the aircraft, refueled it, and continued their wait for clearance to proceed. Four days later, on the 3rd of October, the weather finally cleared sufficiently for them to

The B-24 named *Big Cow* seen from Jim Setchell's Mosquito named *The Spook*. (Bill Setchell)

proceed. They were married up with a B-24 Liberator bomber with better navigation capabilities than their own and took off at 12:50 local time, following in trail of the B-24 with the curious name of *Big Cow* painted on its snout. Blui 1 was only 776 miles from Goose Bay, but it took them over four hours to get there. Greenland was anything but green—windswept and cold.

With full fuel tanks they took off the next morning, again behind *Big Cow*, which continued to be their lead, this time heading for Meeks Airport in Iceland. Iceland appeared green compared to Greenland. They sat for another three days at Meeks before heading on October 6 southeast to Prestwick Airport in Scotland. Here they parted with their B-24 lead to proceed on their own. They didn't know why it took so long, but they did not receive clearance for another nine days to proceed to their next staging base, St. Mawgan in Cornwall, England. The turnaround at St. Mawgan was fairly quick, and two days after their arrival, on the 17th, they departed for Casablanca, Morocco, a nearly-six hour flight mostly over water. The following morning they took off from Casablanca, the last leg of their long journey, for a four-and-a-half-hour flight across North Africa, landing at La Marsa airfield, near Carthage, at twenty minutes after three o'clock in the afternoon. La Marsa was a typical dusty desert airstrip, which at one time had been used by the Germans. Destroyed

Destroyed Luftwaffe aircraft along the runway at La Marsa air station. (Bill Setchell)

and damaged German aircraft littered the field. A lone Me 109 fighter, apparently undergoing routine maintenance, had been left behind when the Germans had to hurriedly flee the airfield.

Jim settled into his new assignment and found himself appointed commander of the 3rd Photo Reconnaissance Group. New and eager, he aimed to set an example for his men and started flying operational missions soon after taking command. The 3rd Photo Group was part of the 90th Photographic Wing (Reconnaissance) which in addition to the 3rd Photo Group had four additional groups equipped with a variety of aircraft modified for photographic work including the F-8 Mosquito, F-5 Lightning, and B-17 and B-25 bombers. Jim Setchell's group only flew the Mosquito and eventually transitioned to the F-5 Lightning, which he had trained in at Peterson Field.

The commander of the 90th Photographic Wing was Colonel Elliott Roosevelt. Roosevelt was rated a bombardier/navigator, not a pilot, because of poor eyesight. Although he flew numerous combat missions, it was always in the capacity of a navigator. In his diary Jim Setchell recalls a mission he flew with his boss to Algiers. "Flew Spook to Algiers November 10, 1943, with FDR Jr. Stayed all night at Hotel Argo. Went to nightclub that closed at 8:30. Dancing strictly prohibited. Terrible champagne for 225 Francs per bottle." As the old

The dinner table as described by Lieutenant Colonel Jim Setchell—the President of the United States at La Marsa while visiting his son Elliott, surrounded by his generals. (Bill Setchell)

saying goes, "War is hell." Then on December 7 Jim, being Elliott's tentmate, found himself in select company. Reads his diary, "Attended supper with President, Harry Hopkins, Generals Eisenhower, Spaatz, Curtis, Smith and Norstad, Colonel MacDonald [Spaatz's intelligence chief], Colonel Karl 'Pop' Polifka," and others. Such diversions were indeed a rarity. Jim was there to fight in a bloody war. As a matter of fact he understood his role all too well and would fly the most dangerous missions assigned to his group himself, instead of sending his young and less experienced lieutenants.

In January 1944 the 90th Wing, including its 3rd Group, moved from Tunisia to San Severo, Italy. As part of the wing's move Colonel Polifka assumed command of the wing, relieving Colonel Roosevelt. San Severo was one of many airfields near Foggia, from where the 15th Air Force launched its B-17 and B-24 bombers against targets in southern Germany.

The target areas to be photographed that Jim briefly referred to in his diary entries were heavily defended by German flak of all calibers. For the missions he flew on January 16, 17, and 22 he was awarded the Distinguished Flying Cross.

The citation accompanying the award of the DFC reads, "A major tactical problem was the location of well camouflaged guns that were

Colonel Karl "Pop" Polifka, a legend in the reconnaissance community, awarding the Air Medal to Jim Setchell at Severo airfield, Italy. Jim had just landed in *The Spook*, his navigator Jerome Alexander behind him. (Bill Setchell)

taking a costly toll of Allied troops. Faced with the urgent need to find the locations of the German guns so they could be knocked out and many lives saved, Lieutenant Colonel Setchell, as commanding officer of the 3rd Photo Group, proposed to fly missions to locate the guns at 10,000 to 12,000 feet—less than half the normal operational altitude and well within range of all enemy antiaircraft guns. Three missions were flown on January 16, 17 and 22 in an obsolete Mark IV Mosquito, the only aircraft available with camera equipment suitable for the task. The flak was intense and accurate. Lieutenant Colonel Setchell, knowing full well the importance of his mission, flew faultless flight-lines straight through the thickest of enemy defenses over Formia and Gaeta, Italy. The next day, 17 January, a similar mission was planned, and again Colonel Setchell took the assignment. This time his aircraft was hit repeatedly over the battle lines of Casino and the Volturo River. Colonel Setchell completed the mission before limping back to base with gaping holes in his aircraft. Then on January 22 a similar mission was flown over Anzio harbor and the airdrome at Nettuna. The pictures obtained on these three

Anzio Annie (Leopold), a giant railway gun, along with another (Robert), was used effectively against the Allies at Anzio. Jim Setchell flew several missions to locate these guns so they could be destroyed. They never were, but were captured in June 1944. (Author)

missions were of vital importance to the Fifth Army and resulted in the saving of many lives, as well as contributing substantially to the advance of our armies. . . ." Jim was lucky to have survived. It was a time when American and British forces landed at Anzio, a drive that soon stalled, turning into a bloody battle, pounded by some of Germany's heaviest guns, guns which Jim had been tasked to locate so they could be destroyed.

In the months to come, Jim Setchell flew his share of combat missions, including two missions to Cairo photographing German positions on the island of Crete, and two missions into the Soviet Union photographing targets en route and on the way back. By September 10, 1944, Jim had transitioned to the F-5 Lightning. His group still flew the Mosquito, but as for *The Spook*, it had met its end on August 19, 1944, when the aircraft was destroyed in a crash landing after returning from a combat mission. Jim's diary tells the story of what happened next:

"Departed San Severo on September 10, 1944, in F-5 number 123. Landed at Bari and had fuel topped off. Flew on the deck, weather clear and hazy, towards the island of Corfu. Approached my first target on the deck over the water, dropping my tanks four minutes offshore. Passed over the harbor of Piraeus, pulled up to 300 feet as I crossed the coastline and started my cameras. The target for a planned airborne drop was easily visible. I crossed directly over it, with front and right oblique cameras operating. There were about forty large seaplanes in the harbor and several active transports on Kalamaki airdrome. Saw no flak, but after passing Kalamaki airdrome the plane lurched violently to the right while passing over a target. Trimmed to the left and noticed a large hole in the right rear tail-boom, probably made by 20mm flak. The right rudder must have sustained some damage as well, causing the plane to swing to the right. The lower cockpit window was smashed, inflicting several cuts on my right arm and hand. After trimming to the left, the plane operated OK. Apparently neither engine had been hit. I skirted hills and proceeded to my second target. Again I approached from over water on the deck and pulled up to 300 feet as I crossed the coast, starting my cameras. Many people were on the beach. After passing Khalkis harbor the temperature on the right engine suddenly hit the peg. Looking at the engine I saw fire under the right engine, rapidly spreading along the entire length of the boom. The cockpit was filling with smoke, making it impossible for me to see the instrument panel. I pulled the emergency canopy release, put down the left window and ditched the plane. The plane landed very well, then swung sharply to the left before stopping, twisting my right shoulder. I unfastened my safety belt, picked up my dinghy and first aid kit and stepped out on the left wing. Then I pulled the Mae West cords and stepped off the wing into the water as the plane sank nose first. I was about 50 yards off shore. Salt water made cuts on my arm and hand very painful. I floated fine in the Mae West survival jacket and decided not to inflate the dinghy. I noticed people on shore and waved to them. A boat approached with two men in it, stopping about 50 feet from where I was. I shouted, 'Americano, Americano.' One of the men fingered a mean looking gun, but he finally came toward me and pulled me into the boat.

"They were Greek fishermen. We then pulled in my dinghy and parachute. We reached shore, and several people put their arms

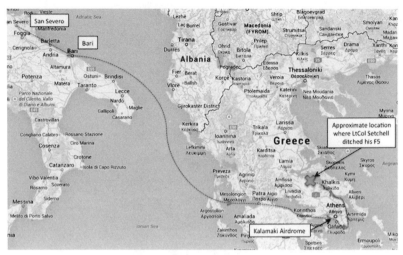

Colonel Setchell's route from San Severo, his base, to Bari, to Kalamaki airdrome, where he was hit by German AAA and eventually had to ditch his aircraft—F-5A-10 #42–13123. (Bill Setchell)

around me, smiled, saying 'Americano.' Three or four men had old rifles with gun belts across their chests. They escorted me up a winding trail to a church, announcing proudly that they were partisans. In the priests bedroom I removed my wet clothes while the priest bandaged my arm and hand. They gave me native clothes to wear, and I ate a good meal—goat, potatoes, brown bread and raisin wine. After an hour's rest in the priest's bed, complete with clean sheets, I awoke from pain in my shoulder and hand. The priest brought in my clothes, which had been dried and pressed. About dark, a doctor arrived and told me in English that I was to spend the night in his house. He rebandaged my arm and hand and massaged my shoulder which hurt intensely. I slept that night in a comfortable bed and fully realized how fortunate I was. I had asked the doctor about contacting English or American forces, and while he claimed he had no knowledge of their whereabouts, he assured me that the partisans would see to it that I was taken care of properly.

"The following day, September 11, I spent the morning talking to two Greeks from nearby towns who had lived in America. They emphatically assured me that I was safe and would not be turned over to the Germans. In the afternoon I talked to the doctor who was remembering more and more of his English. He had been a political

Major Leon W. Gray, C.O. of the 5th Photo Reconnaissance Group, flying out of San Severo, inspecting damage to his F-5A after returning from a combat mission. This is the aircraft, #123, Jim Setchell flew when he had to ditch it on September 10, 1944. (Bill Setchell)

prisoner of the Germans for two months during which time 40 or 50 prisoners from his camp were shot daily. He had studied medicine in Vienna for seven years, and his former professor, who was now in Athens in an official capacity, had obtained his release. A few days before my arrival, the Germans had come and taken most of his furniture, silver and things he was not able to hide before fleeing into the mountains with the rest of the villagers. I walked around his property noting that he had an old Ford truck and tractor. He informed me that we were leaving early in the morning.

"On September 12, at 0400 hours, the doctor, two partisans and I started along a narrow rocky road. After about a mile we met up with a two wheeled cart which carried us over a very rough road to Ata. We rested for an hour, sitting in a small sidewalk café. A large crowd formed to look at the American. Pictures were taken with the partisan chief who sported a full beard, three gun belts, four knives, a rifle with a bayonet, binoculars, big tassels on his shoes and a funny little round hat. He said that the uniform and most equipment had been taken from Germans he had killed. He seemed a comic figure until the doctor told me that his brother and two sisters had all been killed by the Germans. I gave the partisan chief an American dollar bill as a souvenir and he gave me some German money he had taken from one of his victims. We continued on a motorcycle which had been left behind by the English. When we arrived at Lev, people lined the streets, clapping their hands, giving me flowers and fruit. I sat in the town square drinking ouzo with three men who had lived in America. People crowded around wanting to know when the American and British armies would arrive. Small children marched by with wooden guns singing partisan songs. Being stared at by the multitude was getting tiresome and I was glad when the doctor told me we were leaving for another town for lunch.

"After about an hour's ride on the motorcycle we arrived in the small town of Akos. Here I watched a parade. More flowers and fruit, and I was prodded to make a speech from a little balcony with a Greek interpreter by my side. That evening we had a wonderful dinner of fish, macaroni, chicken, potatoes, salad, wine, fruit and olive oil cake. The cake took all my democratic spirit and stomach to get it down. I was informed that the girls of the town had made it especially for the American—so down it went. I asked where the Germans were and was told that none had been reported in the area for days. I walked around the town. Saw the damage that had been done by German naval ships when they shelled the town after a fight between the Germans and the partisans. After a short motorcycle ride and a three hour mule trip up a mountain trail we arrived at the small village of Ka. The doctor and I stayed in a simple peasant's home, ate some kind of stew from a common pot. No plates. We slept on the floor with plenty of beautifully colored blankets. The next morning I was served black bread and goat cheese for breakfast. The doctor told me that there was some sort of Allied military mission nearby. We learned it had recently been attacked and withdrawn, so we returned to the doctor's home."

Dorothy, Jim Setchell's wife, had not been told of him being missing and shot down. The familiar Western Union telegram was instead
sent to his father in early October 1944, who re-sent it to Dorothy.
No one wants to see a telegram like this:

THE SECRETARY OF WAR DESIRES ME TO EXPRESS HIS
DEEP REGRET THAT YOUR SON LIEUTENANT COLONEL
JAMES F SETCHELL HAS BEEN REPORTED MISSING IN
ACTION SINCE SEPTEMBER ELEVEN OVER GREECE.
IF FURTHER DETAILS OR OTHER INFORMATION ARE
RECEIVED YOU WILL BE PROMPTLY NOTIFIED. J A
ULIO ADJUTANT GENERAL.

"On the 14th of September I helped the doctor make a cast for
a partisan who had been shot through the thigh. In the afternoon
I watched him remove the eye of a Russian partisan who had been
wounded in a fire fight. I couldn't last out the operation and got out of
the room just prior to passing out. I spent a couple of hours listening
to the rantings of a communist who spoke very poor English—but
he helped kill time. In the evening I watched the doctor dress the
arm of a villager. He had removed the man's shattered hand in the
woods at night by lantern light while the Germans were in the village.
Had a good supper of chicken. Saw pathfinder flares from planes
probably bombing Athens. The doctor advised me we were leaving
again early in the morning. A motorcycle driver arrived claiming
that many Dakota planes had landed at the mission site. I went to
sleep with high hopes of soon being on my way back to Italy.
    "On September 15 we departed at 0500. Passed through several
villages. Partisans on horseback directed us down roads to avoid
German troops. We rode along a railroad track while a train loaded
with German troops passed. After a three hour mule trip we arrived
at the mission. There I was met by a British major, an Australian
captain and interpreters. Sent a radio message to the 90th that I was
safe. During the morning saw 60 B-24s passing overhead. The next
day the doctor left for home. I walked part way down the trail with
him, very sorry to part company. A sincere friendship had sprung
up between us and I felt a great indebtedness toward him for the aid

The C-47 Skytrain, the military version of the versatile DC-3, was used extensively in the ETO, from dropping paratroopers to towing Waco gliders on D-Day, to mundane deliveries of whatever kind. It was an indispensable aircraft. Referred to as Dakota by the British. C-47s at Fassberg air base, Germany, during the Berlin airlift in the spring of 1949—my mother and ten-year-old sister Ingrid behind of one of the Airlift C-47s. (Author)

he had given me at great risk to himself. Had a conversation with the British major. His job was sabotage, distributing air dropped guns, ammunition and supplies, and keeping his station one jump ahead of the Germans. A sergeant gave me fresh clothes and toilet articles. What a privilege to properly clean my teeth. He also bandaged my arm and hand which were healing nicely.

"Slept the night on a pine bow bed. Very cold at night, but had plenty of blankets. Food has been excellent—cooked American style without olive oil. Sent another radio message to Cairo regarding evacuation point for me. The next day, September 20, I drank our last ouzo and we ran out of sugar. Waiting for the next plane to arrive and a messenger who had been sent to Athens for supplies. Athens is the best supplied city in Europe. Plenty of whiskey, chocolate, cigars. Members of the station often put on civilian clothes and spent several days in Athens mingling with the Germans. Forged passes are prepared and the only real danger is of being picked up when the Germans decide to gather a few hostages. What a strange war.

On the 21st an F-5 flew directly overhead making slight vapor trails. So near and yet so far. That evening a Dakota dropped off three men and supplies from Italy.

"I helped round up chutes and supplies. Partisans and goat herders tried to steal everything. The major announced that the mission would move the next day, September 23, and that I would be in the advance party. Up at 0600 for a four hour hike down the mountain to a fishing village. Got in a fishing boat and after about four hours of rowing the fishermen decided the wind was too bad and turned around. Had a fish supper and slept on the floor of an old shack. Rats running around and over me all night. Very little sleep. In the morning the British major arrived with no news. He is very friendly and said if I wanted to take a boat to Turkey he would accompany me to the coast. The next day the major told me that all boats heading for the coast of Turkey had been captured by the Germans. It's early on the 27th of September. We are up at 0630, but the mules weren't ready until 10:00. The major gave me ten gold sovereigns for which I gave him useless American paper money from my escape kit. I also had a parachute for bartering purposes. Walked about a mile out of the village when a charcoal burning bus picked us up and delivered us to Yer. An old woman on the bus gave me some green olives and cheese. At the coast the sea was too rough and we had to wait.

"The next morning I spent two hours picking up shells along the beach to keep from going slap happy. Tired of people standing around and staring at me. On the 29th I boarded a fishing boat. The schooner passed close to a town occupied by the Germans. Everyone was alert looking for German boats. We finally reached Galax. Went to the home of a lady who was the Greek wife of an Englishman, and had lived in India. I'm in heaven. Tea with maple sugar and grapes as soon as we arrived. Someone to talk to in English. Wonderful supper. Then listened to Victrola music before going to bed in an elegant bedroom. Paid one gold sovereign and parachute panels. Next morning we walked and rode mules to Levireki. Every house destroyed and burned. Spent the night in a priest's house and collected an army of fleas. Paid with parachute panels.

"On October 3 we arrived at the English mission headquarters. Had tea and cakes. Wonderful to sleep in a real bed, fleas terminated.

Paid for mules with one gold sovereign, waiting for a plane to arrive. After four weeks in Greece, even Italy will look good—no plane by October 8."

That day Colonel Polifka, Jim Setchell's boss, wrote a brief letter of encouragement to Jim's wife Dorothy. Dear Dottie, I am sorry I was unable to write to you these details before, but I was unable to do so because of the necessary time lapse which we must allow for, and beside, I was hoping by allowing a little time I would not have to write you. Jim's last mission was a low level mission in the Athens area in making final preparation for the recent invasion of Greece by two British divisions. The only opposition anticipated was a heavy concentration of 40 and 88 millimeter anti-aircraft on one of the coves. Here the heavy assault landing was to be made. I believe that Jim probably received a crippling hit on this run and hope that he was forced to crash land in the vicinity. I fully expect to send him home to you on thirty days leave before Easter as we have been fortunate in having everyone of our people who have crash landed in this particular operational area return to us within four or five months time. I will not offer you condolences as I feel positive that Jim is okay. Sincerely, Karl.

"October 10 was rainy and cold. An American captain arrived with three American enlisted men to be evacuated, as well as three American OSS men, two with fever and one with a broken leg. No plane. On the 12th the weather was very good, but we learned there would be no plane tonight, nor on the following day. Much shooting at night and hand grenades being set off to announce the liberation of Athens after almost four years of occupation. All English and Americans went to the local café where we sat with the villagers drinking great quantities of ouzo. Listened to many Greek songs— *You are my sunshine; Down by the old mill stream; Show me the way to go home.* On the 14th four Me 109s passed over, flying east in a wide formation at 500 feet. At 1300 a Halifax circles several times, but didn't land."

On October 23 Jim Setchell finally managed to get a ride on a Red Cross truck to Lamia, escorting the American with the broken leg. The roads were terrible, bridges were blown requiring detours through rough mountain country. Finally, on the morning of

October 25 they reached Athens. The American with the broken
leg was cared for at a Red Cross hospital, and Jim found luxury accommodations in the Grand Britain Hotel. Life in Athens seemed
normal, as if there was no war going on. The following day he got a
ride to Kalamika Airdrome and caught a ride to Bari, Italy, just across
the Ionian Sea, accompanied by wounded British paratroopers on
stretchers and four war correspondents. His odyssey, which never
took him further than 100 miles from Athens, ended practically
where his plane had crashed six weeks earlier.

In a letter to Dorothy, on November 4, 1944, after returning to his
unit, Jim writes: "Darling Hag, Pop [Colonel Polifka] returned yesterday from his trip to the States and what a celebration we had last
night. He brought three bottles of bourbon, which we consumed with
the greatest of ease. Since my return I have been busy with physical
checkups and interrogations from various headquarters regarding
my experiences. For security reasons I have been taken off combat
flying, so now must do my flying over friendly territory. No more
flak or fighters, and of course goodbye to most of the thrills and fun.
All I can tell you now of my trip is that my plane was hit by flak,
caught fire, and I landed in the water. I had the laugh on lots of the
boys when I got back because most of them swore it was impossible
to successfully land a P-38 in the water without it immediately going
to the bottom. I got out of it before it went down. My several weeks
of wanderings in the mountains, and how I finally got back to Italy
are, of course, secret. But you'll know the whole story after the war."

Lieutenant Colonel James F. Setchell survived the war and returned to his wife and young son after nearly two years of combat,
decorated with the Silver Star, the Distinguished Flying Cross, four
awards of the Air Medal and the Purple Heart. Before war's end
Jim was promoted to colonel and continued to serve as operations
officer of the 90th Reconnaissance Wing in Italy. In 1958 Jim was assigned to the Industrial College of the Armed Forces at Fort McNair,
Washington DC. His studies were cut short by a brain tumor. He
died in 1960 to join the many flyers who had gone west before him.

General Doolittle writes in his autobiography, *I Could Never Be So
Lucky Again*, "Our photo reconnaissance group, under Colonel Elliott Roosevelt, developed the capability to take radar photos, which

Lt/Colonel Jim Setchell in Italy, after his return from Greece. Good to be alive. (Bill Setchell)

was particularly useful when the target areas were clouded over. If we saw a target being built up, we didn't want to bomb it until the enemy had spent considerable time in the construction phase, then we would take it out. The reconnaissance flights and their resultant radar photos permitted us to select targets, determine the best time to attack, and, afterward, determine how much damage had been done. This photo capability was greatly enhanced as the resolution on our radar screens improved. Elliott did a splendid job for us in North Africa and continued to show his leadership qualities in England. My only worry about him was that he was absolutely fearless and flew on some very difficult missions. I was greatly concerned that he would be killed and I would have to explain to the President why I let him do some of the things he did. I almost broke his heart when I took him off flying."

AL TUCKER

P-38 LIGHTNING/GLOSTER METEOR/P-80 SHOOTING STAR

The lucky ones were brought to Barth to rot in a Kriegie kamp,
to live each day and at night to lay in a room that's cold and damp.
I'll bet there's less of home's comforts here than you'll find in all creation,
but for all that, it'd be really rough, if it weren't for our Red Cross rations.
—AUTHOR UNKNOWN

The training for F-5 Lightning reconnaissance pilots was done at Peterson Field, Colorado Springs, Colorado. Most P-38 Lightning fighter pilots were trained at Santa Ana, California, now the Santa Ana municipal airport, and Williams Field near Tempe, Arizona. Albert "Tuck" Tucker and Robin Olds, both West Pointers, class of 1943, went to Williams for pilot training. Their stories of young men going to war to serve their country are, to say the least, inspirational.

Recalled Al Tucker when I interviewed him, "My father was an army officer. His home was Lexington, Virginia. He was born and raised there, and I feel like I grew up in Lexington, because my father would send my mother and us children to Lexington for the summer each year. As a consequence I thought I grew up as a Virginian; although I was born in 1921 in Lexington, Kentucky. Of course my father, being an army officer, was stationed at various army posts in the country. I got my fascination for aviation at Fort Benning, Georgia, which for years was the location of the army's infantry school. Each military specialty had a particular post which specialized in a particular arm—such as infantry, armor, artillery, and so on. That would have been back in the early thirties when I was there as a young boy, about eleven, twelve years old. The infantry school had to have some aviation, so they had a flight of O-25 observation planes. To my amazement I saw lots of airplanes while I was there, fighting planes as well, which demonstrated to the infantry what they could do. I was absorbed with the spectacle of watching these planes fly, I loved it, and decided right then and there that I was going to fly some day.

"My dad's response was, 'You can fly if you want, that's your business. But you have to graduate from college first.' Well, I agreed with that. And since I had to go to college, that was the rule, I decided I may as well go to the army college, at West Point, and then I would be able to join the people I was going to fly with. I did that. Got into West Point after going to a prep school and passing a slew of tests. I entered the Point in 1940, which would have been the class of 1944. But Pearl Harbor happened in December 1941, and four days later Germany declared war on the United States. The war was on, so the army decided that we would graduate in three years rather than four. By the way, my father was not a West Pointer. He graduated from the University of Virginia.

"While at West Point it was also decided that those of us who wanted to go into aviation would get our flight training while we were there. So, I got all my flight training before I graduated from West Point. I received my wings a day before I was commissioned in the United States Army as a second lieutenant. There was a small field at Newburgh, New York, where we trained. A civilian field had been taken over and they lengthened the runways, built hangars and buildings, all the stuff that goes with a regular airfield operation. As a result of me being a qualified aviator, I did not have to march in my graduation parade. Instead I, along with several other classmates, flew over it. The day I got my wings General 'Hap' Arnold, the commanding general of the Army Air Forces, pinned my wings on. And then the next day, since I now was a pilot, I flew over my graduation parade with my first passenger, the crew chief of my AT-10 volunteered to fly with me. It was a tremendous formation of AT-10 and AT-6 aircraft that did a fly-by that day, about 60 to 80 aircraft. After the parade flyover we landed back at Newburgh and were driven back to West Point. That afternoon they had the graduation ceremony. But the president of West Point got sick and couldn't come. At the

Newly promoted 2nd Lieutenant Al Tucker in 1943 with his proud parents. (Al Tucker)

last minute they got General George Marshall, from VMI, to do the honors, and he shook my hand that afternoon. So, I am quite proud of the fact that two very important people had shaken my hand within the span of two days—Generals Arnold and Marshall.

"Also, I want to mention, that during my third year at West Point we got about twice as much flying time as the average pilot trainee. So we were well prepared for what lay ahead. Those in the flying cadet program barely got 200 hours flying time spread over six months— while I got a little over 300 hours, including instrument training. You could hardly fly through the bad winter weather without such training. The average trainee got little or none of such training. As a result, the losses in training and later in combat as a result of a lack of instrument training were colossal."

Stephen E. Ambrose, the well-known writer about World War II, in his book *The Wild Blue*, writes about training losses. "It was at Coffeyville that [George] McGovern [senator from South Dakota in later years] saw his first pilot killed. The officer had pulled up too fast on takeoff and stalled into a nose drop. 'He just hit the runway—just bang. I was standing not too far from there. The fire engines were out in what seemed to me to be nothing flat. But when they pulled him out of the plane his body was just like a lobster.' Cadet Charles Watry wrote that an accidental death led to a cadet saying, 'That is the hard way out of the program.' One of his classmates was practicing S-turns along a road. A twin-engine plane was doing the same thing. They had a mid-air collision. One of the propellers of the twin-engine craft cut off the tail of the classmate's plane, which crashed, killing him. In total, the AAF lost 439 lives in the primary flight schools during the war. In basic school there were 1,175 fatalities, while in advanced training—flying bigger, faster airplanes, with more complicated training—there were 1,888 deaths."

"Twelve of us were lucky enough to be sent to P-38 training," Al Tucker continued. "I think half my class of flyers volunteered for P-38s, but only 12 out of about 200 applicants were picked. Among the people who went to P-38s was the great Robin Olds. We were buddies at the Point, and all the way through flight training and P-38 training. As a matter of fact, because we were regular officers [vice reserve officers, which most of the flyers in the Army Air Forces were] we went through P-38 training about two or three times. As regular officers, the rules stipulated, we couldn't be sent to duty anywhere in a capacity less than flight leader. Wisely the squadron commanders overseas wouldn't accept us new guys as flight leaders without combat experience. So, we had to find a way to get over into the war. Robin and I found a sergeant who prepared for us a request for orders. The sergeant gave the request to his lieutenant, who gave the request to his captain, and the captain took it to the colonel—who said OK. Not only for Robin and me, but the other ten as well. We walked out of the place with orders in hand, sending us to Europe—not as flight leaders, but as regular pilots. They made it legal by sending us to one final fighter group that was forming up in the United States. It was the last to go as an organized fighter group rather than just replacement pilots going to existing groups. We joined that last group—the 479th Fighter Group forming up in the United States. All of us were at the same level—amateurs without any combat experience. I became a flight leader. The group commander didn't mind, because he hadn't been a flight leader either. We were all amateurs—and that was a mistake. We got a few drills of how we were supposed to behave over there in England, how we were supposed to fly, and how to find our home base among hundreds. There weren't many aids to navigation in those days."

Of course, the 479th was the outfit that Dave Schilling refused to take as its commander when Hub Zemke broached the offer to him, so Zemke took over this "lame-duck" outfit, as everyone seemed to refer to the 479th, and gave up the 56th Fighter Group, a P-47 outfit better known as the Wolf Pack, to Dave Schilling.

"Once we arrived in England," Al continued with his story in our interview, "we had to get used to talking on the radio. We would call for a 'steer.' And we had a homer. The homer was the radio in the tower that steered you. I am sure it was all great fun for the British, because this whole radio bearing scheme was RAF designed. We had to fit into it, get used to their way of doing things. Most of the voices we heard would be hard to read British/Scotch brogues. We must have messed them up a little bit with our Yankee talk. At least I hope so. When I called for a steer, at least three other stations remote from each other would listen and draw a bead on you, draw a line on their charts, and then, by telephone pass those bearings to whoever was acting as the coordinator. Where the lines crossed, that's where you were. They would call back and say something like, 'Yank, you asked for a steer. I say old chap, I see right where you are.' He'd then give you a heading to get you to your airfield. That's the only radio aid we had to navigation. Then we had to get used to what the countryside looked like. It was beautiful and navigable when you could see it. But you had to get used to flying very low. We weren't restricted to any particular altitude in those days. We flew at any height. I have to marvel, with all the air activity over there, I don't understand why there weren't just volumes of collisions, especially for the bombers. When the bombers would take off in the morning, starting about four o'clock, it would take them a couple of hours just to join up. And it might be overcast. And I don't know how they got away with it. We would hear them drone overhead for hours before we even got out of bed."

Said Colonel David Taylor, a B-17 pilot, in my interview with him: "I remember one particular bad mission. I was looking at my best friend flying next to me, off my right wing, and he was looking over at me. I still remember the look on his face. Then he took a direct hit. His aircraft exploded. There was nothing left for me to see. On many of our missions, the killing started before we got going. On bad-weather days—and there were many of those in England—we called them crash-and-burn days—after take-off we were to assemble over a radio beacon near our base. In theory it was a good procedure. In practice, it left a lot to be desired and we never fixed the problem throughout the war. As we took off, the lead aircraft made a spiraling left turn until breaking out of the overcast and then waited for his squadron mates to join up. Unfortunately, there were numerous bases nearby. As we spiraled up to altitude, our turns got wider and wider, like an inverted cone, and in time our cone would overlap with the cone of another base. The aircraft crashing into each other never knew what happened. On take-off I frequently could see the bodies of my friends strewn across meadows, hanging over fences. Others burned to death in the inferno of a crashing aircraft. Do you know what a human body looks like after it has burned in an air crash? A little black ball which you can hold in your hands. That's all that's left of a man." Dave paused, the recollections of tragedies flitting past his inner eye as if they happened yesterday. He frowned. His eyes shone brightly.

The Mighty Eighth War Diary, by Roger A. Freeman, notes that between June 1942 and May 1945, more than 6,500 B-17 and B-24 heavy bombers were lost over Europe. One in six, more than a thousand aircraft, were lost to accidents rather than enemy action. The Eighth Air Force heavy bomber force in England was maintained at a strength of two thousand aircraft.

Bob Hoover recalled during my interview with him: "We didn't do much flying while in England, with the English winter weather being what it was—rain, snow and more rain. If not rain then heavy cloud layers and morning fog obscured the countryside. When a pilot was vectored in over an airfield, ground control would shoot up a green flare to let him know he was over the field. Then pilots would circle down slowly until they broke out of the clouds to land. That

Typical European flying weather was lots of clouds, rain, interrupted by occasional days of sunshine. A Red Bull P-38 in flight. (Martin Frauenheim)

kind of flying alone was scary enough, but there was a hill near the runway, and if the pilot's circles were too wide, he crashed into the hillside." Every day flying took its toll.

"We were assigned to RAF Station Wattisham," Tucker continued, "in County Suffolk, near Ipswich, near the mouth of the Thames River. We were about as close to the English Channel as you could get. Close to the other side as well, a very short flight across the Channel. A major from another group came over to brief and lead us on our first combat mission. A good thing, since we were all amateurs. The major took us around in a couple of big formations over England to get us used to flying over England. Then he led us over the Continent a little bit, not far, but just far enough to get shot at so we knew what flak looked like. Then we were turned loose. I flew twenty-two combat missions—and was shot down on my twenty-second. One of those was a tremendously exciting mission. It was on the 5th of June 1944. Late afternoon before D-Day. We knew something big was going to happen because we were ordered quite suddenly to go down to the flight line for briefings. As we approached the flight line, we could see our airplanes being painted with big white and black

Lieutenant Al Tucker being strapped into his P-38 Lightning fighter by his crew chief at RAF Station Wattisham, United Kingdom. (Al Tucker)

stripes over the wings. We ended up flying top cover on D-Day, the 6th of June 1944. It was raining. The visibility was poor. An ugly day to be starting a battle. I was just aghast at the spectacle below me. I saw many boats in the water—it seemed like there were thousands. And they were all getting in line. It looked like rivers of boats heading for the Channel, one behind the other, like marching in a parade. These streams of boats then joined up into a great mass. I thought, 'Oh, my God, I wouldn't want to be on the other side, with that coming at me.' On the other hand, what a target they were. We just orbited over the Channel; didn't go over land. Our orders were to shoot down anything that was at our flight level or below us. The Luftwaffe never showed. We flew several of those missions that day and the following day. They used P-38s for this task because everyone knew what a P-38 looked like. And the other side had nothing like it. As we were circling at 4,000 feet, I watched battleships hurl their gigantic shells against the enemy. The shells came past us fairly close. I could clearly see them traveling through the air.

"Then I flew several escort missions to Berlin. On one of those missions I finally got to see an enemy airplane, but we were not permitted to leave the bombers. I learned the Luftwaffe had a policy at the time, to avoid a lot of losses unnecessarily, not to attack bombers with fighter escort. Instead they chose another bomb group without escort. So we didn't experience any air-to-air combat. Robin and I just had a ball flying the P-38.

"The twenty-second mission was my last. It was a day that we didn't have a mission assigned, the 22nd of June. We were playing volleyball when a sergeant in a carry-all drove up and told us to go down to the airfield right away for a briefing. 'They have some kind of mission for you all.' We quickly got into our flight gear and headed down to the briefing room. There we learned that 9th Air Force wanted us to take out a railroad bridge just north of Paris. We were assigned to the 8th Air Force. Our mission was fighter escort for bombers. The 9th was responsible for supporting the ground forces. On this day the 9th didn't have enough resources to do it on their own, so they asked the 8th Air Force for help. I wished I had dropped a bomb in the P-38 before, that was going to be our mission, but none of us ever had. I had seen it done on newsreels. At the briefing we learned that my squadron was to fly top cover for the other two squadrons in our group. Each of their airplanes would carry a 1,000 pound bomb under each wing. In addition, the group commander, accompanied by three other pilots from his staff, was coming along as well.

"A combat squadron consisted of four flights of four. But our lead squadron this time would have five flights of four because the group commander and his staff were coming on this mission as well. Added up, that came to a total of 72,000 pounds of bombs carried by 36 aircraft. My squadron shouldn't have carried any bombs, but someone higher up decided that we could carry a couple of 100-pounders under each wing and still be able to provide top cover. And if some Messerschmitts should show up, we'd pickle them and be ready to defend our friends down below. As soon as we destroyed the bridge, the idea was, every flight was to hit the deck and return home on a preassigned heading. And strafe any targets of opportunity on the way back. Off we went. As I remember, it took us about an hour and a half to get there. The whole group went into orbit over the target to get a good look at it. Then the number one squadron went down, five flights in trail, led by the group commander. I looked down. Bombs were going off all over the place. Most landed on dry land throwing up huge geysers of earth. The fuses had been set with a 14-second delay, which explained why so much dirt was thrown up into the air obscuring the target itself. Some of the bombs hit the water—that was spectacular to watch. Pretty soon all the bombs had been dropped—and it looked to me like the bridge hadn't been hit. It was an open girder railroad bridge, so there really wasn't any floor to the bridge. Even if a bomb had hit the bridge it would have gone right through, or skipped over that girder and blown up somewhere else, with that 14-second delay set into the fuse. To me the bridge looked perfectly fine after dropping 72,000 pounds of bombs. My squadron leader, Major Keller, called over the radio, 'Hey, group, this is Keller.' By the way, we weren't supposed to be talking on the radio. 'That bridge looks like it is still standing. You want us to go down and have a crack at it?' With little hesitation the group commander responded, 'Yea, Keller, you might as well have a crack at it too.' So, Keller over the radio calls, 'OK, Blue Cross Gang,' that's us, 'it's going to be flights in trail. Follow me. Here we go.' Keller had the flight in front of me. Robin Olds had the flight behind me. And he had the fourth flight behind him. As soon as Keller got going down, and as soon as I got going down, I began to see what I would describe as golf balls coming up at us. Once I got to the POW camp I learned from more experienced flyers that the 40mm round had a glow behind the back side of the shell. And it caused a halo to appear around the shell which can be seen when the shell is in your line of sight— meaning the shells were coming straight up at us. We were looking right down the barrels of the guns shooting at us—seeing golf balls coming up at us. Everything happened very fast. I didn't respond to the first one. The next shell hit my right engine right on the spinner of the propeller; knocking the spinner off. The airplane shook violently as the shell penetrated through the engine longitudinally. The engine stopped running, throwing fire back into the airstream. I knew I was hit bad, but here I was in a dive, and I figured I might as well finish the dive. Everybody went down the same chute, one right after the other. On the way down, in addition to seeing the golf balls, I saw two airplanes going in—one blew up in the air. The other one blew up when it hit the ground. Robin saw this too, and he saw me getting hit. Robin was the only one in our squadron who used his head. He pulled his flight out to the right under a lot of fire and then he approached from a differing heading and dropped his bombs. His guys survived. When I got out of the POW camp and I met up with Robin, he said to me, 'Tucker, you did what you were told. I didn't.' Ours was an example of how not to fly a combat mission. Everything we did was wrong, from the bomb fusing to the way we attacked that bridge. Why was it allowed to happen? Our training was terrible. That's how I got shot down."

Robin Olds, in his book *Fighter Pilot*, reflects on those grim days. The 479th Fighter Group took some heavy losses soon after the D-Day landings: "Our losses were dispiriting yet not devastating. Lieutenants Kuentzel and Grdenich failed to return from a mission. They'd been trapped atop an overcast topping out near 28,000 feet. When last seen, both aircraft were in a steep spiral headed for the ground near Rouen. Just three days later, more bad news. This time four were lost, including my pal Tucker. He was hit by flak while returning home on one engine. Canella, Ilsley and Lutz went down too, lost forever, but it turned out that 'Tuck's Luck' held, and Al survived to sit out the rest of the war in Stalag Luft I. Those of us who survived those days went on to fly with an appreciation of life that can be known only by those who have been in combat. Laughter was as profound as sadness. Friendships deepened. Every moment of each day felt exactly right, and the edges of time seemed tinged by light."

"After I got rid of my bombs," Al Tucker recalls, "I peeled off to the right and headed home. No time to be scared. Just doing what I could to stay up in the air. I flew on the deck. My wingman stayed with me until we got to Reims where he saw me get shot down. We were flying at treetop level. I recall clipping the tops of trees. My good engine went through them with no problem. Beyond the forest there was a ridge line. I thought I saw some fence posts running along the top of the distant ridge. As I approached, I realized the fence posts were changing elevation because I was going higher too. They weren't fence posts, but gun barrels. I had trouble climbing. The props on the dead engine were bent forward. I couldn't feather them. They dragged me down. The most speed I could get out of

The German V-1 'Buzz' bomb, could be launched from the ground, ships and aircraft. Shown at an enemy aircraft exhibit at Wright Field in 1945. (Author)

A computer generated picture of a British Spitfire in the process of tipping the wing of a V-1 to cause it to crash. Most V-1s were taken down by AAA using American proximity-fused ammunition. Release of such fusing was tightly controlled by the Combined Chiefs of Staff in Washington to assure that there was no chance proximity-fused ammunition fell into German hands. (Hans Ulrich Gaserow He 111 pilot)

my good engine was about 190 knots. But if I did any climbing I lost airspeed rapidly. I was slowing down as I approached the AAA guns on the ridge line. I was now under 150 knots. The airplane wouldn't steer between the guns, but dragged me right over a gunpit. I could see three men behind each of the guns. They were Oerlikon, Swiss,

20mm guns with two barrels each, firing alternately. They hit my wing fuel tank. The airplane was on fire and all I could do was belly it in. I could see and feel the flames. I pulled the power back. The P-38 settled down nicely and held together until I jumped out. I ran for my life. The ammunition in the nose was exploding as the aircraft burned. Very quickly a platoon of infantry arrived. What appeared to be a sergeant came up to me and said, 'For you ze var is over.' He spoke very good English, of course with a heavy German accent. I had landed right in the middle of a V-1 launch site.

"A car appeared and took me to their headquarters. From then on I was in the hands of the Luftwaffe. The Luftwaffe fired the V-1s, but apparently the security guards were Wehrmacht—army. They first took me to a jail in Lille. There I got a little bit of an interrogation by a sergeant. Whoever he was, he was a commanding presence. He towered over me by about a foot, and I am over six feet tall. I objected to him taking my class ring. 'You can take my watch, things off my uniform, but not my class ring,' I protested. I don't speak German but I understood everyone of the expletives he uttered very loudly into my face. The following day I, along with other POWs, was put on an old fashioned passenger car from the turn of the century which was hooked onto a freight train. The car was full.

People were sitting on the floor, laying in the overhead baggage racks. For some reason I got to sit by the window. I thought that was nice. I opened the window to breathe in the fresh air. A woman in a railroad uniform sat opposite from me. She was a good looking gal, probably in her thirties. She looked very serious. She had a bag of cherries, it was the season, and she began to eat the cherries one by one, very slowly, deliberately. I was hungry and salivating. Oh, those cherries looked so good. I thought she was expressing contempt when she looked at me. It got me irritated. I began to resent her, thought it was pretty nasty of her to be sitting there eating those cherries in front of my face, knowing that I was hungry. Then, without changing her facial expression, she rose to leave—and handed me the bag of cherries. There was a lesson for me to learn from this experience—not to judge people too quickly. A couple of times the train stopped and we had to get out, but we were lucky and didn't get attacked by our own fighters. It took about a day and a half to get from the jail in Lille to Frankfurt. In Frankfurt we got off the train and were loaded on a bus which took us to the Luftwaffe interrogation center at Oberursel.

"Our briefings had been very accurate about what to expect if we were captured and sent to Oberursel. They knew much about us, but we also knew their interrogators by name. I was interrogated by one of their very best—Herr Scharff. His winning ways were charm and gentleness. He was so helpful and encouraging that it was easy to 'spill the beans.' I was there for about thirty days. One of my West Point classmates who had been shot down the day before me was confined with me for the last ten days. We quickly determined that they probably expected us to talk to each other, so we didn't, only whispered. We looked all over for the 'bug' that we knew had to be somewhere, but never found it. In later years I learned that the bug was indeed there, concealed in the overhead light fixture, which wasn't reachable by us. Every cell was wired to a central listening point, so anything said was recorded. During the interrogations I stuck to the name, rank and serial number response. I tried to show no surprise when Scharff mentioned something that I thought was a guarded secret. I tried to control my body language as well. Eventually both my friend and I were shipped to an intermediate POW camp before we were sent to Stalag Luft I at Barth. Barth was a resort town on the Baltic Sea between Rostock and Stralsund, about 100 miles north of Berlin. But on the eve of our leaving Oberursel the German interrogators put on a going away party for us—hard to believe, but they did. They were all smiles, had hot tea for us, were very gracious. And then they gave us a briefing of what they knew about us. It was quite dramatic how much they knew about our organization and us individually. Information they shouldn't have had. Where did they get it? I have no idea.

"Three months after my capture I finally arrived at Stalag Luft I. I received a letter from the sergeant who had taken my West Point class ring during my initial interrogation. The letter read, 'Dear Lieutenant Tucker. I am sorry that this process of interrogation took so long. I want to return to you the enclosed personal items. I hope they reach you in good health.' I got my ring back. Some of my fellow POWs received similar letters and had personal items returned to them.

Stalag Luft I ID tag issued to POWS. Al Tucker's number was 7938. By the end of the war the camp housed nearly 9,000 POWs, including Hub Zemke and Gabby Gabreski. (Al Tucker)

There was a level of civility practiced by Luftwaffe personnel—not the case with the Gestapo [Secret Police] and the SS [Hitler's personal security force—Schutz Staffel]. The SS would inspect our camp about once a month. When they came, the Luftwaffe guys were more afraid of them then we were. The SS officers looked like something out of a Hollywood movie. Pompous peacocks, running around looking as mean as they could.

"Once I was on a Red Cross detail, allowing me to go from compound to compound, distributing Red Cross parcels among the prisoners—a credit to how well the Luftwaffe tried to treat its American and British prisoners. They did everything according to the rules. They exhibited no meanness or animosity. As the war came close to its end, we were in the last piece of territory still controlled by the Germans. There was a small airfield right next to our camp. What was left of the Luftwaffe flew out of this little field against the Russians. We watched them take off and land, and were cheering for them. Every day there would be fewer and fewer of them. They could have flown fifteen minutes north, to freedom in Sweden—but they didn't. They'd take off to the north, then turn around and go southeast toward the Russian lines. We could hear the artillery. Some didn't make it back; others crashed when they attempted to land their damaged aircraft. It was for us a tremendous spectacle to witness the principle of 'duty, honor, country,' as practiced by German fighter pilots. I admired their discipline and what they did in a totally hopeless situation.

"All the Luftwaffe camp guards were wounded on the eastern front. Many of our aces were in my camp at Barth. Gabby Gabreski and Hub Zemke. Zemke was a hero to us. He spoke both Russian and German. It came in handy when the Russians finally arrived. 'Hub' also managed to work out arrangements with the German camp commander—how they should manage their final days, which were obviously coming. Hub apparently promised them to put in a good word for them when the time came. In return, he expected them to reciprocate by leaving the lights on for us and keep the water running once they left. Gabby Gabreski became the informal commander of an adjacent compound. I was in compound North 2, and the last one that was set up was North 3, where Gabby was. We had no overall American camp commander—we were in command of ourselves and the Germans respected that. As for food, the Germans shared their food with us to the extent that they were required to, which was augmented by the Red Cross parcels. We in fact ate better than our German guards. The food they fed us was what they ate—horse meat, beef from animals killed by shrapnel. The bread, *Kriegsbrot*, was durable stuff. They stacked it outside like bricks. A German sergeant received a quarter of a loaf of bread a day, a little bit of margarine, and a quarter of a length of blood sausage. That was his ration for the better part of a day. He received a cooked meal, soup, once a day. To some extent we ate better than the guards did. I didn't smoke, so I traded my cigarettes for candy bars.

"We had a pilot from Wright Field, Gus Lundquist, he was a test pilot. Gus was designated to get one of those Fw 190s at the airfield next to our camp ready once the Germans left. Bob Hoover, however, who arrived in the camp toward the end of the war, got impatient and decided he couldn't wait. Bob managed to get to that airfield, found a German crew chief and got him to start an Fw 190 for him. He flew west and was home free. He was the first out of our camp."

The story of how Gus Lundquist, who retired from the Air Force in the rank of brigadier general, ended up in Stalag Luft 1 is quite interesting in itself. In *Test Flying at Old Wright Field*, he wrote: "During 1943 we received several captured German and Japanese aircraft at

Stalag Luft I POW camp—Bob Hoover sitting front row, fourth from right. (Bob Hoover)

Wright Field, including the Me 109G, the Fw 190G, the Ju 88, and the Japanese Zero and Betty, all of which I was able to fly and evaluate. I did a great deal of flying in the Fw 190 in late 1943 and early 1944. Although not quite in the class of our P-51, I found the Fw 190 to be a first-class fighter plane. Like the P-51 it was a pilot's airplane, with an excellent cockpit layout, good visibility, excellent control response and maneuverability. Another interesting program was testing the modified Spitfire IX, then flying it across the Atlantic. It took a few stops, to prove that the Wright Field engineers had given it a bomber escort range. They had indeed accomplished this mission but in doing so had turned a beautiful flying machine into an absolute clunker. While at Boscomb Down I flew most of the RAF operational and experimental aircraft they had, including the Typhoon II, the Spitfire XXI, the Tempest, the Whirlwind, the Defiant, several training and bomber aircraft and a captured German Me 210 and Heinkel 111. In 1945, I did extensive testing of the Me 262 at Wright Field. The engines did not hold up well when operating near the redline limits and I had to make a couple of single engine landings."

Boscomb Down was the British counterpart to Wright Field. The British allowed Gus Lundquist to fly any aircraft he wanted to fly, but what Gus really wanted to do was fly a few combat missions. His host agreed to his request. Inexperienced as Gus was flying combat, he was shot down on his third mission, ending up at Barth along with Hub Zemke and Gabby Gabreski. While at Barth, and with little else to do, Gus talked about flying the Fw 190. Bob Hoover took advantage of the opportunity, gaining a level of familiarity with the 190's cockpit layout. Once Hoover got into one of the German abandoned airplanes, he wasn't a total stranger to the situation.

"Although Bob Hoover was the first to fly out of Barth, mind you, in a most unusual way, we soon followed," Al Tucker recalled. "The 8th Air Force came for us in a massive armada of B-17 bombers. A small party had arrived earlier in a couple of C-47s and set up an approach control system, tower, and so on at the German airfield. When they were ready, here came the B-17s. It was the most beautiful demonstration of formation flying with four-engine airplanes I'd ever seen. Combat group after combat group came in. They used an inactive runway where they stopped and we got on. Twenty of us were loaded on each B-17. The B-17 had a crew of nine, they were all onboard as well. Every crewman of course insisted on making this flight—because this time there would be no flak. So the rest of us had to squeeze onto that airplane. It was the most crowded flight I've ever had, but also one of the most enjoyable flights I've ever made. Our pilot took us over Essen, to allow us to see what their bombing had done to a German city. It looked like the end of the world. I couldn't figure out how Germany was ever going to survive that. We didn't go back to England, but to camp Lucky Strike in France, near Cherbourg. My reaction to Lucky Strike was, Holy Mackerel, I just got out of a prison camp, now I am back in a prison camp. Ugly, ugly, ugly. I managed to get out of there the third day I was there.

"There was a second lieutenant in charge of this tent city. He required us to hold inspections every morning to ensure our bunks were properly made up, and so on. Then we had to go to lectures and listen to how sorry they were that we were all undernourished, and all the suffering we had to go through. We got pretty sick of all this, including the dear Red Cross ladies who were constantly expressing how sorry they were that we had been treated so badly. We survived. Didn't need to listen to all that stuff. We just wanted to go home. The

The legacy of war—Berlin. Major cities all over Europe suffered a similar fate. (Laufer)

ladies clung to us, walking around with pitchers of eggnog, wanting us to drink that stuff. I hated eggnog, even with bourbon in it. They didn't have any bourbon of course. On the third day a C-47 landed. My tent happened to be quite close to the airstrip. Sure enough the pilot was a member of my former P-38 squadron. He immediately recognized me. We shook hands. He had come to Lucky Strike to pick up someone. I said to him, 'You got to get me out of here. This place is terrible.'

"'Sure I will,' he said. 'But first I need to talk to this major to pick up someone else.' So I hung around the airplane. When he returned, by himself, with a serious look on his face, he said he had bad news for me. He was ahead one class of me at the Point, and duty, honor, country, and never tell a lie was chiseled into all of us. So he told me what he thought he had to tell me, but he didn't tell me what I had to do about it. So he told me what the major had said, 'No sir, he can't go.' Then he walked away. I knew what he was really telling me. Nobody was watching, so I just got on the airplane. In back I removed an access panel and hid in the area behind it. There were wires running through the area which operated the rudder and the elevators. But I fit into the space. Soon I heard voices. The airplane

Camp Lucky Strike was just another US Army tent city, established soon after the D-Day landings and the capture of Cherbourg. (Fred McIntosh)

took off. Once we leveled off, I got out and introduced myself and got a big hero's welcome. I was still a first lieutenant, but my friend was a major by now. He was a lieutenant like me when I saw him last. We landed at RAF Honington, a former P-38 base that had converted to P-51s. There was someone there that I knew, Sam Phillips, who met me as I arrived. He went on to become a four-star general and commanded the Air Force Systems Command in the seventies. Sam was a major, had a staff car, and was a squadron commander. I wore prison garb. Sam said to me, 'We got to get you some clothes to wear before we do anything else.' Sam took me somewhere and got me a uniform to wear.

"Then Sam drove over to where his squadron airplanes were lined up in front of a hangar. Shiny new Mustangs. They were no longer in revetments; the war was over. Sam asked, 'Would you like to see mine?' Sure. So he stopped in front of his airplane. He got up on the right wing. Sam's crew chief came over to see what was going on. He got up on the left wing. Sam says, 'You want to fly it?' Hell, yes. They strapped me in. I hadn't been flying for a year, but no problem. The cockpit was similar to the AT-6, built by the same people. I was right at home. I guess I flew for about an hour and a half. I looked

Freed American airmen at Stalag Luft I after the German guards departed. Well armed with German rifles and Luger pistols. Al Tucker is the guy in the middle, a head taller than all the rest. Camp Lucky Strike reminded them all too much of where they had just come from. (Al Tucker)

around for somebody to joust with, a fighter pilot compulsion, but couldn't find anyone. When I looked down I saw all those haystacks. I made a simulated strafing run on one of the stacks. I turned on the gunsight, I pulled the trigger. After all I was a combat pilot. All six guns fired. I didn't know the plane was armed. The tracers set the haystack on fire. I hurried back and landed. Sam wasn't there, but the crew chief was. He saw I fired the guns, they had been taped over. He said, 'Lieutenant, here is what I am going to do. I am going to rearm those guns and clean them myself and nobody in Ordnance is going to know those guns were fired.' I was grateful. I was afraid I was going to get court-martialed. The next day they ferried me back to my old base, and I was back with Robin Olds again.

"What happened next was weird. They couldn't pay me because I didn't exist as far as the paymaster was concerned. They didn't have any orders on me. The finance officer said, 'Don't worry about it. Any time you need money just come over and I'll give you partial pay.' This way I could purchase a new uniform. I became civilized again. Got checked out in the Mustang, but never mentioned my experience over at Honington and setting the haystack on fire. We were training to go to the Pacific in either a long range P-51 or P-47. We flew P-51s and P-47s, and practiced gunnery and dive bombing. We had a young pilot, he was an ace. He and another were in disagreement if it was better to dive straight down at a target or approach at an angle. He chose to demonstrate diving down vertically and flew right into the target. A very sad experience." [Most likely the result of Mach tuck leading into the Graveyard Dive.]

"I didn't fly with Robin as much now, he was a squadron commander and I was just a fly-boy. We also had a B-26, and I loved flying it. I hadn't flown for a year while a POW, and I tried to do all the flying I could. All this fun flying came to an end when the atom bombs were dropped on Japan and the war in the Pacific ended. We then received orders to deliver all the remaining fighters in the UK to RAF Burtonwood where they were smashed. I did three or more flights a day. Since they were going to be smashed up at Burtonwood, we flew them with the throttles wide open. No worry fouling the plugs or what have you. No one else volunteered to fly the P-38s. I did and flew every one I could. Well, we jousted with each other on the way to Burtonwood and I bested the P-51 in the P-38 every time.

"After returning home I did a short tour of duty in our first jet, the P-80, at March Field, near Riverside, California, with my classmate and friend Robin Olds again. While I was there, a British officer joined our squadron—Peter West. Surprisingly, soon after Peter arrived in California, I received orders to go to England. It was in October 1948. I was assigned to Peter's squadron, part of 12 Group, at Horsham St. Faith flying Meteors. Robin Olds was assigned to Number 1 Squadron, also flying Meteors, in 11 Group at Tangmere, and became its squadron commander. That was quite a distinction. At Horsham I met a British flying officer by the name of 'Paddy' Harbison. Paddy and I became close friends."

Paddy, as he was called by his friends, retired in the rank of air vice marshal in the Royal Air Force, a three-star general officer equivalent. He married an American TWA stewardess, flight attendant today, while he was assigned to March Air Force Base as an exchange officer, and eventually made his home in Arlington, Virginia. Paddy Harbison flew the Spitfire and Mustang in World War II. He was a member

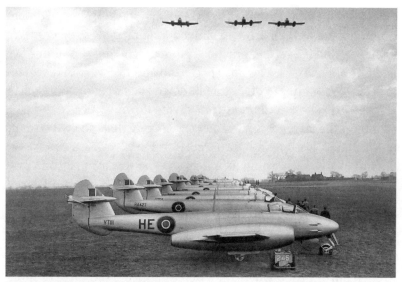

Meteors at RAF Tangmere, 1948. Robin Olds was assigned to Tangmere and Al Tucker to Horsham St. Faith; both flew Meteors. (Al Tucker)

of a group of retired flying officers who referred to themselves as the Old Bold Pilots, and met most Fridays for lunch at the Army Navy Country Club in Arlington, Virginia. It was my great pleasure to be part of this group of quite famous airmen and test pilots including men like Kenneth Chilstrom, Whitey Feightner, Fred Ascani, "Hot Dog" Brown, Gene Deatrick, and others. My chance meeting with Al Tucker and subsequent interview revealed his friendship with Paddy Harbison. They had not seen each other for years. So it was my great pleasure to have Al and his daughter as my guest at the Army Navy Country Club—to the great surprise of Paddy Harbison.

"At RAF Horsham I flew the Gloster Meteor jet," Al Tucker continued. "First the Meteor III, then the Meteor IV. My flight leader and I discovered that it was a great airplane to fly formation aerobatics. We developed a two-ship routine. Our squadron leader saw us doing it and insisted that we fly a three ship formation—with him as the lead. Well, he was too ham-fisted. So, what to do? I was selected to give him the bad news. Surprisingly, the squadron leader took it rather well. We became really good at what we were doing. The group commander saw us, and he called the air marshal com-

Air Vice Marshal Paddy Harbison, center sitting; Rear Admiral Whitey Feightner sitting to Paddy's left; Colonel Ousley on Paddy's right; Colonel Eugene Deatrick on the right standing. (Author)

manding. Air Marshal Trail came down to see us. He liked what he saw and designated us the Royal Air Force Meteor Demonstration Team. So I did little work for the rest of my exchange tour, other than practicing and flying demonstrations, including a performance for the king and queen of England. Paddy Harbison left about halfway through my tour of duty and went over to the US to fly the F-80, later the F-86, with the First Fighter Wing at March Air Force Base. When I finished my tour of duty in England in 1949, there was Paddy welcoming me back to March Air Force Base.

"I stayed with the First Fighter Wing. The wing moved to Palmdale for a couple of months, then we moved to Griffith Air Force Base in New York state. Robin Olds, my old friend and classmate, and I were in the 71st squadron. Robin was my squadron commander for the second time around. It was a great friendship we had, going back to our days at West Point, then P-38 training at Williams Field in Arizona. At 'Willie' we trained in the P-38 together. It wasn't really a P-38 we were flying then, but something called the P-322."

Robin Olds in his book *Fighter Pilot* wrote: "There were some major differences between the two, although they looked alike. For

Paddy Harbison climbing into his Spitfire while stationed at RAF Manston during WW II. (Paddy Harbison)

one thing, the props on the 322 rotated in the same direction, as opposed to the counter-rotating engines in the P-38. The oil and coolant flaps were manually controlled. You flew with one eye on the temperature gauges, constantly adjusting settings for every phase of flight by sliding levers back and forth to keep the values in the green. The P-322 lacked the turbo-superchargers of the 38, and its performance at altitude was pathetic. These particular aircraft had been built for the Brits, who wisely refused to accept them."

Al Tucker recalls: "Robin and I flew formation in the 322, doing aerobatic maneuvers as a two ship. Unfortunately we were seen doing it and turned in, resulting in a severe reprimand for the two of us. But I think it was really an expression of admiration for the flying the colonels saw us do." Robin Olds, Al's best friend and West Point classmate, saw that occasion a little differently. "Al Tucker, Lou Nesselbush, Charlie Walker, Hank Rosness, Buck Coursey, Don Mc-Clure and Bob Orr went through fighter training with me. They had advanced to the P-322, when within a short time, the reality of this business hit our group of eight. Bob Orr was flying solo, crashed and died. It stunned us, but it was reality in the life of a pilot. We would often dog fight among ourselves. It wasn't exactly against regulations, but it couldn't be ignored when two of us jumped a stray P-322 which turned out to be our squadron commander. That afternoon seven of us were lined up before the desk of a very livid major. We received a royal chewing out and wondered if this was the end of our fledgling careers. Finally, the major said, he knew the ambush had been carried out by one of us and asked who had done it? He was astounded when Al Tucker and I stepped forward and confessed. He didn't know quite what to say. I guess he had never heard of the honor code. We had learned that officers do not lie, cheat or steal, or tolerate those who do. We simply did what we had been conditioned to do. He sputtered a bit, and I think he admonished us not to do it again.

"After the war," Al continued, "it was natural for us to team up whenever we could. Robin had gotten me out of a terrible supply job I had been assigned to right after my return to the United States. He got me to fly the P-80, which was so much easier to fly than a piston airplane. So there were Robin and I doing our usual stunts of old, but now in a jet airplane at March Field. The colonel saw us doing it. Before long, the group commander was watching our routine. Then the general came over to take a look at us. Then we got another classmate, Ted Carnes, to fly with us. The general liked what we were doing, and before long we found ourselves being sent to the Cleveland Air Races in the fall of 1946. Robin Olds, Ted Carnes and I flew out to Cleveland in our P-80s. The airplanes had been lightened, the guns removed, and tuned to a fine pitch."

Robin Olds and Ted Carnes were flying for the 1st Fighter Group. Captain Kenneth O. Chilstrom, my dear and longtime friend who only recently went west after 101½ years of life, and Gustav Lundquist, the Wright Field test pilot who had managed to get himself into Stalag Luft I, were in the race from the Wright Field flight test division. Gus Lundquist and Al Tucker had served time together at Stalag Luft 1 at Barth—here they meet again, but under more civil circumstances. Lundquist was going to win the race, flying Ken Chilstrom's P-80. This is how Ken Chilstrom described the event to me. "I had been prepping three of our new P-80s for at least a month for the Cleveland races. Jack Sullivan, Gus Lundquist and I were going to fly in the race. The First Fighter Group from March Field also sent three guys, headed by Robin Olds. When the time came, Gus

The Wright Field flight test crew at Cleveland in front of one of their three P-80s. Ken Chilstrom 2nd from left. (Ken Chilstrom)

looked at our three airplanes and said to me, 'Ken, I think I'll take that one,' and he pointed at my airplane. Gus outranked me, so I flew his airplane instead. As we raced down the track, we were wing tip to wing tip. Going into the third turn, I was indicating about 515 miles per hour, right on the deck, full throttle to 101½ percent when the boost goes out on me. I couldn't move the stick and I am in a turn. All I could do was pull back and I was out of the race. Robin Olds, who was a fierce competitor, had turned off the engine regulators on his planes and flew his engines at 109 percent. Olds was right on Gus's wing. It was like they were flying formation, but Lundquist won the race—in my airplane. Not one of the engines from the 1st Fighter Group could fly back home. They over-temped their engines and ruined the blades. When Robin landed his P-80, he flamed out immediately after touchdown."

"In addition to the race," Al Tucker recalled, "we did loops, and rolls and barrel rolls for the spectators. Then, just to break things up a bit, we had a drill where Ted and Robin went up in a two-ship and criss-crossed each other, while I dove from higher up down toward the runway from the north while they were flying east west. I then pulled straight up. There was a bit of an overcast. I disappeared from

Al Tucker in front of his F-86 Sabre Jet after the 1st Fighter Wing converted from the F-80 to the F-86—so much easier to fly than the P-38, Al recalled. The United States Air Force became an independent service in September 1947. Fighter designations were changed from a P prefix to an F prefix; F-80 rather than P-80. (Al Tucker)

view going through the cloud deck. When I popped out at the top, I just pulled the power back, flipped over and came straight back down through that same hole. The people loved it, I was told. We formed up and landed. So, somehow, Robin and I probably contributed to getting the Thunderbirds off the ground as our premier Air Force demonstration team. That evening there was a big party attended by Group Captain Sir Frank Whittle, the inventor of the Whittle jet engine. He gave a talk. When I was in the restroom, several people entered. I heard a British voice saying, 'I certainly would like to meet that young chap Tucker.' I dried my hands and introduced myself to Frank Whittle, 'I'm Tucker, sir.'"

ROBIN OLDS

P-38 LIGHTNING/F-4C PHANTOM

Oh! I have slipped the surly bonds of Earth
And danced the skies on laughter-silvered wings;
Sunward I've climbed, and joined the tumbling mirth
of sun-split clouds, and done a hundred things
You have not dreamed of, wheeled and soared and swung
High in the sunlit silence. Hov'ring there,
I've chased the shouting wind along, and flung
My eager craft through footless halls of air. . . .
—JOHN GILLESPIE MAGEE JR., *HIGH FLIGHT*

During the Vietnam War in 1968 I was flying out of Takhli Royal Thai
Air Force Base in Thailand. For me it was a war without focus, except
for Robin Olds. Robin had gone home by the time I got there, but he
reminded me of the great fighter pilots on both sides in World War
II. I knew many of them by name as a kid, and they inspired me to
one day be like them. The world had changed by the time my time
came, except for Robin. He was a man I could look up to, inspirational, the kind of guy you'd follow anywhere just to be near him. Any
book about the P-38 that doesn't include Robin Olds would obviously
be incomplete. He flew that airplane against the best the German
Luftwaffe had to offer, the way, many years later, he would fly his F-4
against the North Vietnamese—with skill and imagination. When he
passed on June 14, 2007, his book *Fighter Pilot* was unfinished. His
daughter Christina, in the spirit of her father, finished the job—and
all of us aviators thank Christina for doing that. The following story
is largely based on excerpts from *Fighter Pilot*—Robin's story.

"With second lieutenant bars and new pilot wings I joined seven West Point classmates with orders to Williams Field, Arizona, for training in the P-38 Lightning. Al Tucker, Lou Nesselbush, Charlie Waller, Hank Rosness, Buck Coursey, Don McClure and Bob Orr went through fighter training with me. We all became members of the 479th Fighter Group and went to war together. One was killed, two became POWs, one almost finished a tour but quietly disappeared, two finished and went home, and the remaining member went on to fly two tours and became a twenty-two-year-old major and commander of the 434th Fighter Squadron. That was me.

"The P-38 would wait a bit in our training. First we had to fly the AT-9, a twin-engine of dubious performance. The intent was to introduce trainees to the rigors of twin-engine flight before meeting the P-38. It wasn't a P-38 we were to fly, but a bird named the P-322. There were some major differences between the two, although they looked alike. The generally accepted belief was that the P-322 was a more dangerous airplane than the Lightning, at least for the pilot. Within a short time, the reality of this business hit our group of eight. Bob Orr was flying solo, crashed and died. We never knew how it happened. It stunned us, but it was reality in the life of a pilot. We had lost five classmates back at the Point in training accidents before graduation, and wearing wings didn't keep it from happening now. I'd had to learn how to deal with it.

"After gunnery training at Matagorda, Texas, we ended up at Muroc Field, the current Edwards Air Force Base and flight test center. The P-38s were incredible. Our days were filled with the wonder of the machines, even though the bulk of them were bent and battered. There were D-models and E-models. There were even some early C-models. Each was unique, with instruments never in the same location, the throttles, mixture, and rpm controls mixed around on the power quadrant, and switches all over the place. Each switch had a placard that hinted at a bewildering variety of functions, mostly mysteries to us, and I suspect also to our instructors, as they seldom mentioned them. The differences, however, could sometimes be quite frightening. On take-off you'd be looking forward, reach to reduce the power and rpm, and suddenly realize you were pulling back the mixture controls, which of course could shut down the engines if inadvertently pulled back too far. Accidents were common. One morning we were outside the quarters playing jungle volleyball when two P-38s pitched out above us for landing. We never knew who he was, but the second of the two rolled into his bank and kept right on rolling until he smashed into the ground not five hundred feet away.

"After the game I flew my scheduled flight and then joined some others for a truck ride to the other side of the base for lunch. The road crossed the west end of the runway, where we had to stop for two birds taking off. One never got airborne. With smoking brakes he sailed right past our noses and on out into the desert. There the nose gear collapsed; the pilot got out, turned and waved to us that he was alright. Little did we know we hadn't seen anything yet. Coming back from lunch we found two more P-38s nose up off the same end of he runway. That made four accidents so far. On the first flight of the afternoon there were two bailouts reported. Soon after that, someone tried to land with one engine out and botched it. He went bouncing off the east end of the runway and out onto the dry lake bed. There he stopped when the gear collapsed. Toward late afternoon, two trainees had a midair collision. Neither survived. Flying for the rest of the day was canceled. Nine accidents in one day were going to be hard to explain to the higher-ups."

In time Al Tucker and Robin ended up where they wanted to be—in England fighting for their country. They were assigned to the 479th Group based at RAF Wattisham, the last P-38 Group to be formed in England. It seemed like it was Muroc all over again. "Crazy Lieutenant Canella cheated death when he ran his plane into the ground at 400 mph, staggered back up into the air, dragged across the roof of a warehouse, plowed through a pile of bricks and tar barrels, and then walked away unscathed from a burning wreck. Captain Walker, commander of the 436th, spun in on May 25. He had been test firing his guns and when last seen was at 800 feet on a single engine and burning. It was a blow to his squadron. My own plane arrived that same afternoon, a brand new P-38-J15-LO, just under twenty hours of flying time on her. My first combat mission was anticlimactic. I saw a few halfhearted puffs of flak but sure loved the hot-metal smell of my new P-38. On the second flight of the day we went on a patrol sweep over France and I damn near passed out from lack of oxygen."

The group didn't see much action over D-day, June 6, 1944, or the immediate days thereafter. "The third week of June started with a bang. Make that several. A B-17 bellied into a field about 500 yards from the officers' club. The crew escaped except for the tail gunner who didn't get out. News came that Lieutenants Kuenzel and Grdenich had failed to return from a mission. They'd been trapped atop an overcast topping out near 28,000 feet. When last seen, both aircraft were in a steep spiral headed for the ground near Rouen. Just three days later, more bad news. This time four were lost, including my pal Al Tucker. He was hit by flak while returning home on one engine. Canella, Ilsley and Lutz went down too, lost forever. But it turned out that 'Tuck's Luck' held, and Al survived to sit out the rest of the war in Stalag Luft I.

"Finally! Victory for the 479th at last! On the fifth [of July] Jeffrey drew first blood from the enemy when he found a Fw 200 Condor taking off from the Chateau-Bernard Airdrome and shot it down before anyone else could get close. The O club scene that night was memorable! The following day Lieutenant Tipps got the squadron on the board again by downing an Me 109. The rest of us were itching to continue the streak and were frustrated as hell by weather socking us in for days. Gleason and I got some jollies blasting an ammunition dump on the fifteenth, but we both limped home with damaged ships. We were lucky. Both P-38s were full of holes, mine from flak and Gleason's from debris that was blown into the air when the dump went up.

"By August we had all changed. Combat does that. The group had made progress since our arrival in early May, but the price had been high. We'd lost three of our flight commanders, both of my roommates had been shot down over Holland, and many pilots were KIA or POW. Nearly half of the original 434th Squadron was gone. The other two squadrons in the group had suffered similar attrition. Our original group CO, Kyle Riddle, was lost to flak on May 10. No one was immune. We who survived had gotten smarter about combat. Our salvation appeared with the arrival of Colonel Hubert 'Hub' Zemke, who replaced Colonel Riddle as CO two days later. In May, both of Zemke's wingmen, flying P-47s, were shot down by Luftwaffe ace Guenter Rall, who in turn was shot down by 56th Group ace Joe

Powers in the same dogfight. He jumped at the chance to command the 479th because he wanted to fly the new Mustangs. His 56th Group had P-47s, which were increasingly focusing on ground attack. He knew we were converting to P-51s. Hub was our kind of guy, aggressive, smart, relentless and determined to hit the Luftwaffe where it hurt. He was already a triple ace and had created legends in the 56th, like Gabreski, Mahurin and Johnson. We in the 479th knew about their exploits and were in awe of their skill and good fortune.

"On his first day at Wattisham, Hub put up a sign on the door of his office:

KNOCK BEFORE YOU ENTER.
I'M A BASTARD TOO. LET'S SEE YOU SALUTE.

The young pilots got a huge charge out of that." The day finally came for Robin when he saw "two dark shapes fly across the road left to right about a mile ahead of me. I turned right to cut them off, got right down on the grass, pushed the mixture into auto-rich, rammed the props to high, and shoved the throttles to the wall. The cut-off angle was good and I could see I would be coming in behind the bogeys in short order. I still didn't have a positive ID, but every instinct told me they had to be German. Instinct is no good when you are coming up behind a target with a 20mm and four 50 caliber guns armed and ready to shoot. It is particularly no good when your adrenaline is pumping. Patience, patience. I am closing fast, there isn't much time left. I pressed rudder and slipped the pipper on the trailing aircraft's left wing. Another second, and suddenly I could see the Iron Cross on the side of the lead plane's fuselage. I squeezed the trigger. The wingman's bird lit up with strikes, spewed heavy smoke, rolled inverted and hit the ground with a huge explosion. I had to get the other 190 before he gained an advantage on me. He made a violent left break the moment his wingman was hit. I followed, staying inside the turn, knowing my left wingtip was no more than 20 feet off the ground. The G-forces came on hard but I was scarcely aware of them. I flew the pipper slowly through his fuselage, pulling ahead, trying to get about a 100-mil lead. I pressed the trigger in a short burst and watched as strikes moved down his fuselage. Perfect!

A Fw 190 armed for ground attack. Like the P-47, it had a radial engine, but not the punch of a P-47. The aircraft shown is on display at the National Air and Space Museum, Udvar Hazy Center, in Chantilly, Va. It was one of the aircraft brought to the U.S. by Colonel Watson. (Author)

Another burst, more strikes, and he suddenly pulled straight up. The canopy separated and the pilot came out as though he had a spring in his seat. His chute opened immediately and he swung under it. I had pulled up with him and rolled inverted in time to see his aircraft hit in the middle of a farmer's field. I rolled into a hard left bank and watched through the top of my canopy as the Jerry landed close to his burning aircraft.

"The flight home was uneventful. I hoped my camera had worked. The camera in the P-38 was mounted in the nose right under the 20mm gun. It jiggered and bounced like crazy when the guns fired. Sure enough, my briefing was met with obvious skepticism. Then Colonel Zemke walked into our squadron ready-room. He came up to me as I snapped to attention, looked me in the eye, and said, 'You don't know how lucky you are, Captain. I just got a call from the 355th Group. They were passing overhead and saw your engagement, the whole thing. Your claims are confirmed.' I don't remember if I whooped out loud in the colonel's face, but I sure was whooping inside!"

Robin was going to cheat death many more times and by the time he got ready to go home his tally of enemy planes shot down had risen to thirteen. He would add four more kills to his record during the Vietnam war for a total of seventeen. But there was one particular mission that nearly cost him his life—it was the P-38 nemesis, compressibility. Seeing a P-51 in distress below him, Robin "rolled inverted and pulled the nose almost straight down. Airspeed built rapidly. Suddenly, my P-38 gave a shudder and the nose tucked further down. I pulled back on the control yoke. Nothing. No feedback. No elevator response. Just looseness, and the nose tucked further down. Damn it! It was compressibility, that dreaded phenomenon we had been warned about. Few pilots had ever recovered. None ever bailed out. There'd been smoking holes out in the Mojave Desert as mute testimony to the warning.

"Down, down I went, the throttles in idle, prop pitch full forward, the aircraft shuddering and shaking as the shock wave tucked the nose and blanked my tail. Through 18,000 . . . no response, down . . . down . . . down . . . I held the yoke just on the point of burble and cranked a tiny bit of back trim on the elevators. Anything I could get might make a difference. The bird seemed to respond. Through 12,000 and the response increased a little. The nose slowly started to rotate from the vertical. Down, still down, too fast to think of bailing out. No time anyway. As the air grew denser, the control response increased, but the ground was coming up and I wasn't recovering. I kept milking the elevator back, back, and all of a sudden I had full bite. The G-forces came on like a sledgehammer. Something exploded behind me with a horrible, rushing, tearing roar. I tightened my gut muscles and screamed to keep the blood from rushing from my head. The world turned gray. Looking down two dark tunnels as my eyesight went dark, I could barely see the ground. It was close, and I was going like the hammers of hell toward a huge brown plowed field. The nose came slowly up and then to the horizon. I had made it! I was dimly aware of the field furrows flashing just under my wing, scarcely 20 feet below. God that was close. I was alive. My P-38 was flying but this boy had enough for one day." Mach tuck leading to the proverbial Graveyard Dive—Robin lucked out. Robin Olds's experience was very similar to what Franz Roedel experienced in his Me 262 when he entered the critical mach number for his aircraft, like Robin, pulling it out of its fateful dive just feet off the ground. As Robin put it after landing, "Life was sweet, I was alive."

The war in Europe ended on May 8, 1945. "Life at Wattisham took on a form of normalcy for the rest of the summer. The news about going to the Pacific for the invasion of Japan was reinforced by the assignment of some fourteen brand-new P-47Ms to my squadron. Part of our time was spent ferrying aircraft to Liverpool or to a base called Langford Lodge near Belfast. I took a P-38 over there one beautiful day. The bird had less than 20 hours flying time on it and even smelled new. Before I had even finished signing all the transfer paperwork at Langford, a scruffy bunch of workers cut the tail booms off with acetylene torches and pushed it off to a trash heap. I nearly cried at a waste of a wonderful airplane."

The war soon ended in the Pacific, and that August, Robin Olds, now a double ace fighter pilot, went home having survived both the enemy and his beloved P-38. Olds was my hero in the Vietnam war, not just mine, but every one of us young flying officers loved Robin, a man we could unabashedly look up to. He was a fighter, a man with no pretensions. Only days after his death on June 14, 2007, I received an email from a friend, a tribute to Robin, written by a young F-4 pilot, Bob Hipps. Wrote Bob: "When I was checking out in the F-4 at Nellis in 1967, our class was shown a film of Colonel Olds's 'New Guy' speech to the folks at Ubon. Imagine our disappointment when our class arrived there in October '67 only to learn that he had gone home. When I finally got to meet him a few years ago, when he was the guest speaker at a Seymour Johnson Mini-Reunion, I informed him that I had a bone to pick with him. He gave me a strange look and asked what my problem was. I told him that it was because he was gone when I got to Ubon—and I never got to fly with him. He laughed heartedly and said, 'You'll just have to wait until the next war.'

"Fighter pilots used to say that there was a glass case in the A-Ring of the Pentagon. It was built to the precise dimensions of then Colonel Robin Olds, who would be frozen and displayed wearing his rankless flight suit, crushed fore and aft cap, gloves, and torso harness with .38 and survival knife. Beside the case was a fire ax beneath a sign reading, 'In case of war, break glass.' It was something of an exaggeration, but it contained an element of truth. Robin Olds was built for war. And he was born to fly. It was imprinted in his genes."

Robin Olds was the kind of leader that all of us airmen could follow wherever he chose to take us.

LLOYD WENZEL

P-38 LIGHTNING

LIGHTNINGS IN THE SKY

Oh, Hedy Lamar is a beautiful gal, and Madeleine Carroll is too.

But you'll find if you'll query, a different theory among the men of a bomber crew.

For the loveliest thing of which one could sing this side of the Heavenly Gates,

Is no blonde or brunette of the Hollywood set—but an escort of P-38s.

Yes, in days that have passed, when the tables were massed with glasses of scotch or champagne,

It's quite true that the sight was a thing to delight, intent on feeling no pain.

But no longer the same, nowadays, in this game, when we head north from Messina Straits,

Take the sparkling wine—every time, just make mine an escort of P-38s.

Sure, we're braver than hell; on the ground all is swell—in the air it's a different story.

We sweat out our track through the fighters and flak, we're willing to split up the glory.

Well they wouldn't reject us, so heaven protect us and, until all this shooting abates,

Give us courage to fight 'em and—one other item—an escort of P-38s.

—T/SGT. ROBERT H. BRYSON, KIA, WWII MTO

Captain Lloyd M. N. Wenzel, a P-38 fighter pilot, suddenly found himself deeply involved in a program, Project Paperclip, no one wanted to explain to him when he was first assigned to it. He was told that he didn't have the necessary security clearance. Perhaps what Captain Wenzel had going for him was that he was young and unbiased, had experienced war, and, not the least of his attributes, he was a Texan, raised in a land where one could stretch out one's arms without touching another person, a land where earth and sky merged on a distant untrammeled horizon—and he spoke German.

"I was born on June 3, 1922, in Seguin, Texas," Lloyd began our interview, "a small town thirty miles east of San Antonio. Seguin, named after Juan Seguin, a Mexican who sided with the Texans against General Antonio Lopez de Santa Anna, sits on the line where the black soil of the north meets the sand of the south. Germans who settled this area picked the black soil for their farms to grow cotton. Seguin had a big German community when I was a boy. Then you were either a German, or you were a 'raggedy,' that's what they called non-Germans. The Germans were very neat and kept their barns and houses painted. Other places, to them at least, looked raggedy compared to their own. My paternal grandmother was six years old when the family immigrated from Germany, shortly after Texas broke away from Mexico. They settled in the little town of Waldeck, about sixty miles from Austin. The local authorities were eager for farmers to settle the land. My grandmother's father was made a very attractive land offer, bought a farm near Waldeck, and started to grow cotton. When my grandmother was still in her teens, she married. Soon after her wedding, her fellow rode off to fight in the Civil War. The guy had one of his legs shot off and died on the way home.

"My paternal grandfather too came from Germany, but as an indentured servant. A Texas farmer paid his way over and he had to work for the man for three years to pay him back. That man's farm happened to be right next door to the farm of the young widow whose husband lost a leg in the war and died. The two married and had five sons. My uncle Albert, as the oldest, inherited the farm; uncle Gustav and uncle Otto became carpenters; uncle Adolf became a blacksmith, and my dad, Robert, the youngest, wanted to go to college to become a schoolteacher. When he told the old man about his plans, his father locked him in the corncrib and told him to shuck corn until he got that foolishness out of his head. My dad had severe hay fever and nearly died shucking that corn. That night my grandmother dragged him out of the crib and saved his life. The old man finally relented, even letting my father ride his horse to school. Dad never did get a college degree, but he got enough college to teach school in Seguin for fifty years. Actually, he had retired by the time World War II came along, when the school board called on him and said, 'Robert, you've got to teach again.'

"My mother was half German, half English. Her parents too were farmers. I have a sister eleven years older than I; she taught me to speak German. Randolph Field was about fifteen miles from Seguin and my dad and I would ride out there occasionally and look at the airplanes. When they officially opened the field, General Pershing came down from Washington for the occasion. I went over to watch the ceremony. It was all very exciting for a young lad. Once an airplane made a forced landing on my grandfather's farm and we got to look at that broken-up airplane. My grandmother made refreshments for the pilots until someone came to pick them up. I felt awed by the flyers. Maybe, some day I could be a flyer, I thought. My best friend and I frequently rode our bicycles to Randolph Field, right into a hangar, and looked at the airplanes and kicked the tires. There were no fences or guard posts. A couple of times I sat in the lap of a sergeant when he ran up the engine. It was a BT-8, a single engine trainer. Soon I was building model airplanes, and in the Boy Scouts I went after the aviation merit badge. I sat around for hours with my friends talking flying. Airplanes became and remained an important part of my life.

"I spoke German like nearly everybody else. As a boy you couldn't work in a grocery or drygoods store in Seguin if you couldn't speak German. There were just too many people who only spoke German. Willie and Lena Foss were my folks' best friends. They were on the school board. Willie passed away while I was away in the war. When I came home in June 1945, my father and I went to see Mrs. Foss. My German was so rusty, I spoke in English to her. When we left, my dad said to me, 'What's the matter with you, Lloyd? Don't you have any manners? Speaking English to that old lady and putting that burden on her. You should have spoken German.'

"I attended Texas Lutheran College in Seguin with the intent of getting enough credits so I could apply for aviation cadets. You had

A BT-8 Seversky basic trainer at Randolph Field, Texas. It's possible that Lloyd Wenzel as a youngster sat in this very aircraft fantasizing about becoming a pilot. The BT-8 was the trainer Hal Watson flew as well. (Ruth Watson)

to have two years of college to get into the program. When the war came, my mother was intent on not letting me go. When I turned twenty in June of 1942, I applied anyway. On August 13 I went to take my test at Fort Sam Houston in San Antonio. I passed the written but flunked the physical. I had an undescended testicle. 'If you don't have that corrected, it can become malignant,' the doctor said. I must have looked so disappointed that he said to me, 'You really want to fly, don't you?' I said, 'Yeah, I always wanted to fly.' Said the doctor, 'Listen boy, I'll put your file up here,' and he stuffed my folder among some books on a shelf above his head. 'You remember where it is, because I will examine thousands before you get back. Have the thing removed and if you can get back here in two weeks I'll continue to process you. Otherwise, you'll have to start all over again.' I phoned my doctor at home from the major's office and set up surgery for the next morning and had the damn thing taken out. After I could walk again, my friends accompanied me to Fort Sam Houston and carried me up the stairs to he doctor's office so I could get sworn in. Because they cut me open in the groin, I wasn't supposed to walk up stairs and had to be carried up. I used to tell people it cost me my right ball and sixty-five dollars to join the Air Corps. My fellow cadets gave me the nickname 'Stud.'

"It wasn't until 1943 that I received a pilot training class assignment, 43K. I thought I would be going to a cadet training center in San Antonio, but they threw me instead on a train and sent me to Santa Ana in California. I wanted to be a B-17 pilot because my scoutmaster flew B-17s. He was highly decorated and came home on military leave from the Pacific before I went off to California. I listened to his war stories and wanted to be just like him. But once I got to California I saw the P-38 fighter and that changed everything for me. The P-38s would come in low, dive toward the end of the runway and then peel up and over, doing a complete vertical 360-degree turn, and land. In the early P-38s they had the coolers for the turbo superchargers in the leading edges of the wings, and there were two little square holes near the tip of each wing allowing the air to escape. In the high humidity of California, those P-38s would pull two big streamers off each wingtip as they went up and over and came in to land. I decided, to hell with the B-17, I want to be a P-38 pilot.

"In flight training I first flew the PT-17, a beautiful Boeing biplane, and then the BT-13, known as the Vibrator for all the noises it made. Next came the AT-9, a twin-engine high-performance aircraft, and then the RP-322. The RP-322 was a twin-engine P-38 ordered by the British before the start of Lend-Lease in early 1941. Once Lend-Lease came into effect, the Brits canceled their order and those airplanes [some of them] were converted to American specifications and configured as trainers. I got about ten hours in that airplane. After I was awarded my pilot wings, I was assigned to an RTU in California. I found the airplane a high-performance beast and if you didn't pay attention it would kill you quicker then the Germans could. I was lucky. The training outfit I went to had a bunch of North African campaign veterans from the 82nd Fighter Group, guys who had combat experience flying the airplane in North Africa against Rommel's Afrika Korps. I remember one of them. Captain Albert Wolfmueller, from Fredericksburg, Texas—another German. He was strafing, and didn't see some high-tension lines. As he pulled up, a line caught his tail and flipped him over on his back at about ten feet off the ground.

The PT-17 Stearman trainer, the US Navy version known as the PT-13 Kaydet, was a solidly built aircraft, designed by Stearman and built by Boeing. Many modernized Stearmans are still flying to this day. This PT-17 Stearman is being flown by Al Tucker with his father in the front seat. (Al Tucker)

He controlled that airplane and recovered. Quite a feat. Albert was the son of the owner of the Wolfmueller bakery in Fredericksburg.

"We finished training in March 1944 and were outfitted for deployment to the Pacific. Everything was hush-hush. When we arrived in San Francisco, they had us turn in all that Pacific stuff and we drew European stuff instead. We got on a train to New York and crossed the Atlantic on the liner *Mauritania* in five days. There were only three P-38 groups remaining in England when I arrived—the 474th, the 370th, and the 367th. I was assigned to the 474th Fighter Group. We were in the IX Tactical Air Command, IX TAC, of the 9th Air Force, commanded by Lieutenant General Hoyt S. Vandenberg. [Vandenberg became the second Air Force chief of staff in 1948, succeeding General Carl A. Spaatz.] Major General Elwood R. Quesada commanded the IX TAC. All three P-38 groups were slated to convert to P-51s or P-47s. Because of its longer range, they wanted the P-38 in the Pacific. My group petitioned General Spaatz [Then commander United States Strategic Air Forces in Europe, the latter-day USAFE] to let us keep on flying the P-38. He approved our request. We were the only group to fly P-38s out of England onto bases in Germany.

"November of 1944 was colder than hell. I had fifty-two combat missions by then. We were in Florennes, Belgium, and experienced heavy losses. On one mission we lost eight out of twelve aircraft. Most of our losses were due to anti-aircraft fire. By D-Day the Luftwaffe was pretty much beaten down, but the ground fire was fierce. The 88mm radar-directed gun was a mean gun and could shoot you at 30,000 feet. My squadron, the 428th, was authorized fifty-five pilots and twenty-five airplanes. We lost twenty-eight pilots in less than a year. We sustained the heaviest losses in the 474th Fighter Group. The 430th squadron had the least. Their commander had combat experience in North Africa and flew a little less aggressively than we did. Near the end of the war it was announced that a fighter tour in the IX TAC was seventy missions. We moved to Euskirchen, then to Langensalza—deep in what would become the Russian Zone of Occupation. After I flew my seventy-second combat mission, my group commander wanted to see me. I trotted into his office and he said, 'You've got five months in grade, Wenzel. In a month I can promote you to captain, if you stick around, that is.' I said, 'No sir. I want to go home.' He replied, 'No, I won't let you go home. You stay.' 'Well, if I stay I want to fly.' He looked at me, shook his head, and said, 'Wenzel, you are through flying combat. You can run an orientation for our replacements and teach them formation flying and tactics, but your combat flying days are over.' I was kind of glad he said that. I didn't want to fly any more combat. I was sick of it.

"Once I got back to the States, in June 1945, I had orders to go to the Pacific. Two days before I was to ship out for San Francisco they dropped the atomic bomb. I was at home on leave and right near Fort Sam Houston. At Fort Sam Houston they told me, 'Things have changed. If you want to get out, you can. But you have to decide right now.'

"So I phoned my wife. We talked and agreed for me to stay in. I was ordered to Luke Field, near Phoenix. All of my old friends were there. For reasons unknown to me I was selected to report to the Air Technical Service Command at McClellan Field in Sacramento overhauling B-26 Marauders. On July 29, 1946, I received orders directing me to report at once to Wright Field, Dayton, Ohio, for duty with T-2, Intelligence. I asked, 'What is Intelligence?' Nobody

P-38 pilots, October 1944, Florennes, Belgium. R-L: 'The Stud' Lt. Wenzel; 'The Holt' Lt. Holt; 'The Kid' Lt. Rankin. Holt and Rankin were killed in action soon after the picture was taken. (Lloyd Wenzel)

knew. Personnel phoned Wright Field and nobody had an answer. At that time Project Overcast, renamed Project Paperclip on September 3 [1945], was classified and no one who knew anything about it talked. Over the four years I was to spend at Wright Field I did just about everything that had to do with the German *Wissenschaftler*, scientists, under Air Force control. I picked up their families at the port of New York when they began arriving and escorted them to Wright Field. I even became their paymaster in 1947. Shiploads of scientific documentation began arriving that had been collected under Operation Lusty by Colonel Watson and his people in Germany. We had the German scientists go through the piles of paper and throw out the trash and assemble what remained into a technical library. I was just a fighter pilot thrown into this thing because I spoke some German.

"I don't recall anymore the contractual issue that arose about this time, but it was of a critical nature and I found myself right in the middle of the Paperclip mess." Captain Lloyd Wenzel, the fighter pilot, suddenly found himself in the awkward position of having to write a contract, to make American citizens out of enemy aliens. General Donald Putt, the commander of Air Materiel Command at

P-38 pilots of the 474th Fighter Group taking a break on the tail section of a former Luftwaffe Me 110 night fighter. (Lloyd Wenzel)

This is what happened to the P-38s at Langensalza once the war ended in Germany. They were crushed and buried by German POWs. (Lloyd Wenzel)

Wright Field, had Wenzel up to his office and told him, "You're in charge, Wenzel. The Germans are your people. Write a contract and get it signed by the Secretary of War or his authorized representative. And I need to remind you—do it fast!"

Lloyd Wenzel, on the right, the fighter pilot who never dreamed that one day soon he would serve as an intelligence officer in a highly classified program—Project Overcast/Paperclip. (Lloyd Wenzel)

"I was terrified," Lloyd confessed to me. "So, I, a fighter pilot, took an old supply contract and spread it out on my living room floor. I cut and pasted and made a contract out of it, and into the contract I wrote the terms of Project Paperclip. It was a personal services contract, and had to be approved by the Secretary of War or his designated representative. Colonel Watson, who had brought the German jets to this country, was the executive to the Assistant Secretary of War for Air. I reviewed the contract with General Putt. He felt that what I had was 'good enough.' The general said to me, 'You have to go to Washington and get the Assistant Secretary for Air to sign this thing. If you get into trouble,' which I was sure I would, 'call this guy,' and General Putt handed me a piece of paper with Colonel Watson's name on it, and his room number in the Pentagon.

"I went to the Pentagon with my 'raggedy' contract in my briefcase. My first stop was a major, a contract specialist, who had been cleared for Project Paperclip. She said, 'I know what you are trying to do, captain. But what you have here doesn't even qualify as a contract. Now get out of my office, I don't have any more time to waste on you.' I called Colonel Watson. General Putt had already talked to him.

Wenzel, on the left, standing in front of the 428th Fighter Squadron Intelligence shack, December 1944, Florennes, Belgium—never thinking that Intelligence would be his postwar future. (Lloyd Wenzel)

Watson said, 'Come on down to my office right away, I'm in a hurry.' I went to his office and started telling him about my contract when he interrupted me. 'That sounds good, Captain. What do you have to have to get out of here?' I have to have the Secretary's signature. 'Where?' said Watson. I opened up the contract. 'Right here, sir,' pointing to the place where I wanted the Secretary to sign. 'Come with me,' Watson muttered, and we entered the Secretary's office. 'This is Captain Lloyd Wenzel from Wright Field on the German scientist program, Mr. Secretary. He has drawn up a contract for the Germans. It's very critical that we get them on contract so we can proceed with their employment and get them out of that enemy alien status. We need your approval, sir.' The Secretary replied, 'What do I need to do?' 'Sign here,' Watson said, handing the Secretary a pen and holding the signature element in front of him. The Secretary signed and I returned to Wright Field. That was it. Without Watson we would have never moved forward on this.

"There were just too many people dragging their feet. All but one of the German scientists took us up on our offer and signed the contract. The State Department continued to drag its feet. No one seemed to understand that we had to keep the Russians from getting these people. No one seemed to understand how important these people were to our national security. I had a couple of real fine young women working for me who kept track of the details and kept the immigration visas coming. Once we figured out what State wanted, we pursued things with vigor. Each scientist ended up with a dossier a foot thick. The main thing was that we had to prove that they were not Nazis. Once immigration visas were issued, the scientists and their families had to leave the country to shed their enemy alien status. So we took them up to Niagara Falls, New York, drove them across the bridge into Canada and the Canadian authorities stamped their papers. Then we turned around and had them readmitted to the United States, this time as legal immigrants.

"All the scientists had several job offers from academe or private industry. Some, like Dr. Hans von Ohain, the inventor of the Jumo 004 jet engine, went to work for our government and in time became the chief scientist of the Wright-Patterson AFB laboratories. When I left the Paperclip project in 1949, I remained at Wright-Patterson as a student at the Air Force Institute of Technology. The German professors who were still around tutored the hell out of me in the evenings. I graduated in 1951 and became a procurement officer."

Colonel Lloyd Wenzel served in the United States Air Force for thirty years. He spent much of his air force career in contract management and procurement, being one of the early directors of the F-15 program. After Lloyd's P-38 experience in Europe, he never flew a fighter again other than to maintain his flying status in varied aircraft. This was a common experience in the post–World War II world where there was a surplus of flyers, the key ingredient for a nascent airline industry. Most ended up doing something other than earning their pay flying airplanes.

FRED McINTOSH

P-38 LIGHTNING/P-47 THUNDERBOLT/TA 152

P-47

They told the kid, a 38's the thing, it's got two props and guns that sing.
It's got plenty of range, and can carry a load, and it's a friend to have on a
combat road.
But, the kid looked up and said in revolt, "You take your 38, I'll take a
Thunderbolt."

—LT. E. C. BUCKLEY

Frederick B. McIntosh, Fred, was a gung-ho fighter pilot if there ever
was one. Like many other Americans, he was of German heritage.
"My stepfather's name was Heinrich Warnholz," Fred said laughing
when I interviewed him some years ago. "I was born on June 8, 1918;
don't remember when my mother married Heinrich. I was still very
young. She changed her name; I kept mine. People and things in my
life were pretty much German. Eleanor Volmer, my twenty-some-
year-old high school German teacher, was from Berlin. I picked
up her accent. Years later in 1945 when I was retrieving captured
Luftwaffe aircraft, Germans frequently asked me if I was a Berliner.
After high school I went to work for the Pacific Gas & Electric Company in Oakland. I graduated on Friday, and on Monday night I
was digging ditches for the gas company for fifteen cents an hour.
I worked nights, and went to school during the day. In college I
took Navy ROTC with the idea of becoming a naval aviator. When
I applied for flight training, the navy recruiter told me that a junior
certificate just wouldn't do. I had to have a college degree to get into
naval aviation. I went across the street to the army recruiter who

didn't care what my educational pedigree was, and signed me up with the Army Air Corps, Class of 43C." Lloyd Wenzel was in 43K, a few months after Fred.

"I reported to Santa Ana," Fred continued, "in southern California, no more than a wheat field then and a bunch of tents. Next came Thunderbird II, again a new airfield near Phoenix with few amenities. But there at least we didn't have to sleep in tents. After graduation in March 1943 I went to Williams Field near Tempe, Arizona, where I spent a year as an instructor pilot in the P-38 Lightning. Whoever set the date for the invasion of the Continent must have foreseen the need for replacement pilots. Four-hundred of us from Training Command were picked to 'volunteer.' When we arrived in Florida we were introduced to the P-47. Hell, you could just look at that airplane and tell it wouldn't fly. We all signed up for P-38s. We got about four hours flying time in the P-47 and then were sent to New York and put on a seventy-two-ship convoy, mostly tankers, heading for Europe. Sitting on the tankers were fighter planes. We didn't see any P-38s, but we saw lots of P-47s and P-51s. When we got to England, we second lieutenants were met by several 'bird colonels,' commanders of P-38 fighter groups. Some of us thought this kind of odd and we trotted over to Intelligence to take a look at some mission summaries for different types of combat aircraft. What fell out for me was that for every P-47 lost, they lost two P-51s, in round numbers, that is. And for every P-51 they lost two P-38s. You didn't have to be a blackjack player to figure out the way Jimmy Doolittle [Who commanded the 8th Air Force at the time Fred arrived in England] was running the air war. The first airplane to stay out of was the P-38, the second the P-51. I didn't know what they were doing with the P-47, but I decided that airplane was for me after all.

"I arrived at the 56th Fighter Group at Boxted, near Colchester, on June 5, 1944. I was assigned to the 62nd squadron. They had been in England almost a year and a half by that time. The 56th Fighter Group was the most successful group in the 8th Air Force. It had more aces than any other outfit—Gabby Gabreski, Hub Zemke, Dave Schilling, Walker Mahurin, Fred Christensen, Gerald and Bob Johnson, Joe Powers, Paul Conger, Leroy Schreiber, Jimmy Steward—not the actor bomber pilot—and many more. Zemke was our group commander

The TA 152 was Kurt Tank's final upgrade to the Fw 190. It saw very limited action and only one TA 152 was returned to the United States. It currently is in storage in a disassembled state at the National Air and Space Museum. Fred was the only American to fly the TA 152. (Fred McIntosh)

through the invasion. Schilling was Zemke's deputy and my squadron commander. Schilling and I took a shine to one another. I flew twenty-five missions on his wing." Colonel David C. Schilling was the eighth highest scoring American Army Air Forces ace in World War II, with 22½ victories.

"Zemke then went to a down-and-out P-38 outfit," Fred continued, "to shape it up, the 479th Fighter Group at Wattisham, part of our wing, the 65th. They were scheduled to receive P-51s. Zemke transitioned into the P-51 and ended up bailing out over France when his aircraft iced up and spun into the ground. Zemke escaped by the 'skin of his teeth,' as the old saying goes, and ended up as a guest of the Germans at Stalag Luft I, near Barth, Pomerania. Schilling took over the 56th when Zemke left. Both Zemke and Schilling were full colonels in their twenties.

"I learned to love the P-47, it was a tough little airplane. I once flew one through the trees and made it home. Gabby Gabreski tried the same thing and ended up in Stalag Luft I along with Hub Zemke. When Stalag Luft I was liberated toward the end of April 1945, they brought all the POWs from Barth to Camp Lucky Strike, near Le Havre. On May 4, I got word that Zemke and Gabreski were at Camp Lucky Strike and I flew over in a Martin B-26 'Widow Maker' and flew them back to Boxted."

A German 88mm anti-aircraft gun, radar guided, like the one that nearly took McIntosh down, and had taken down thousands of Allied aircraft before him. (Author)

Fred McIntosh stayed on in Europe, becoming part of Colonel Harold Watson's team recovering German technology. While Watson focused on finding German jets, such as the Me 262 and Arado 234, to take back to the United States, Fred led the team that focused on recovering the best of Germany's conventional aircraft such as the Heinkel 219 *Uhu* night fighter. Another that took a little doing for him to find and lay his hands on was Professor Kurt Tank's last upgrade to the famed Fw 190, the TA 152. The Brits had some of them and eventually Fred got one to take back to the United States. "I am the only one of our team who flew the TA 152," Fred recalled with great pleasure when I interviewed him. "It was one of the best airplanes I have ever flown. I flew it a couple of times out of Aalborg, Denmark, against a P-51 and both times I ended up on the tail of the P-51. It was a very good airplane with all the kinks of the Fw 190 worked out of it." All the German jets retrieved by Watson and his team, who went by the name of "Watson's Whizzers," and Fred McIntosh's haul ended up on the British aircraft carrier HMS *Reaper* headed for New York harbor. Watson, with Fred as his copilot, returned to Wright Field in

The Ju 290 *Alles Kaputt* at Paris-Orly airport, France, on July 28, 1945, just prior to their departure for the Azores, Bermuda, then Wright Field, Dayton, Ohio. Watson standing, third from left, McIntosh was his copilot. The aircraft had "Tokyo" fuel tanks, giving it considerable range. (Fred McIntosh)

a German Ju 290 four-engine transport quite appropriately named by them *Alles Kaputt*. One hell of a way to end a war.

McIntosh didn't forget his old outfit, the 56th Fighter Group at Boxted. In early 1945, flying at 30,000 feet in his P-47, Fred's plane became the target of German radar directed AAA fire. Shrapnel shattered the canopy and shredded his parachute. Blood spurted from his ears. The cold air stopped the bleeding, but he couldn't hear. He pulled out of the formation and another P-47 led him back to Boxted. The doctors took out about a third of his teeth, he told me, and put a temporary plate in his mouth. So, while at Merseburg airfield in Germany, his base of operation, he received a call that his permanent plate had arrived at Boxted and for him to come and have it installed, so to speak. "Better come and get it quick," Fred was told, because they were packing up to go home. So he grabbed a German pilot, Heinz Braun, who had flown the Heinkel 111 before. The He 111 was a Battle of Britain vintage plane. "So, Heinz Braun and I flew the Heinkel over to Boxted. I chose the 111 because our airmen at Boxted had complained that they fought two-and-one-half years in the war and didn't even have a souvenir to show for it. I told Watson that I would fly the He 111 over so the men could field strip it for souvenirs. After we landed in England, I helped disconnect the batteries, so the men could field strip it." What was left of the airframe remained at Boxted for years.

Fred McIntosh was released from active duty in 1946, and like so many of his fellow World War II flyers, he was recalled in March 1951, after North Korea invaded the South. Colonel Hal Watson, who by this time had established the Air Technical Intelligence Center, ATIC (called FTD, the Foreign Technology Division, when I served there in 1975–78, now named the National Air and Space Intelligence Center, NASIC) at Wright-Patterson AFB, got ahold of McIntosh and put him to work setting up a school for technical analysts. In July 1951 the better part of a MiG 15 was recovered and the MiG parts were shipped to Wright-Patterson, where Fred's team of analysts put the MiG back together again. Recalled Fred: "We found that the MiG had a wing-flutter problem. The Russians had solved it simply by putting a cast iron slug in the tip of each wing. A single man could hardly carry the weight, it was that heavy.

"When the engineers had done their preliminary analysis, and our girls had typed up the report," McIntosh told me, "Watson flew to Washington to present his report on the MiG to the Air Force Chief of Staff, General Hoyt S. Vandenberg. Watson took a cast iron weight along and put it on General Vandenberg's desk. When the

A vintage Russian MiG 15 at the Bradley Air Museum at Bradley Field, Hartford, Connecticut. (Author)

guys with the slide rules finished their analysis, their findings were within 5 percent of the actual performance of the MiG."

Fred ended his Air Force days in 1961 in the rank of lieutenant colonel, flying the B-47 Stratojet. He flew 104 combat missions in the P-47 Thunderbolt in Europe. He said to me, "Flying German planes for Watson was one of my life's highlights. A time I never forget."

CHARLES A. LINDBERGH

SPIRIT OF ST LOUIS/P-38 LIGHTNING/P-47 THUNDERBOLT/F4U CORSAIR

To really live, one must almost die.

—UNKNOWN

The agreed-upon first priority among the United States and Great Britain was the war raging in Europe and North Africa. There also was a war going on in the Pacific; however, it was the second priority in terms of overall planning and resource commitment. Germany was deemed much more dangerous than the threat posed by the Empire of the Rising Sun. While Europe and North Africa was principally a land war, the opposite was true in the Pacific. This was an ocean war. Here the Imperial Japanese fleet had to face the combined allied fleets, and it very soon became a carrier war. Additionally, the decision had been made to keep American and British submarines out of the Atlantic, so that if a submarine was detected it was by definition an enemy submarine. However, American submarines raised havoc with Japanese shipping in the Pacific, and in no small part contributed to the rapid decline of Japanese combat capabilities. General Douglas MacArthur, a West Point graduate, a combat general who had served in World War I, led American and Allied forces in the Southwest Pacific area. Fleet Admiral Chester W. Nimitz commanded the South and Central Pacific land and naval forces. After initial setbacks, using an island-hopping campaign, MacArthur and Nimitz pushed the Japanese to the brink. Information in any war is the key to success. The breaking of the Japanese naval code gave the United States unprecedented insights into Japanese fleet movements.

Charles A. Lindbergh posing by the *Spirit of St Louis,* an instant American hero. The *Spirit of St Louis* is on display at the National Air and Space Museum in Washington DC. (Author)

The breaking of the German Ultra code provided similar access to strategic decisions and enemy movements in Europe. However, tactical operations required daily observation of the enemy—and the F-4/5, the reconnaissance versions of the P-38 Lightning, were really good at doing that. The aircraft had long range, a great asset in the Pacific, and operated well at low altitudes.

The F-4/5 reconnaissance aircraft flew with their nose armament removed, and instead sported a sophisticated array of cameras. General George C. Kenney, the commander of the 5th Air Force in the Pacific, was very much aware that the European war was number one in terms of getting the aircraft he needed. So, when the P-38 ran into problems in Europe, Kenney was willing to take all he could get. In the Pacific the P-38, and its reconnaissance variants the F-4 (based on the P-38E) and the F5 (based on the P-38G/J and L ver-

Feldmarschall Hermann Goering, in 1938, awarding Lindbergh the *Verdienstkreuz Deutscher Adler* by order of the Fuehrer, Adolf Hitler. Lindbergh's close association with the German leadership was to become a problem for him in the future once war broke out. (Minnesota Historical Society)

sions) did a marvelous job, after a little help from an unexpected source—Charles A. Lindbergh. The same Lindbergh who had flown the *Spirit of St. Louis* in a thirty-three and one-half hour crossing from New York to Paris. Landing at LeBourget airfield on May 21, 1927, at 10:24 p.m. Lindbergh was an instant American hero and was returned to Washington in triumph aboard the cruiser USS *Memphis* on June 11, 1927.

Lindbergh was a captain in the Army reserve. He was received by Calvin Coolidge, the President of the United States, promoted to full colonel in the reserve and awarded the first Distinguished Flying Cross for being the first to cross the Atlantic.

Lindbergh, in the 1930s, frequently visited German aircraft factories and test centers. He met with German aircraft designers and test pilots, such as Willy Messerschmitt, Kurt Tank, and Ernst Heinkel; expressed his admiration for the Germans and their policies and was personally decorated by Hermann Goering, Germany's air force commander. As a result of his close association with the Germans, once war broke out, the erstwhile hero of the *Spirit of St. Louis* became a social outcast, and men such as General Arnold, the Army Air Corps chief of staff, distanced themselves from Lindbergh. A. Scott Berg, in his book *Lindbergh*, quotes Lindbergh from his personal journal, "Now that we are at war I want to contribute as best I can to my country's war effort. It is vital for us to carry on this war as intelligently, as constructively, and as successfully as we can, and I want to do my part."

After doing volunteer work at Ford, testing P-47 Thunderbolts, Lindy, as he was called by friends and admirers, was asked by the president of the United Aircraft Corporation to participate in the evaluation of the gull-wing F4U Corsair. Writes Scott Berg in Lindbergh, "Trained as a fighter pilot and frustrated at not having seen action, Lindbergh participated in maneuvers and mock combat. . . . taking his plane up and engaging in a high-altitude gunnery contest against two of the Marines' best pilots. The forty-one-year-old civilian outguessed, outflew and outshot both of his opponents, each practically half his age." One thing Lindbergh knew was how to fly. "On January 5, 1944, Lindbergh conferred with Brigadier General Louis E. Wood of the Marines, in Washington, about the possibility of going to the South Pacific for a survey of Corsair operating bases in the combat zone. The next day Lindbergh was told he could proceed."

In late April 1944, Lindbergh left San Diego for Hawaii, Midway, Bougainville, eventually arriving at a Marine Corps base in the Pacific to test fly Corsairs. He flew patrols and on rescue missions with Marine Air Group 31 and, "Upon learning that Lindbergh had actually fired his guns when he was over Japanese held Rabaul, a Marine colonel dressed him down. Another chimed in, with a wink, 'it would be alright for him to engage in target practice on the way home.' From then on the military looked the other way." Before returning home Lindbergh wanted to fly combat in the twin-engine P-38 Lightning to be able to compare the F4U with the P-38. It just happened that an old friend, General Ennis Whitehead, was there to facilitate his endeavor, telling him to head for Hollandia where P-38s were being flown.

Writes Scott Berg in *Lindbergh*, "On the afternoon of June 26, Lindbergh knocked on the shack-door of Colonel Charles Mac-Donald, the commander of 'Satans Angels,' the celebrated 475th Fighter Group of the 5th Air Force. Entering the colonel's quarters, Lindbergh offered his name; but McDonald engrossed in a game of checkers, did not catch it. Lindbergh explained that he was interested in learning about combat operations with P-38s, and that General Donald Hutchinson, the Task Force Commander, had said MacDonald was the man to see. The Colonel and the deputy commander remained guarded in their conversation and focused on their game, while the tall intruder dressed in khakis just stood there. At last MacDonald asked, 'What did you say your name was, and what phases of operations are you particularly interested in?'

"'Lindbergh,' he replied, 'and I'm very much interested in comparing range, fire power and your airplane's general characteristics with those of single engine fighters.' His eyes still on the checkerboard, MacDonald realized that the only way the intruder could get his answers was by flying the plane; and the tall man was not wearing any kind of wings. After a few more moves, he asked, 'Are you a pilot?'

"'Yes,' he said, which prompted MacDonald to take a closer look at the forty-two-year-old man with the receding hairline standing there. 'Not Charles Lindbergh?'

"'That's my name,' he replied. MacDonald forgot his checkerboard and began talking airplanes. The men quickly became friends; and Lindbergh who had but eight hours flying time in a P-38, was invited on a four plane 'anti-boredom flight' the next day to Jefman and Samate. Once Lindbergh left the shack, MacDonald's deputy said, 'My God he shouldn't go on a combat mission. When did he fly the Atlantic? He's too old for this kind of stuff.' MacDonald thought their visitor seemed fit; besides, commented Major Thomas B. McGuire Jr., the Air Force's second leading ace, 'Who would be flying on his wing? I'd like to see how the old boy does.'

"The next day they all saw, as Lindbergh not only mastered his plane, but four hundred miles deep into Japanese territory—weaving through black puffs of ack-ack—also successfully strafed an enemy barge in Kaiboes Bay. After several more days of bombing missions, the crew of the 475th had noticed that Lindbergh's plane invariably returned with much more fuel than any of the others. One evening, MacDonald introduced the new recruit to the rest of the pilots at a briefing in the thatch-roofed group recreation hut; and he asked Lindbergh to explain why that was the case. In his flat midwestern tones, Lindbergh said that by raising the manifold pressure and lowering revolutions per minute, the engines would consume less gasoline, gallons that could be translated into time in the air and an increase in combat radius. The initial reaction from his audience was of disbelief and disrespect, cracks about grinding their engines down. 'These are military engines,' Lindbergh replied, 'built to take punishments. So punish them.' Then he added, that if any man felt uncomfortable about adopting this method, he should not. 'You're the captains of your own ships,' he said. 'You must make the decisions. After all, you know more about flying your planes than I do.' But over the next few weeks, the three squadrons of Satan's Angels learned otherwise, as they stretched their six-to-eight hour missions to ten hours, allowing them to surprise the Japanese with attacks deeper into their territory than expected."

Increasing the P-38's range by leaning the fuel mixture, lowering the revolutions per minute and raising the manifold pressure was a big deal. John R. Bruning in his excellent book *Race of Aces*, describes events in a little more detail of how this was achieved. Writes Bruning, "On July 3, Lindy flew with Mac [MacDonald] again on a squadron level patrol. They found no Japanese planes and took to strafing luggers and barges again—the same sort of thing that got Lynch killed and Bong badly shot up. During the strafing runs, several of the pilots reported critical fuel states and headed for home. Lindy's wingman also ran low on fuel. He pulled up over the strafing patterns and orbited, waiting for the rest of the planes to finish as he tried to maximize his fuel economy. When Lindbergh realized he was gone, he radioed him and ask how much gas he had left. 'About 175 gallons.' Lindbergh did the math. He had plenty left to get home safely, if he managed it well. He told the pilot to set his engine RPMs to sixteen hundred, set his mixture to auto lean, and slightly increase manifold pressure. The young aviator did as Lindy suggested and made it home with 70 gallons to spare. When the group checked Lindy's tanks, they found he had 260 [gallons] still in his tanks.

"That night, Lindbergh talked of fuel-management strategies to the other pilots. At first, Mac thought the idea was crazy. Leaning out the fuel mixture while keeping the RPMs low and the throttles advanced seemed like a perfect way to foul spark plugs and damage the engine's valves. Two days later MacDonald went to see Lindbergh's plane. The group's mechanics had stripped the engines to see how much damage his fuel strategy inflicted. To everyone's astonishment, the plugs were clean and the valves remained in perfect condition. That sold MacDonald completely. He became an evangelist of Lindy's technique, realizing that it could extend their range so significantly that it could have strategic implications on the drive to the Philippines." And so it did.

According to Scott Berg writing in *Lindbergh*, "'In the days that followed,' MacDonald would later recount, 'Lindbergh was indefatigable. He flew more missions than was normally expected of a regular combat pilot. He dive-bombed enemy positions, sank barges and patrolled our landing forces on Noemfoor Island. He was shot at by almost every anti-aircraft gun the Nips had in western New Guinea.' By then Lindbergh had logged more than twenty-five combat missions and close to ninety hours of combat time. On July 10, 1944, Lindbergh received a message from Australia requesting his presence. It was signed, 'MacArthur.'

"Lindbergh was introduced to General Richard K. Sutherland, MacArthur's Chief of Staff, with whom he discussed his method for increasing the combat radius of the P-38s. Sutherland was so astonished by Lindbergh's report—that a radius of 700 miles could be reached—he insisted that Lindbergh talk immediately to General MacArthur himself. After exchanging cordial salutations, MacArthur—looking younger than Lindbergh expected—asked if what Sutherland had just told him was true. MacArthur said, 'It would be a gift from heaven if that could be done.' MacArthur also said Lindbergh could do any kind of flying in any plane he wanted. Lindbergh returned to New Guinea where he spent much of his time teaching fuel management. On July 28, 1944, Lindbergh joined up with the 433rd Fighter Squadron, as observer in the number 3 position of an

MacArthur and senior staff members on a field visit, his personal aircraft, a converted B-17 bomber, behind him. (Barney Dobbs)

eight-plane sweep. Their mission was to bomb and strafe targets of opportunity.

"Although the Japanese were rumored to have strong flying forces in the area, the skies were clear. Suddenly, the radio squawked that another fighter group had spotted enemy aircraft nearby, a *Sonia* that was successfully eluding two American P-38s, whose pilots had run out of ammunition. As Lindbergh dove through a white cloud and black anti-aircraft bursts of smoke, Lindbergh got his first sight of a Japanese plane in the air—closing in head-on, with their combined speed close to six-hundred miles per hour. 'Of all the attacks it is possible to make on a Japanese plane,' MacDonald would later explain, 'the one liked least is the head-on pass, for there you and the enemy approach with tremendous speed, each with guns blazing. There is always a good chance for collision, even though both of you try to avoid it, and against a Japanese one could never be sure to what lengths his suicidal tendencies would push him.' Lindbergh fired for several seconds, seeing his machine gun tracer bullets and 20mm cannon shells pelt the *Sonia*; but a collision seemed unavoidable. As the *Sonia* zoomed closer to Lindbergh, he pulled back on his controls with as much force as he could exert. There was a violent jolt, with but a five-foot cushion of air between them, as Lindbergh successfully banked to safety and the *Sonia* succumbed to a vertical dive into the sea.

"At another private meeting with MacArthur in Brisbane, the General told Lindbergh of his recent conference with the President [Roosevelt] in Hawaii. MacArthur was otherwise interested in all Lindbergh had to say about his mission to the Pacific, especially in his success increasing the combat radius of the P-38 by almost 200 miles. MacArthur asked how many Japanese planes he had shot down, and Lindbergh told him of his experience off the south coast of Ceram."

Increasing the P-38's combat radius from 500 to 700 miles was a game changer for the P-38 and its subsequent employment in the Pacific region. However, the P-38's most famous combat mission had already been flown on April 18, 1943, a year before Lindbergh's influence extended the combat radius of the Lightning. To quote from *Lightning Over Bougainville—The Yamamoto Mission Reconsidered*, by R. Cargill Hall: "Early on the morning of 18 April 1943, Admiral Isoroku Yamamoto, commander-in-chief of the Japanese Combined Fleet, waved to those nearby at Lakunai Airfield, Rabaul, New Britain Island. Then he turned and entered a Mitsubishi G4M1 Betty bomber. The flight was to bring the Japanese leader southeast from New Britain to front line bases on Ballale and Bougainville Islands. There he would meet the emperor's soldiers and sailors who faced Allied forces, confer with their commanders, and return.

"Just after 9:30 on the morning of 18 April 1943, a tight formation of sixteen Lockheed P-38s roared across a beach some 30 miles northwest of Buin, on Bougainville, in the northern Solomon Islands. Led by Major John W. Mitchell, commanding officer of the 339th Fighter Squadron [347th Fighter Group/13th Air Force], they had departed Fighter Two, a rough airstrip near Kukum, Guadalcanal, some two hours before. Staying well to the west of the Japanese island strongholds at Rendova, the big Lightnings had flown over 430 miles, skimming the waves of the Solomon Sea to avoid detection.

"First Lt. Douglas Canning, a twenty-three-year-old Nebraskan, was the first to sight the quarry. He broke the long radio silence at precisely 9:34, calling out, 'Bogeys, 11 o'clock high.' Three miles away a flight of eight aircraft, six Mitsubishi A6M3 Type 32 Zeros and a pair of G4M1 Betty medium bombers, was approaching its destination, Ballale Island, off the southern tip of Bougainville. Spotting the Americans, the pilots of the Zeros jettisoned their drop tanks and turned to meet the attack. The two bombers dove for the safety of a nearby fighter airstrip at Buin, Bougainville.

"It was over in less than ten minutes. The Zeros claimed a single victim. Lieutenant Ray Hine. But the Japanese had paid a heavy price. The returning Lightning pilots reported three Zeros destroyed, [but none actually were]. One of the Bettys had splashed down in the Ocean. A column of black smoke rising above the jungle canopy marked the spot where the second Betty had come to earth. United States Army Air Forces pilots had intercepted the Admiral's flight and, in one blow, decapitated Japanese military leadership in the Pacific. That blow, like the failed invasion and loss of aircraft carriers at Midway Island ten months earlier, was one from which wartime Japan would never fully recover."

The P-38s that intercepted Admiral Yamamoto's flight were very close to the extreme limit of their range—500 miles. Lindbergh's procedural change, to raise the manifold pressure and lowering revolutions per minute, reduced fuel consumption and extended the radius of the Lightning to 700 miles. Writes Scott Berg in Lindbergh, "Bombers had been requesting fighter cover over Palau for some time, but they had repeatedly been refused on the grounds 'that the distance was too great and the weather too bad.' Lindbergh's mission to Palau refuted such excuses. Within days, the top brass had done an about-face."

Aside from giving the P-38 'legs,' Lindbergh had worked diligently for some time before going to the Pacific to deal with hypoxia. The prevailing attitude at the time was that there were no symptoms for a flyer to warn him that his oxygen supply was insufficient and that he was about to pass out. Spending time in a one-of-a-kind pressure chamber at the Mayo Clinic [Flying jets in the postwar world routinely at or above 40,000 feet, I and my fellow flyers periodically had to take a 'chamber flight,' which allowed us to identify our symptoms, warning signs that we were experiencing oxygen deficiency], Lindbergh learned his symptoms and quickly put his experience to actual use. On one test flight of a P-47 Thunderbolt, according to A. Scott Berg in *Lindbergh*, he wrote, "Lindbergh ran short of oxygen without warning—at 36,000 feet. The gauges indicated otherwise; but he sensed too late that something was happening 'to clarity of air, to pulse of life, perception of eye,'" as Lindbergh later put it. 'He grew aware,' he would later write, 'of that vagueness of mind and emptiness of breath which warn a pilot of serious lack of oxygen.' As the dials in front of him faded and began to black out, he shoved the stick forward, diving as quickly as possible. Senseless, except for a vague awareness of a shriek outside his cockpit, he fell 20,000 feet before full consciousness returned and his thought process was restored with the increasing density of air. Shortly after landing, a mechanic informed Lindbergh that the plane's pressure gauge was reading fifty pounds too high and that his oxygen tank had simply run empty at 36,000 feet. As a result of Lindbergh's study, Ford modified its oxygen equipment [for the P-47], thereby saving countless lives." The P-38 Lightning was unpressurized.

Lindbergh is and always has been an American aviation icon. Before the United States entered World War II he had advocated neutrality and not to provide weapons of war to Britain. He was an active pacifist. He was accused of being a Nazi fellow traveler, and when the President questioned his suitability of being a colonel in the United States Army Air Corps Reserve, he tendered his resignation. However, he stated in his letter of resignation according to Scott Berg's *Lindbergh*, "I will continue to serve my country to the best of my ability as a private citizen." And so he did.

BARNEY DOBBS
AND ALLEN BLUM

P-38/F-4/5 LIGHTNING/B-26 INVADER

The accusation it was made: of course it was denied.
They said of the germ bombs I'd dropped, and about it I had lied.
A bomb that's filled with fleas and flies, dear Lord, I've never seen;
but men for propaganda's sake can sure be mighty mean.

—BARNEY DOBBS

Captain Byron Alexis Dobbs Jr. was born in Phoebus, Virginia, on January 14, 1920, under the muzzles of the quiet guns of Fort Monroe and across the bay from the Norfolk Navy Yard, and just outside the gate of Langley Field. His father was a carpenter. When the depression hit, his family barely managed to stay alive, moving from one relative to another, always chasing the next dollar or the next meal. Said Barney Dobbs, "One summer we stayed on my grandmother's forty-acre farm. My dad got a contract from the Heinz Company to grow pickles. I recall riding the pickup loaded with cucumbers down to their plant. The job only lasted for the summer, but that gave us enough money to make it through the winter. Eventually in 1933 we settled in Birch Run, a small village in Michigan. Both of my parents were from Michigan. I graduated from high school in 1937. After high school I tried to enlist in the Navy. They wouldn't take me because the doctor said I had hammer toes. Two years later, in 1939, when Hitler marched into Poland, I tried again, but this time I went to the Army recruiting office. The doctor who examined me asked, 'Is there anything else I should know about your health,

The Seversky P-35 was jointly designed by Alexander P. deSeversky and Alexander Kartvelli and in 1937 it was the best there was in the Army Air Corps inventory. It was all metal, had a retractable landing gear and an enclosed cockpit. By the time the first of an order of seventy-six were delivered to the 1st Pursuit Group, the aircraft was outdated and subsequently the P-38 Lightning was delivered to the 1st Pursuit Group renamed the 1st Fighter Group. (Barney Dobbs)

Barney?' Well, I always tried to be honest, so I told him the Navy had turned me down in 1937 because I had hammer toes. 'I don't care which way your toes point,' the doctor said, 'as long as there are five on each foot.'

"I was given a choice of Chanute Field in Illinois, Hickam Field in Hawaii, or Selfridge Field, Michigan," Barney told me when I interviewed him. "I chose Selfridge Field, where I was assigned to the First Pursuit Group. I selected Selfridge because I had met a real cute redhead from Clio, the next town down the road. It was at Selfridge where my life truly began. They had P-35s there. At night I would go and sit in the cockpit of a plane and think about flying. I dreamed of being a pilot. When I sat in one of those planes, I was on top of the world. The officers were gods to me. They treated us real well, and I did everything they told me to do. In 1940 I went to technical school at Lowry Field in Denver, Colorado. Here, for the first time in my life I really studied hard. I wanted to do well. By 1941 I made corporal. A big deal for me, and my pay was increased to forty-two dollars a month."

"After tech school I was sent to the Louisiana/South Carolina Maneuvers with the First Pursuit Group. Here, among other things, I learned about black widow spiders. A bite from one resulted in a fairly serious operation which brought down my parents and that cute redhead from Clio—now my fiancee. Kay has followed me around the world ever since. Later that year I was promoted to staff sergeant, and I applied for enlisted pilot training after the attack on Pearl Harbor. I was accepted. I attended flying schools at Ryan Field near Hemet, California; then Minter Field near Bakersfield, and finally Williams Field near Phoenix, Arizona. While at Minter, after passing my forty-hour check ride, I convinced Kay to marry me. So on September 26, 1942, the day after Kay's eighteenth birthday, we were married in the Minter Field chapel. I sailed through advanced training at Williams in Class 43B, got my wings and was promoted to flight officer. I ended up at Peterson Field in Colorado Springs, where I checked out in the P-38 and the F-4/5, the reconnaissance versions of the P-38. What a beautiful airplane! Seven months later, after only forty hours in the P-38, we were considered combat ready by our instructors. At Peterson I met Horatio Holton and Allen Blum, friends for life. All three of us were assigned to the 8th Photo Reconnaissance Squadron somewhere in the Pacific. Allen Blum was good at keeping a daily log so I'll let him tell his, Holton's and my story."

Writes Allen Blum in his diary: "I was getting a little sack time at Peterson Field. It was Sunday, July 25, 1943, waiting for a Link trainer scheduled at 1800 when the phone rudely interrupted my sleep. The terse command to report to the orderly room immediately gave us a clue of what was coming. That was at four o'clock in the afternoon. About half the guys could not be located. Our first orders were to board a Transcontinental Airlines flight at 1030 that evening. Of course a lot of bitching ensued and since accommodations could not be obtained, we were finally told to report the next morning at 0800. Of course that night was a hustle for Jo [his wife] and I to get my junk packed. What to take and what not? The next morning, 26 July 1943, we loaded up into Flight Officer Barney Dobbs's car, who lived right across the street from us, and had found out that our plane didn't leave until three o'clock in the afternoon, so we had plenty of time to clear the base. I said goodbye to my swell little wife.

We had just been married on June 5, not knowing if I'd get to see her for a long time or not. Dobbs and I planned to meet our wives at Hamilton Field, near San Francisco, just in case we had a few days to spend there.

"We arrived at Hamilton Field the next noon and found that our whole group was short on shots. They gave us the first series and we had to wait five days for the second series. I called Jo and Kay [Dobbs] right away and had them get on the next train westward bound. In the meantime we were busy getting our supplies—jungle kits and life rafts attached to parachutes, impregnated gas proof clothing and more. It made us realize we were going to war. The good news was that we were to fly to our destination rather than going in a convoy, as we had assumed. After two days Kay and Jo arrived. From then on until the morning we left we spent every minute together. The girls stayed at the Field with us during the day until 1600 hours at which time we were free to go into Frisco. We took in Fisherman's Wharf for seafood, the International Settlement for entertainment, and stayed at the Sir Francis Drake Hotel. Sunday, August 1, 1943, came and at about 1100 we went to the swimming pool at Hamilton Field. When we checked in with the orderly room, we learned that we were scheduled to leave sometime that night. It wasn't until the next morning that we actually left. We said goodbye to our wives and boarded a big B-24 cargo ship, also known as a C-87."

"On Monday morning, August 2, 1943," Dobbs continues, "our group loaded on a B-24 with secret orders and instructions not to open them until two hours into our flight. My close friend Al Blum and I speculated where we were going. When we ripped open the envelopes, we found our destination was Amberly Field, Brisbane, Australia. We landed at Hickam Field, Honolulu, Hawaii. The island was blacked out at night, but we could still see some of the destruction from the Japanese raid. The next morning, August 3, we headed for Canton, a tiny island in the Phoenix Group. Once we arrived we were surprised to see that all it was was a tiny coral reef, so small that one could take in the whole island standing in one place. We stayed there for eight hours. Then took off at midnight for Nandi in the Fijis. There we had breakfast—eggs and wieners. Al consumed seven eggs and I don't remember how many wieners. We barely finished eating

A C-87 transport. A converted B-24 bomber without its guns. It was widely used in the China/Burma theater of operations to fly the "Hump," the Himalayas. (Author)

when we loaded up again, this time heading for New Caledonia, which we made in time for dinner. In the meantime we crossed the equator, the international dateline, and jumped ahead a day. Once we arrived in Brisbane we were told our final destination—the 8th Photo Reconnaissance Squadron at Port Moresby, New Guinea—*The Eight Ballers: Eyes of the 5th Air Force* was our somewhat lengthy but appropriate handle. Al and I stayed in Brisbane two nights and thought they were crazy when they issued us six blankets each. But after the sun went down we discovered the reason—though it was August, it was midwinter down under.

"In Moresby they were glad to see us. Their numbers were pretty well depleted. We lived in tents, and our comfort depended entirely on how hard we worked at it. Lumber was near impossible to get, but Al and I managed by hook and by crook to build us a little hut with a tent for a roof. At least we had a clean place to put our feet in the morning. The air was so humid our B-4 bags began molding after only a few days. Cigarettes absorbed so much moisture they were barely smokeable. There were five or six landing strips in the area identified by their distance from Port Moresby—three mile strip, five mile strip, seven mile strip, and so on. We were to fly the F-5, the photo version of the P-38 fighter. Al Blum and I stayed together as much as we could throughout our tour, flying missions all over that part of the world. I spent thirteen months flying eighty-eight combat missions from Australia and New Guinea, fighting mosquitos, malaria, jungle rot and Japanese. Al flew 100 combat missions. Al kept a diary of our day to day experiences. Years later, he sent a copy to me and on the cover page he wrote, 'I occasionally reread it Barney [Dobbs], I can still feel the anxieties, fears, frustrations, satisfactions, joys, memories of friends and comrades, sadness when someone didn't return, and the many other emotions of a shavetail involved in the greatest transition of his life—from farm boy to combat pilot.'

The diary of Al Blum depicts in great detail the day to day life of airmen living in rudimentary circumstances in the jungles of Asia, fighting a war where death is arbitrary, and going home is a dream that may or may not come true. Writes Al Blum:

21 August 1943—In a few days I went on my first combat mission with Flight Officer Ludke—one of the old pilots—and of course I was plenty nervous. We always fly in pairs—one to watch for the enemy, while the other does the photo work. Sent three of the old and three of the new pilots to Charters Towers, Australia, for fighter training. Our new policy was to have pursuit ships in our squadron to escort photo ships.

28 August 1943—My second mission was to Wewak with Captain Foster, our squadron commander. I didn't see the Zeros coming up after us, although they were only 3,000 feet below us. Captain Foster said he could see the red spots on their wings, and he didn't like it when I told him I didn't see them. Can't blame him, since I was his cover. Several nights later I got orders to get ready to leave for Marilinian, about 35 miles from the nearest Japanese base at Lae, and had only been occupied about two weeks by Yanks. Found that I was to be quartered with the 44th Fighter Squadron. Our planes arrived that evening and the next morning.

1 September 1943—I flew my third mission with Lieutenant Sykes to Wewak. Clouds covered the target. Didn't get any pix.

Came back by Alexishafen and Madang which were clear and then on to Moresby to deliver the film and reload. We had no facilities for processing film at Marilinian.

2 September 1943—The next day Lieutenant Duke and I ran a recce over the Markham Valley from Nadzab to Lae. I took pictures of the whole valley; Duke did the coastline from Lae to Hopoi, but clouds covered it. This was all in preparation for a big Aussie and American landing at Lae. 15,000 Aussie troops landed and were covered by P-39s, P-47s and P-38s. The operation was a success, even though they were opposed by 13,000 Japanese. Our part in the show was to fly to Wewak to see if the Japanese had any plane concentrations there—also to watch for Japanese planes approaching Lae.

4 September 1943—5th mission. I SNAFU'D, my oxygen mask broke. I was at 17,000 feet when I began to feel woozy. I checked my oxygen hose and everything seemed to be OK. In another minute or so I was really feeling weird. Then I found a hole in my mask. I called my escort and he went on while I peeled off to get some air at a lower level.

5 September 1943—The Aussies landed 1,500 paratroops in the Markham Valley at Nadzab. It was a beautiful sight to see—the transports covered by P-47s and P-38s. B-25s went in first to strafe ground positions and lay smoke screens.

6 September 1943—Major Hocutt, A-3, gave me the Hollandia mission. I had one fighter escort along. We got there, but the target was covered with a thin layer of stratus clouds. I was ready to turn back, but changed my mind. Right over the airfield was a hole in the clouds. I got the pictures, then headed home. Didn't meet any Japanese nor was there any ack-ack. I was quite apprehensive until I learned of the results of my mission—success. I was the first one to fly this mission successfully. Our operations officer, Captain Guerry, put me in for the Distinguished Flying Cross.

L-R Lt. Landin, Doc Robertson, Horatio Holton, Tom Farmer, Dick Shipway, Bill Gailfus, Byron Dobbs, Thadeus Jones in front of one of their F-5s at Nadzab in 1943. (Barney Dobbs)

7 September 1943—Had three red alerts last night. The first was the only one when bombs were dropped. We suffered no damage—bombs missed the strip and the camp.

8 September 1943—The only excitement today was right here at the camp. Lieutenant Haigler and I were washing up in the creek at about 1100 when we heard some shots ring out fairly close—just below the first bend in the river. We wondered what they were but thought no more about it. That afternoon we learned that several engineers were bathing just below us when a Japanese soldier rose up out of the weeds and took a pot shot at one of them, hitting him in the shoulder. Of course they started running, went to the military police squadron, who wouldn't believe them. They borrowed guns and went back. They found him and got him with automatic fire. He evidently was a pilot who had bailed out near there and had been wandering around. They found his bed. There also was a second one. So there must be one more wandering around somewhere.

9 September 1943—Did a recon mission of Malahang, Lae, Hopoi and Nadzab at 8,000 feet.

10 September 1943—Rained all night. Our dirt runways are fair, which is to say they are about a foot deep in mud.

13 September 1943—My baptism of fire. Duke flew to Moresby yesterday and I was down at Ops awaiting his return. About 10:30 I looked out and saw the linemen running for cover. I then looked over my shoulder and saw a beautiful formation of eleven bombers and thirty Zeros directly overhead. We headed for the slit trenches just as the bombs began bursting. At first we thought they might have hit our camp area, but as it turned out they had just missed. I am now a strong believer in slit trenches and will no longer just lay in bed at night when a red alert is sounded.

14 September 1943—We got orders last night to return to Moresby, which made everyone plenty happy. Got to Moresby and the first thing I heard was that our C.O. Taylor was missing. This was a real shock. He was enroute to Moresby from Dobodura and evidently ran into some bad weather. This evening I had to help sort and pack his personal belongings to be sent home.

15 September 1943—Went on a mission to Wewak to cover damage done on a strike. Had fighter escort but at Kerema just as I was putting on my oxygen mask the snap broke—so I had to return. No mission credit.

16 September 1943—Went on another mission to Wewak to cover this morning's strike. Was to pick up my escort at Marilinian. He never showed. Ops told me not to go without an escort. On yesterday's raid on Wewak B-24s shot down 38 Japanese fighters and 16 probable. P-38s shot down nine with six probable.

18 September 1943—Duke and I took off for a mission in the Markham Valley—Boana and Finschafen. Mission successful— no opposition.

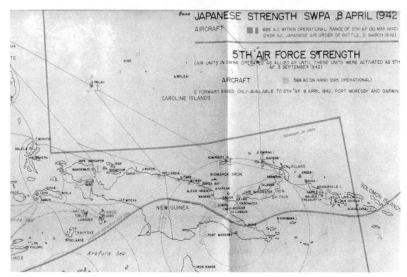

The map displays the locations mentioned in this narrative such as Wakde, Hansa Bay, Wewak, Rabaul, Port Moresby, and so on. (Source: United States Strategic Bombing Survey, The 5th AF in the War Against Japan, June 1947)

19 September 1943—Mission to Dumpu to get low obliques of an old landing strip. Didn't have an escort. Japanese dropped a few bombs here at Moresby last night but scored no hits.

20 September 1943—Had to pack up to go to Dobudura to relieve two pilots who've been there for a couple of weeks. We keep four pilots there to run a visual recce of New Britain every day.

21 September 1943—Started out with Dobbs to New Britain but just as we got there the diaphragm on my oxygen regulator busted and I had to come back. Oxygen seems to be my Waterloo.

24 September 1943—Got orders to bring 8th Photo Detachment back from Dobudura. Packed up and a C-47 brought us back home.

26 September 1943—Did some mapping for the engineers between Finschafen and Sailor. Also mapped Long Island.

29 September 1943—Farmer and I started to make the circuit—
Ramu Valley, Madang and Cape Glouster, but had to return due
to weather, as did all the other ships that started out today.

4 October 1943—Scheduled for Rabaul today. Just got to Gas-
mata when my right engine started acting up. The turbo regulator was out, and the higher I got the less it worked. Jones and
Bateson flew my escort.

7 October 1943—Jones, Bateson and I started for Rabaul again
but ran into a front about 20 miles out to sea off Cape Ward Hunt
so had to return—no pix.

8 October 1943—Ludtke with Holton and Bateson as escorts
went to Madang to check up on some convoy activity. Just out
of Madang they were jumped by Zeros. Bateson failed to return.
They didn't see him get hit, so he may be safe in the Markham
Valley. My orders came through today awarding me the DFC.

10 October 1943—My 16th mission. Walt Langdon and I took
off for Madang. At 18,000 feet started through a cloud deck on
instruments. I hadn't turned on boost pumps yet and was flying
close to the lead ship so as to keep it in sight. About that time my
left engine gave out. I immediately turned on the boost pumps,
but lost sight of Walt. I came out beneath the cloud deck while he
continued on until he got on top. Tried to call him on the radio,
received him OK, but couldn't transmit. We got the pix of Madang
and Alexishafen and started for Finschafen. Over Finschafen, at
24,000 feet, I saw two planes approximately half a mile away.
They peeled off toward me. I immediately dropped my tanks and
pushed the throttles to full RPM in a slow climb toward home.
Was able to outdistance them. Love that high altitude foxhole.

13 October 1943—17th mission. Started for Rabaul with Holton
and Loos for escort. Ran into a front about 20 minutes out of
Rabaul. Had to return with no pix. My hydraulics went out, so
I had to hand pump my landing gear down—talk about sweat!!

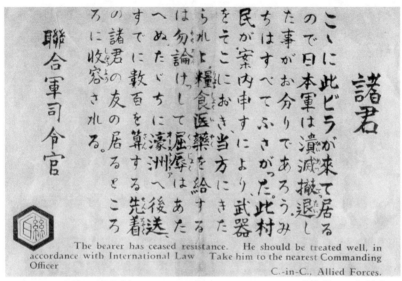

聯合軍司令官

諸君

こゝに此ビラが来て居る

この事が日本軍は潰滅撤退し

民が案内すべてふさがった。此

ちはすべてふさがっり。武器村

たはすべてふさがった。此村

のでお分りであろう。

The bearer has ceased resistance. He should be treated well, in accordance with International Law. Take him to the nearest Commanding Officer

C.-in-C., Allied Forces.

Every survival kit included documentation of this nature—it never worked. (Barney Dobbs)

14 October 1943—My first combat leave to Sydney. What a time. How one does appreciate hot showers, soft beds, thick steaks. It all costs a lot of money, but it is worth it. About 50 Pounds, $150, for the week. Bad weather delayed our return for several days. Met six replacements for our squadron. Good to see some of the old boys from Peterson Field's 10th Squadron. Now for a couple of days of rest and back to work again.

30 October 1943—Took two fighters for escort from the 39th Fighter Squadron and started for Kavieng in New Ireland. My first try at this particular target. Couldn't reach it because of frontal activity. New Britain was also closed out. On our way up landed at Lae for gas. Two short months ago we wouldn't fly over Lae under 30,000 feet, now we are landing here. You should see the destroyed Japanese planes—fighters, bombers. Dozens of bullet holes through them all. One bunch of rising suns which have definitely set.

2 November 1943—My 19th mission. Murphy and I took off for Madang Alexishafen and Nubia. Got pix of all the airdromes and returned to base.

5 November 1943—Loos and Rigsby in the fighters and I started for Rabaul after dinner. But weather got so bad over the ranges that we didn't get off the island.

8 November 1943—Two fighters from the 39th and myself started for Rabaul again. One of the fighters, half way there, had to return for some reason. We got there OK and did all the airfields but two, the harbor and the town. Antiaircraft fire was at our altitude but about 100 yards behind us.

12 November 1943—Rigsby and I had to get up at 5 o'clock to board a B-25 bound for Kiriwina in the Tobriand Islands. Southard was there with an F-5 to cover the Navy strike at Rabaul early in the morning. Then Rigsby was to take the plane as soon as it landed and go back to Rabaul to cover a B-24 strike. I went along as a spare. As it was, the weather was bad and no one got photos.

13 November 1943—My 22nd mission. Picked up my fighter escort at Nadzab—P-47s. And if anyone says anything about a 47 outflying an F-5, they're wrong. Got to Wewak, but it was cloud covered. No pix.

15 November 1943—Loos and I did Cape Gloucester, New Britain, then Finschafen. We were jumped by two Zeros at Finschafen. Wasted no time in getting out of there—leaving them in the dust so to speak.

17 November 1943—Flew to Sydney as copilot on a B-26. Picked up furniture and food for the club. Right brake locked on landing blowing out the tire, wrecking the wheel and ruining the nose strut. Took about a week to get repairs. Had lots of fun— flew under the Sydney bridge and got back to Moresby just in time for Thanksgiving dinner. General [George C.] Kenney had been at the squadron in the morning to award medals, I missed mine. [General Kenney was at this time the commander of the Allied Air Forces including the 5th Air Force in General MacArthur's Southwest Pacific area. In June 1944 General Kenney

was appointed commander of the Far East Air Forces, FEAF, which included the 5th, 7th, and 13th Air Forces.]

30 November 1943—Tried to get to Kavieng alone but a front over the Bismark Sea changed my mind for me.

6 December 1943—Orders came through promoting me to first lieutenant.

10 December 1943—Went to Kavieng again without escort but after getting there could get no pix due to clouds covering target.

16 December 1943—26th mission. Erb and I flew a mosaic off Saidor. Met no opposition.

20 December 1943—Captain Moffat went on leave to Sydney leaving me with Operations.

21 December 1943—Another mission to Saidor, but no pix due to clouds.

26 December 1943—Colonel Hutchinson with Colonel Arnell as copilot started out from our airdrome in our B-17 this morning to cover the allied landing on New Britain. It wasn't daylight yet, and there was heavy ground fog. The ship crashed off the end of the strip killing two. There were 17 men aboard of which four were war correspondents. It was a terrible mess. The smell of burning flesh is a very unpleasant experience. Two more men died later in the hospital. I flew a mission to Hansa Bay, but no pix due to weather.

29 December 1943—Today I am 24 years old and flew my 29th mission. I flew a fighter escorting Ludke to Cape Busching.

31 December 1943—We lost another pilot. The last seen of Lieutenant Erb—yesterday morning—his plane was on fire, and he was turning back, but didn't make it. I spent an hour and a half this morning searching for him. His little daughter had just been born a couple of weeks ago. Lt Fairbanks and Colonel Darnell were released from the hospital this morning. They were survivors of the B-17 crash.

5 January 1944—Rigsby, Clark and I started for Kavieng, but just as we got over the range we saw weather building up, so we turned back.

6 January 1944—My second combat leave to Sydney with Captain Loos and Holton. Needless to say, a good time was had by all.

23 January 1944—32nd mission. Gailfus and I went to Manus Island. Got the pix but Gailfus's left engine quit. He landed at Finschafen. I went on to Garove Island and New Britain. Flew a total of 6:45 hours, my longest mission so far.

27 January 1944—Lt. Schultz and I went on a search and rescue mission in the L-5. Found red and yellow panels but no survivors.

29 January 1944—34th mission. Curran, Gailfus and I went as far as Jacquinot Bay on New Britain after going around a front on the Solomon Sea. Curran got pix, but the rest of our targets were cloud covered. We turned back after seeing 4 Zeros attempting an interception. On returning to Moresby we found it was all socked in. We had enough gas to get us to Milne Bay where we waited for the weather to clear.

5 February 1944—Lt Shipway and I started out to cover a big strike at Kavieng. Weather stopped the whole show. It would have been interesting to watch since they were going in at 10,000 feet. There were two groups, 7 squadrons with 4 squadrons of 38s as cover. We were to go in at 21,000 feet.

12 February 1944—Colonel Darnell as my escort and I started for Kavieng, but returned due to weather. Two days ago Flight Officer Davis was lost in weather.

14 February 1944—37th mission. Lt Holton, who now is my permanent flying partner, and I went to New Hanover to search for a reported Japanese convoy. Low cloud cover prevented us from finding it.

15 February 1944—Went to Townsville to ferry up a fighter. Had to wait a week before it was ready.

8 March 1944—Captain Counselman and I started for Hollandia but weather forced us to return.

9 March 1944—Captain Counselman and I started for Hollandia, by going around Finschafen, we got as far as Bagbag Island at about 50 feet over the water. Counselman got lost and I had to bring him back. It sure tickles me to have one of the big dogs get lost. One does learn from experience.

12 March 1944—Holton and I went to Hollandia. Got pix of Humboldt Harbor, Tadji drome, Dagua and Wewak dromes.

15 March 1944—Holton and I started for Hollandia, but no pix due to clouds so got Tadji and Wewak on the way back. Interception was attempted from Boram drome.

19 March 1944—Captain Shipway, Lt. Clark, Lt. Holton and myself with eight fighters for escort took PICS of Wewak at 15,000 feet. Saw 14 Japanese planes airborne but they didn't bother us. Intelligence reported from Manus Island invasion that the Japanese intended to lead a life of ease and luxury. Quantities of beer and liquor were found and Geisha girls with their throats slit rather than let the Yanks capture them.

25 March 1944—Holton and I started to Wewak, but a 20,000 foot ceiling made it a no go for pix.

29 March 1944—44th mission. Holton and I went to Hollandia to cover a strike—the first ones there. Smoke and low clouds prevented photos but they really left a trail of damage. Using 20 pound fragmentation bombs, 16,000 of them, they knocked out 112 planes on the ground and shot down ten more. 60 some fires were seen near and on the runways. No losses to us. Got pix at Wewak, Tadji and Nubia.

2 April 1944—Went to Wewak to cover a strike and look for inland road. Got pix OK.

4 to 22 April 1944—Combat leave to Sydney.

24 April 1944—To Wewak. Got pix of all dromes.

27 April 1944—47th mission. Went to Wakde Island. Got 90 exposures of coastline between Wakde and Hollandia. A six hour mission.

30 April 1944—48th mission. To Wakde Island. Couldn't get mapping on account of clouds. Got Wakde airdrome and several small dromes. This gives me 152 combat hours—halfway home.

6 May 1944—Today ended in tragedy. Lieutenant Walt Langdon, a good friend, was killed in a crash on takeoff this afternoon. He and I spent the morning playing pinochle, then we went to fly a couple of ships that hadn't been flown for several days. I took off first, made my turn, and saw that he was off the ground and turning. I turned my attention to my own ship and then, when I looked around for him to see whether he was joining in formation, I couldn't see him. So I turned back toward the field and then saw the black smoke from a fire. I circled it low and saw one recognizable wing tip. He was killed instantly. The fire truck arrived on time to keep him from being burned. He leaves a wife and 6-month old son. The second crash in a week in our squadron. Who's next?

7 May 1944—49th and 50th mission. Captain Shipway as pilot, me as copilot in a B-25 went to Hollandia. Stayed over night and then with another B-25 went to Bak Island to obtain oblique pix of 20 miles of coastline at 500 feet. Had 15 P-40s for escort. On our run we had to fly directly over a Corvette in the harbor. P-40s strafed it to draw the fire away from us, but he shot anyway, missing us. Got the pix and on our return we sighted a merchant vessel approximately 200 feet long. We both went down and strafed it. Fourteen 50 caliber guns shoot a lot of lead. We went on, P-40s following us saw the ship blow up. Had we known this in time to take a picture of it, we'd have received an Air Medal. Oh well, at least we sunk it. Got a lot of heavy ack-ack at Salmi. The other B-25 received a hole in the tail from it.

15 May 1944—51st mission. Monroe and I to Wakde. Got a full magazine of pix.

16 May 1944—Gailfus and I had the same mission again with 100% coverage.

17 May 1944—Trying out a new camera set-up. A K-22 oblique, 12 inch focal length, for low altitude coastline obliques. Works well. Got pix in the area of Cape Chrysalis.

18 May 1944—Low obliques from Cape Gordon to Hansa Bay.

21 May 1944—This morning we leave for Hollandia to stage our missions from there.

23 May 1944—Monroe and I started out for Baboons but couldn't get pictures due to weather. We are doing our cooking over an outside fire, using 100 octane gas. Had lots of good bacon for a change. Everyone sleeps with their .45 under their pillow. The Japanese out in the hills are pretty hungry and sneak into camp trying to find food. A major in another outfit discovered one in his tent one night.

26 May 1944—Monroe and I once more to Noemfoor Island, Manicure, etc. Couldn't get the first two but got Moemi dromes,

Baboons, Cape Lanamerah dromes and Nabira to make a 5 hour and 30 minute mission.

28 May 1944—Our detachment moved to Wakde Island, 200 miles west. I didn't go. Had to stay so I could test-hop a ship that was in the process of having its engines changed. Found that my chute had gone with our detachment to Wakde, so I had to fly without one. You sure feel naked when you don't have your chute. Probably would have been court-martialed in the States for doing that. Flew the test-hop and then on to Wakde to get my chute, bedroll and other personal equipment. Have to take this bird back to Nadzab tomorrow.

29 May 1944—58th mission. Took off and delivered the ship to Nadzab where I learned the squadron is moving to Bak Island— our next home. A jump of 800 miles into Japanese territory. The Allied landings were only made there on 27 May, two days ago. And there had been more opposition than we figured on. We lost four miles yesterday. On Wakde Island they have been bombed heavily, and one night even strafed with landing lights on. A small group of Japanese made a suicide attack on an Air Corps unit but their own end was all they accomplished. They had bombs tied to themselves as well as machine guns and rifles with fixed bayonets. We'll have plenty of use for a good slit trench when we get to Bak. Two American nurses, presumably from the Philippines, were found in a Japanese brothel at Hollandia. They were nearly crazy from drugs and dope.

30 May 1944—Major Shipway and I did some mapping at Hollandia. This ends my best month so far—49 hours and ten minutes combat time in one month. Today's flight broke the 200 hour mark. Just 100 more to go. [While in Europe the mission count, anywhere from twenty-five for bombers, to eighty+ for fighters, determined when crews/pilots got to go home; in the Pacific, at least for recon pilots, it was the number of combat hours flown—at this time of the war it was 300 hours.]

B-25s were collocated with the F-5 squadrons. The F-5 pilots checked out in the B-25s as time permitted. A B-25 RTU also was located at Nadzab. Although equipped with cameras for photo missions, the B-25s were armed with fifteen .50 caliber machine guns—twelve forward firing. The crew of five included two pilots, crew chief, radio operator, who also served as gunners, and one tail gunner. (Author)

31 May 1944—Another mission with Holton to Hollandia, but could not get there due to weather.

1 June 1944—61st mission. Holton and I got full K-18s of mapping the Wewak area. After finishing, we saw P-47s dive bombing at Hansa Bay, so we entered their bombing pattern and followed them in even though they were only dry runs for us. Some fun.

3 June 1944—Colonel Guerry had me do some personal work for Generals Wurtsmith and Whitehead. It was color stuff of their quarters both here at Nadzab and at Moresby.

4 June 1944—Orders were received awarding me the Air Medal for 25 missions between August and December.

7 June 1944—Flew as copilot with Major Armstrong in a B-25 on a courier mission to Wakde.

20 June 1944—Arrived back from Sydney after a week of good food and hot showers. Everything still as ever in the squadron.

22 June 1944—Went to Wakde Island with the advanced detachment and flew a mission to Babo to cover a strike.

23 June to 22 July 1944—Flew nearly every day, and on July 23 ended up with 303 combat hours and 100 missions. In one three-day period I had to return twice on single engine. The last time was for 4 hours which is quite a while with only one fan. Our detachment moved back to Hollandia because Wakde was too small for all of our planes. One night on the way back from a mission—I delivered some prints to Wakde—in taxiing to a parking place I ran over some shrapnel and cut up a tire. It was too late to get it fixed that night so I had to leave the bird sitting on the taxiway. During the night we had several red alerts and one raid. Bombs destroyed 6 planes and a gasoline storage area filled with 50 gallon drums of aviation gas. Luckily my plane wasn't parked due to the flat tire, otherwise it probably would have been damaged or destroyed. My next to the last mission was to the Halmaheras, 620 miles each way. Got 5 dromes and pix of shipping in the harbor.

23 July 1944—100th mission. Flew my last mission. Will only fly combat zone missions until we go home. No more combat missions. Orders came through awarding me a cluster to my Air Medal.

26 July 1944—Six of us went to Brisbane to pick up six new F-5Es and bring them back. Four were ready. We had to wait for nearly two weeks for the other two.

3 August 1944—My promotion to captain finally came through.

10 August 1944—Flew B-25 for the first time as first pilot to Bak and back—carrying men and supplies. The squadrons are now in the process of moving there.

31 August 1944—Just eating dinner at Nadzab when Dobbs and Holton got in from Hollandia and Bak. They brought with them our going home orders. We are transferred from the squadron to the 91st Replacement Battalion at Finschafen. We went down to ATC operations and found that we wouldn't have too much trouble getting on the manifest for air transportation home. I took an F-5 to Finschafen and got our USAFFE orders authorizing air transportation. Got back to Nadzab and we put in our application for priorities.

1 September 1944—Got up early and found we were scheduled to leave that day at 1400. Got all packed but didn't leave until 1600. Our ship was a C-54, a beautiful thing it seemed to us. I wasn't feeling too well, came down with Malaria. On our way to Guadalcanal I became very sick—chills, fever. Didn't even get out of the ship for supper. From there we flew to Canton Island. The flight engineer took pity on me and put me in one of the bunks in the crew compartment. Finally got some rest and we reached Canton the next morning.

2 September 1944—Took off from Canton to Hawaii. Crossed the international date line and once more it was 1 September. Felt pretty good most of the way. Arrived at Hickam Field around 2200. Had quite a wait there while exhaust stacks were changed on an engine. While waiting, a nurse came around with thermometers. I saw her first and ducked into a latrine until she was gone. I wasn't about to be stuck into a hospital this close to home. Took off on the last leg in the wee hours of the morning. In 13 or 14 hours we should be in Frisco. I happened to be in the crew compartment when the Golden Gate Bridge first came into view. It was about 1600 when we stepped out of the plane in our wonderful USA. Right then and there began the red tape, paperwork and "shoot the bull, pass the buck and make seven copies of everything," which is the identifying characteristic of the Army. Pulled a fast one on the medic who examined me for fever. He stepped out of the room for a minute. I looked at my thermometer which was too high, so I shook it down to normal. Got a good shower, hot water, then a big steak after which we tried to go to sleep. About three in the morning, it seemed none of us could sleep, so we all went back to the mess hall for another steak.

3 September 1944—Got on a train for Fort Sheridan, Illinois, where we are to receive our leave orders. Wired Jo to quit her job and be ready to go to Chicago. Our train passed through Omaha where we had about an hour layover. Then on to Chicago.

Barney Dobbs and Al Blum survived a bloody war; many of their fellow pilots didn't. They were not the same men that had left San Francisco for Australia a year earlier. They changed in ways they had yet to understand for themselves. It was only 1944 and the war in the Pacific still had a year to go before it was finally over.

"In 1946 my wife and I left for our new assignment in Germany," Barney Dobbs recalled wistfully. "I flew the P-61 Black Widow night fighter out of Schweinfurt until the Black Widow was phased out of the Army Air Forces inventory. In 1948 I found myself in Ober-pfaffenhofen where I prepared fighter aircraft for turnover to allied nations. I was quickly drafted into the evolving Berlin Airlift. I was sent to Wiesbaden to fly as copilot in C-47s. I had always flown fighters, and I knew nothing about the C-47 transport. It makes my hair stand up in back of my neck when I think of that time in the C-47. They put us fighter jocks in the right seat. I knew enough to keep the thing right side up. I flew into Tempelhof, landing between five story apartment houses. It was awful. But the GCA radar controllers were superb. I was awfully glad when the airlift was over and I went back to the used aircraft business.

"From Germany I was reassigned to the Military Air Transport Service, MATS, at Westover Air Force Base in Massachusetts. While there I flew C-97 Stratocruisers, the military version of the Pan American double decker airliner. I hated every minute of it. One day while flying a huge four-engine C-97, I surreptitiously joined up with a formation of fighters coming in for a landing. I think they would have court-martialed me for what I did, but a war had broken out in Korea, and I volunteered to be an F-51 replacement pilot. That saved me. Once in Korea I was assigned to K-8, 'Kunsan

The C-97 Barney Dobbs flew looked like the KC-97 air-refueling tankers shown in this picture, except for the refueling boom. The tankers provided fuel, while the transport version carried cargo and people. The C/KC-97 civilian version of the aircraft was the Boeing 377 Stratocruiser made famous by Pan American Airlines. (Robert Hamill)

by the Sea,' as we referred to it, flying the twin-engine B-26 Invader. The B-26 was no fighter plane but the closest thing to it. I soon fell in love with the airplane."

The B-26 Marauder of World War II fame was built by the Glen L. Martin Company of Baltimore, Maryland. It became a controversial aircraft with extremely high wing loading, meaning it had a very short wing to support the weight of the aircraft. It acquired a number of unflattering names over time from "One a day in Tampa Bay" to "Widow Maker." As a result of its various shortcomings it was soon retired after World War II along with the P-38 fighter, another aircraft with a controversial history over Europe. An aircraft with a similar designator to the B-26 was the A-26 Invader, built by the Douglas Aircraft Corporation as a replacement for the A-20 Havoc. The A-26 had its issues as well, however, by the end of World War II those issues had mostly been remedied and the A-26 had earned a level of affection from its pilots. With the original Martin B-26 taken out of service in 1947, coincident with the birth of the United States Air Force that September, the A-26 was redesignated the B-26 Invader. That is the aircraft Barney Dobbs was flying in Korea.

"In the dark early morning hours of February 19, 1952, I skimmed across the craggy Korean countryside at five hundred feet above the ground, intending to be at no more than 200 hundred feet above the terrain in our target area. My crew and I had been to this target before, and we were good at identifying trucks on dark roads with their lights out. If there wasn't anything happening at the location, we had plans for two other sites. I saw the tell-tale shadows of slow-moving trucks thrown up against the side of the road by residual fires from the daylight raids. I pointed the nose of the Invader down the valley and made my first pass. I dropped my bombs to bottle up the trucks. The eight bombs slammed into the lead trucks, blowing two off the road. Explosions lit up a string of trucks reaching back into a tunnel. As I emerged from the valley, banking to my left, I heard a call from a C-47 flare ship asking me if I wanted flares dropped. 'Roger, no flares,' I told the flare ship pilot. I had no time to chat with the fellow. I was busy concentrating on flying my airplane down a dark mountain valley adjacent to the one I had passed through.

"'I can't go home until I drop my flares,' the flare ship pilot continued to badger me. I ignored him. I was lining up for my second pass. I knew I had surprised the anti-aircraft gunners on my first pass, but this time they would be ready for me. I figured they expected me to reenter the valley the way I exited. I made a shallow wide turn instead, flying down the adjacent valley, planning to reenter the way I came in on my first pass but from the opposite side. I was concentrating on my approach to the target with no further thought of the flare ship. I could clearly see the trucks on the winding mountain road. I was lined up, ready to fire my guns, when a bright flare lit up the valley, blinding me, destroying my night vision. To the North Korean gunners I must have looked like a target at their gunnery school. I pulled the aircraft up, cursing the flare ship. I was going to get the pilot's ass when I got home. But first I had to get out of here. Then the flak hit. I felt the impact of the shells as they ripped into the left engine. Fire was everywhere. Get out, I yelled and jettisoned the hatches. The crew chief exited over the right wing. I couldn't see the gunner exit, but I thought he was out when I abandoned the aircraft. My chute opened. I swung once or twice and then I was in the trees. On the ground.

"I was dazed, it happened so fast. The damn flare ship, I thought. I remember unbuckling my chute and how quiet it was. I was alone.

B-26 Invaders getting ready for deployment to Japan. The F-51 during the day and the B-26 at night kept the 8th U.S. Army from being overrun by the North Koreans. (Barney Dobbs)

I looked around for my crew. Only silence. I knew exactly where I was and prepared to make my way back to friendly lines. A river ran down below, and I toyed with the idea of crossing over to the other side to throw off any search party which I knew was going to come to look for me. I discarded that idea and decided to move inland and south. There was a slight moon to aid my travel. I was cold. The snow reminded me that escape was going to be difficult. Someone sure would pick up my tracks. I could hear dogs barking in a village below me. I decided to hide and wait until daylight. I was dressed for the weather and thought I'd be able to stay fairly comfortable if I found a good hiding place. But by morning the dogs had tracked me down. Three villagers escorted me down the mountain and turned me over to soldiers. I didn't know if they were Korean or Chinese. My crew chief was there too. No sign of our gunner. We were kept for several days in the back room of a simple cottage. One day a Russian officer showed up. The Russian was friendly and spoke English well. He loaded me into the back of a truck and to my amazement drove me out to my aircraft. The damn aircraft hadn't crashed. It made a smooth belly landing and was barely damaged. The Russian was a ground pounder and didn't know what questions to ask. What he seemed to want to know from me was what we had in our aircraft that allowed it to belly land without a pilot. I don't know how that airplane landed in a mountain valley without tearing itself to pieces."

For nearly nineteen months Barney Dobbs endured torture and degradation as a prisoner of war of the Chinese People's Army. He was interrogated repeatedly. Barney recalled seven different interrogators who tried to convince him to admit that he was using germ warfare. He was deprived of sleep, food, and water to make him compliant. He didn't break. He was repeatedly put in solitary confinement, including imprisonment in a three-by-six-foot hole in the ground for six months. Finally, his interrogators gave up and put him into an unheated shack with twelve other uncooperative American prisoners. When Barney lay in the hole in the ground, he sought of something to hold onto, to keep his sanity, to be able to endure and survive. He tried to recall every hymn he ever sang in church, and in time he composed his own hymn in his mind, writing it down on paper once he was released:

KOREAN SOLITARY
The accusation it was made: of course it was denied.
They said of them germ bombs I'd dropped, and about it I had lied.
A bomb that's filled with flies and fleas, dear Lord, I've never seen;
but men for propaganda's sake can sure be mighty mean.

Interrogators came and went, their lies were all the same.
"Confess," they said, "and you'll go free, or here you will remain.
God can't help you, he's not real, you're living in a dream."
"Not so," said I, "He's real to me, so go to your extreme."

"An execution is your fate, since you've made up your mind
not to confess and tell the truth about your heinous crime."
So they threw me in a hole, never to return.
And I'm afraid their souls will rest in hell and burn, burn, burn.

The hole was deep, not very long and only three feet wide.
The sun and air through a window came, six inches on each side.
The roosters woke us up at four, the guards came round at five;
they brought us food, twas just enough to keep a man alive.

Fish heads and rice were all we had, sometimes a piece of bread,
but we ate it with God's blessing, who watched from overhead.
Soap they gave us, but water none, tobacco but no fire.
They called it "lenient treatment," but only aroused our ire.

I've seen men come, and seen men go, but some men stayed forever.
They paid the price for that plot of ground near the Yalu River.
I've seen 'em beg and scream and yell for a doctor and some pills,
to stop the dysentery, and drive away their ills.

As I sit here and dream of home and ones I love so dear,
I pray to God that some day soon their voices I will hear.
But if God wills that I remain to die on foreign soil,
then comfort bring to those I love through all of life's turmoil.

As I look 'round me at the foe who's never heard His name,
I wonder where their souls will go when they're through life's earthly
game;
never to have heard His word, nor felt His saving grace,
nor seen the love of Jesus Christ for the human race.

For they are children under God, the same as you and I,
but I wonder where their souls go when their earthly bodies die.
In this land of Commie rule, church bells are never heard,
and folks don't go to Sunday School to study Jesus's word.

Four thousand years they've gotten by with oxen and with hoe,
seems to me that without God, they're progressing mighty slow.

"Humbly dedicated to those who didn't make it."

—BARNEY DOBBS

Major Barney A. Dobbs was shot down on his twenty-second night
combat mission. On September 15, 1953, the last day of the POW
exchange, Barney Dobbs was released. "As they were getting ready

Barney Dobbs's decorations from two wars—including the Silver Star, DFC, Purple Heart, Air Medal, Bronze Star, and an assortment of campaign medals. (Barney Dobbs)

to release us, they assembled us in a large camp, gave us decent food for several days and clean clothes. Then they put us on a train to our final camp. On the last day of the prisoner release, I was put on the last truck. I thought I was going to be left behind. Prior to my release, my wife, Kay, had no idea if I was alive or dead. All she knew was that I had been declared missing in action. As the POWs were released throughout September 1953, each day the names of the latest batch of prisoners to be released were announced on TV. It went on for days, and finally she saw my name. In a cruel hoax, Kay had been told by an early released POW that her husband was killed in an escape attempt. That POW, using a false name, then demanded money for more details. Kay turned him down. I still have the prison suit in which I returned home. My life as a prisoner, although much of it taken up by interrogation and by nine months of solitary confinement, included being harnessed to a cart like an ox and pulling it through the village. Fish heads, barley, and occasionally rice was the food I was fed. I lost fifty pounds. I constantly thought about meat and vowed that when I got home I would open a barbeque restaurant, Barney's Barbeque, to ensure I had a guaranteed supply of barbequed ribs for the rest of my life. Of course that didn't happen. Three month after my release I was back flying airplanes."

Barney Dobbs retired from the Air Force in 1965, after twenty-six years of dedicated service to his country, at Hamilton Air Force Base, near San Francisco, where it all started for him years earlier when he and his friend Al Blum left to fight World War II in the Pacific flying the F-5 Lightning. For his service in two wars he was awarded the Silver Star, the Distinguished Flying Cross, and the Purple Heart—each medal twice, for heroism and wounds suffered in combat. The airplane that remained his favorite was the Lightning.

RICHARD BONG
AND TOMMY McGUIRE

P-38 LIGHTNING

They say he died in glory, whatever that may be.
If its dying in a burst of flame, then glory's not for me.
In the briefing room this morning, he sat with clear eyes and
strong heart,
Just one of many airmen determined to do his part.
But death had the final word, in its log it wrote his name.
For my buddy died this afternoon in glory—in a burst of flame.
—AUTHOR UNKNOWN

The war in the Pacific was a completely different animal from the
war in Europe and North Africa. If you, as a fighter pilot, flying over
Europe or North Africa, got shot down, most likely you would land
on terra firma—not so in the Pacific, an ocean area of immense
proportions, and if you got shot down your chances of landing on
dry land were extremely low. And even if you did, landing in a jungle
had its own life-threatening challenges. There was no formal rescue organization to look for flyers bobbing on their flimsy dinghies
around the ocean. Your fellow flyers, if possible, went out to look
for you, but frequently the weather was too bad and the searches
were unsuccessful. My interview with Chuck Meyers, a young B-25
pilot flying with the 498th Bomb Squadron, the Falcons, captured
the essence of what it was like flying in the Pacific.

"There I am, a nineteen year old, ready to go to war. I had no idea
what I was facing. We only flew our B-25s low level. By low level I

mean I never flew above a target more than fifty feet. More often I was only twenty to thirty feet off the ground. If you are going to survive that kind of flying you have to do it constantly. You can't be flying low one day and at 12,000 feet the next. This was my first combat mission. As we pulled off the target, we were turning in an arc to the left. My pilot tapped me on the shoulder and said, 'Look behind you.' There across the airfield we were bombing and strafing, a B-25 was on fire, pulling a long trail of smoke. Then he just sort of pulled up slowly to about 200 feet, turned on his back and dove into the airfield. My pilot nonchalantly commented, 'He always did fly a bit too high.' I, a 19 year old high school drop out, had never even heard about this kind of flying.

"We moved to Tacloban airfield on Leyte in the Philippines in December of 1944. There was one runway running alongside the beach. It had been used by some navy pilots whose carrier had been sunk. There were wrecks of navy and other airplanes lining the runway, pushed aside into the surf by bulldozers. The strip itself was made of steel matting. The control tower consisted of four or five coconut palms that had been lashed together, and someone built a platform up there, holding a desk and a radio. Coming back after a combat mission was hazardous. You could get killed a number of ways, including standing in the chow line, because the Japanese were still in the nearby jungle. Or you could get shot down by a nervous anti-aircraft crew trying to defend all the ships in the harbor from Kamikaze attacks. We lost about 250 to 300 of our ground crew that way. We flew out of Tacloban, later San Marcelino on Luzon.

"Flying long over water missions were always terrifying. More than one pilot felt his courage fail as he turned back prematurely from an eight or ten hour over water flight, where the loss of an engine or a well aimed flak burst spelled almost certain death. The airmen were briefed that no 5th Air Force crew had ever returned after losing an engine off the mainland of Asia. The loss rate would be the highest of any period in the group's history. Within weeks an entire squadron of planes and aircrews would be lost in areas where there were almost no chances of survival. Each man, whether openly or in the depth of his heart, wondered if the next dawn would bring his death in the depths of the China Sea or on some alien oriental shore. Worse yet, considering the danger of the missions, the targets were slim, the weather was bad, and it was a 'big' ocean.'"

Until the introduction of the P-38 Lightning in late 1942, the principal fighter and reconnaissance aircraft used by the 5th, 7th, and 13th Air Forces was the P-40 Warhawk and the P-39 Airacobra, single engine aircraft, coffins if their engines failed, and barely a match against Japanese fighters. The P-38 made its presence known soon after arrival. The first significant action occurred in the southwest Pacific on December 27, 1942, in the Buna-Gona area, when twelve P-38s attacked a gaggle of thirty Japanese fighters and dive bombers, shooting down two of the bombers and nine fighters, for the loss of one P-38. General MacArthur was less than satisfied with the performance of Lieutenant General George Brett, his Air Corps commander. So, MacArthur turned to the Air Corps staff for a replacement, and chose Major General George C. Kenney to replace Brett. Kenney soon was promoted and assumed command of the Allied Air Forces on August 4, 1942. After a lengthy meeting with General MacArthur, Kenney got the authority to clean house, meaning, he got rid of Brett's old crew—a slew of non-performing generals and colonels, the way he saw it—and brought in his own. Kenney, a World War I veteran with combat experience with the 91st Aero Squadron, believed in the concept of air superiority, nothing less. Kenney at first took command of the 5th Air Force, then in June 1944 MacArthur gave him command of the Far East Air Forces (FEAF) which included the Australians and the 5th, 7th, and 13th Air Forces. What he needed most was a long-range fighter, and the P-38 filled that bill. They may have had issues with the Lightning in Europe and North Africa, but here in the Pacific, a vast ocean area, it was the right kind of airplane—it had two engines. While in Europe they were replacing the P-38 with P-47s and P-51s, Kenney took all the P-38s he could lay his hands on. From a pilot's perspective, the Lightning was above all, a twin-engine life saver. Allen Blum, flying the F-5 reconnaissance version of the P-38, more than once lost an engine and made it home safely on the other one. A single-engine aircraft would have sealed his fate.

General Kenney got directly involved in how the P-38 was employed and used. He was the one who got Charles Lindbergh, a noncombatant with a "history," to fly with the newly created 475th Fighter Group. Lindbergh's power management, at first reluctantly adopted by other flyers, extended the range of the Lightning by 200 miles. Once MacArthur heard of that, he was ecstatic, and rightfully so. It put the Japanese at threat in areas where they thought they were safe from American air power. Not only that, Kenney brought in Eddie Rickenbacker to lift the morale of his flyers. Rickenbacker of course was another World War I flyer, the former commander of the 94th Aero Squadron in France, who downed twenty-six German aircraft, which made him the highest-scoring American of that period. He was awarded the Distinguished Service Cross for his achievement, which later was upgraded to the Medal of Honor. In October 1942 Ricken-backer was visiting bases in the Pacific Theater of Operations, as it was referred to at that time, at the urging of Secretary of War Henry Stimson. On the way to MacArthur's headquarters, the B-17 he was traveling in got lost and had to ditch. After a harrowing experience of twenty-four days on a raft in the Pacific, the raft was finally spotted by a Navy float plane, and he, and others in the raft, were rescued.

Kenney attempted to put a spirit of competition into his Lightning flyers, citing Rickenbacker's twenty-six kills in World War I as a goal to reach, or even better, to exceed. Competition is a good thing in many endeavors; in fighting a war it may have unanticipated consequences—breaking of rules and discipline being two of them. Both Richard Bong and Tommy McGuire would be guilty of both infractions in their endeavors to score the most shoot-downs.

After completing pilot training in California and receiving his wings, Richard Bong was stationed at Hamilton Field, near San Francisco. At Hamilton he learned to fly the P-38 from no less an instructor pilot than Major General George C. Kenney, who was fully checked out in two of the aircraft under his command—the P-38 Lightning and the A-29 Hudson, the latter a useful aircraft when traveling with his 4th Air Force staff. One officer assigned to Kenney's command was Richard Bong, who was flying with the 14th Fighter Group, a training outfit, based at Hamilton Field. Bong soon showed what he was made of buzzing Market Street in San Francisco; and while at it, why not fly a couple of loops around the Golden Gate Bridge. Kenney reprimanded Bong, but he also knew

Bong in front of his aircraft. Putting slogans and pictures of scantily clad young women on the noses of military aircraft was commonplace in World War II. Bong plastered a very large picture of his newly found girlfriend on the nose of his P-38 and her name, in large letters, right next to her picture. Only then followed small Japanese flags for every one of his victories. (Richard I Bong Veterans Historical Center)

that that's the kind of fighter pilot he wanted to train. No surprise, instead of going to Europe, Bong ended up on a B-24, similar to the experience Dobbs and Blum had, and found himself in Sydney, Australia, awaiting further assignment.

When Richard Bong arrived in Sydney he was one of only a few pilots checked out in the Lightning. The 49th Fighter Group was still flying the P-40 Warhawk and the P-39 Airacobra, but by September 1942 the group was involved in converting to the Lightning. Arrival of the new aircraft was slow. Bong was heaven-sent with experience in this in many ways complex fighter. While awaiting the arrival of more Lightnings, 2nd Lieutenant Richard I. Bong briefly flew with another P-38 outfit, and on December 27, 1942, flying in a P-38F, scored his first kills—a Val dive bomber and a Zero fighter. Back with his old unit, the 9th Fighter Squadron of the 49th Fighter Group, now fully equipped with P-38Gs, on July 26, 1943, Bong scored four kills—for a total of fifteen. This led to the award of the Distinguished Service Cross and a precious home leave.

While home on leave in Wisconsin, Bong met Marjorie. As could be expected, once he got back to his unit, he named his aircraft *Marge*, and had her picture painted on the nose of his aircraft. Not a small picture, but one that pretty much covered the front end of his fighter. Bong flew every model of the P-38—first the F, then the G, H, J, and L models, all with different modifications and cockpit layouts. Bong loved the aircraft and was a natural fighter pilot. You can learn the mechanics and subtleties of a fighter to keep you alive in combat, but it takes an instinct like Robin Olds's to be an excellent fighter pilot. Bong had that instinct, and by December 17, 1944, flying a P-38L he shot down number forty over Mindoro Island, his last combat flight in the Lightning. Although no American had more victories than Bong, he considered himself a poor shot, even with a 20mm cannon in the aircraft's nose and four 50 caliber machine guns—he reportedly compensated by flying as close as possible to his victim, and flying through the debris of his kill happened all too often. This reminds me of Gabby Gabreski's flying the P-47 in Europe. His gun camera film shows the same tendency to fly up the tail of his prey, and then ducking the debris that invariably followed. Bong had the same habit as Gabby.

On December 7, 1944, Bong added his thirty-eighth and thirty-ninth kills. The following day, on the recommendation of General Kenney, Bong received the Medal of Honor from none other than General MacArthur himself. Writes John R. Bruning in the July 2020 issue of the *Smithsonian Air & Space Magazine*: "The next day [Dec 8] the press broke the news that Richard Ira Bong, America's ace of aces with 39 kills, not only just surpassed Britain's top ace Johnnie Johnson, but had been awarded the Medal of Honor as well. Four days later, as rain fell at Tacloban, the men of the 475th and 49th Fighter Groups stood at formation as General Douglas MacArthur gave the award to Bong. MacArthur was at his rhetorical best as he addressed his weary, wet aviators, 'The Congress of the United States has reserved for itself the honor of decorating those amongst all who stand out as the bravest of the brave. It is this high and noble category, Major Bong, that you now enter as I place upon your breast the Medal of Honor. Wear it as the symbol of invincible courage you have displayed in mortal combat. My dear boy, may a merciful God continue to protect you.'"

General MacArthur, on December 12, 1944, pinning the Medal of Honor on Major Richard I. Bong at Tacloban airfield, Philippine Islands. (Wisconsin Historical Society)

Ten days later, on December 17, 1944, Bong flew one final combat mission and evened out his score at forty kills. Bong scored his first two victories in December 1942 as a 2nd lieutenant; his fortieth came two years later. By now he had been promoted three times to the rank of major. General Kenney exercised good judgment when in January he sent his Medal of Honor awardee home to the United States.

What to do next after all the ceremonies and savings bond rallies were over? Be a test pilot of course, a choice many aces made on returning from combat; and General Arnold, who was known to love his fighter pilots, tried to accommodate them whenever possible. Colonel Kenneth O. Chilstrom, a close friend of mine, was chief of Fighter Test at Wright Field at the time of Bong's return. While most test piloting was done at Wright Field in Ohio or at Muroc Field in California, later Edwards Air Force Base, some testing was accomplished at aircraft production sites. Bong was assigned as test

Once home again, Bong managed to squeeze his girlfriend Marge into the cockpit of a P-38 for a picture. (Richard I Bong Veterans Historical Center)

pilot at Lockheed's plant at Burbank, California—the site where most P-38s had been produced, and where now the first production models of the new P-80 Shooting Star jet fighter were coming off the line. On August 6, 1945, Bong was scheduled to do an acceptance test of a P-80A. At this point he had just over four hours of jet time, all acquired while testing aircraft—no training to speak of. This was his 12th flight in the P-80. As he began to lift off the runway the plane's power faltered and he was forced to eject. Bong cleared the aircraft, but was too low for his parachute to deploy. The plane crashed. His death was front-page news across the country, sharing space with the first news of the bombing of Hiroshima.

In my personal discussions with Colonel Chilstrom, who had flown every aircraft on the Wright Field tarmac including the P-80, he mentioned to me that you had to manually switch fuel tanks in this aircraft. Taxiing to the takeoff position used up most of the fuel in the initial tank, and if the switch was not made before takeoff it was very likely that Bong's engine would have quit on the takeoff run of fuel starvation. The issue will never be settled to everyone's satisfaction, but whatever the cause, it was a sad day for America to loose one of its combat heroes. The *New York Times*'s headline on Tuesday, August 7, 1945, read:

FIRST ATOMIC BOMB DROPPED ON JAPAN; MISSILE IS EQUAL TO 20,000 TONS OF TNT; TRUMAN WARNS FOE OF A 'RAIN OF RUIN.'

Beneath this headline in capital letters six separate articles were featured—side by side—one of which told of Bong's tragedy: "Jet Plane Explosion Kills Major Bong, Top U.S. Ace." So if it had not been for the fact that Bong's death coincided with the dropping of the first atomic bomb on Japan, his tragic story surely would have been the much-deserved headline of the day. Colonel Chilstrom, in his book *Test Flying at Old Wright Field—From the Piston Engine to Jet Power*, includes a listing of 114 test pilots and engineers who perished testing aircraft over the years, including Richard I. Bong, who was test flying a P-80 jet at the Lockheed plant in Burbank. The P-80 came about after the great disappointment over our first jet fighter, the P-59. As "Rosie" Rosengarten, a senior flight test engineer at Wright Field so succinctly described the P-59, "It could hardly be considered a combat plane—at best it was a good safe airplane, a training vehicle for indoctrinating pilots into the jet age."

The Germans had test flown their Me 262 jet in July 1942; two years later, in July 1944, it flew its first combat mission against a British Mosquito reconnaissance aircraft. It was high time for the Air Corps to make a move. So Arnold turned to the Lockheed Corporation for help. Kelly Johnson, the principal designer of the P-38 Lightning, said, "We can do it," and submitted a design proposal on June 15, 1943. A letter contract was issued by the Air Corps on June 17, and on June 21 Lockheed accepted the contract to deliver an XP-80 in 180 days. Writes Major General Warner E. Newby in *Test Flying at Wright Field*, "The XP-80 was completed and transported to Muroc Field on 13 November 1943—less than 150 days after contract go ahead. Lockheed test pilot Milo Burcham made the first flights, two on 8 January 1944, and achieved a maximum speed of 490 miles per hour." This was as good as it was going to get for the P-80 program for some time.

Major Richard I. Bong flew this P-38J on April 16, 1945, at Wright Field, Ohio. His number two engine exploded in flight before he could complete a scheduled experiment. The aircraft is on display at the Udvar Hazy Center of the NASM, in Chantilly, Virginia. (Author)

In view of German progress on its Me 262, General Arnold went ahead and approved the procurement of 13 YP-80s for service tests. Tony LeVier, Lockheed's senior test pilot, who had also test flown the P-38, along with Chief Test Pilot Milo Burcham, flew the XP-80 tests. Milo Burcham died in a crash of one of the thirteen YP-80s in October 1944. In spite of this ominous disaster, four of the YP-80s were shipped to England to show the troops that we too had a jet plane, not just the Germans. On January 31, 1945, one of those four demonstrators crashed, killing its Wright Field test pilot, Major Fred Borsodi. Test flying was dangerous business, to put it mildly. Another aircraft was diverted to Rolls-Royce for installation of the RB-41 gas turbine power plant, an upgraded Whittle engine [this aircraft too was to crash on a test flight on November 14, 1945]. The remaining YP-80 continued to perform morale-boosting demonstration flights for the 15th Air Force in Italy.

In spite of continuing development problems, General Arnold went ahead with a production order for a thousand P-80s. Optimism and production orders, however, do not make an airplane fly. The

P-80's troubles were far from over. The first production P-80A was accepted in February 1945. General Newby was the chief of the Accelerated Test Branch of the Flight Test Division at Wright Field operating out of Vandalia Field, a satellite base to Wright Field. Newby pushed development and testing of the new jet. Lots of deficiencies showed up and had to be dealt with. Newby recalls, "Early in July 1945 a production test P-80A crashed on take off killing the pilot. Early in August 1945 a YP-80A exploded and crashed killing the pilot. A few days later, on August 6, a black-letter day indeed for the P-80 program, Major Richard I. Bong experienced engine failure on take off. Major Bong, America's top ace and Medal of Honor winner was killed in the accident."

The loss of a national hero triggered strong media, then public and political reaction. Concerns over the hazard of flying jet aircraft reached a crisis stage when the congressional opposition began to allege that jet technology was just too risky to fly if test pilots and our top ace could not safely handle the aircraft. General Arnold was faced with serious political threats to cut back, cancel, or withdraw funding for the jet programs. To forestall that from happening he ordered the suspension of all P-80 flying and ordered his commanding general of the Air Technical Service Command at Wright Field, Major General Hugh Knerr, "to fix the problem." Knerr had served under General Spaatz in Europe, responsible for the technical exploitation of Germany's advanced developments. Knerr was a man both Arnold and Spaatz had full confidence in that he could get a handle on the P-80 problems.

Arnold suggested that five new P-80A aircraft be carefully checked and updated with all possible improvements by the contractor and then expeditiously flown fifty hours each. Arnold's message to General Knerr closed with the profound directive, underlined, "There will not be an accident. I repeat, there will not be an accident." There were no further accidents. "The P-80 series did become a first line fighter and remained so until replaced by the F-84 and F-86 during the Korean War," wrote General Newby. He added, "The P-80's evolution was traumatic."

Thomas Buchanon McGuire arrived at the 49th Fighter Group, 5th Air Force, in March 1943, the same Group that Bong flew with.

When the 475th Fighter Group was created, both Bong and Mc-Guire transferred over to the 475th. By the time McGuire arrived in Australia, in March 1943, Bong already had nine kills to his credit. General Kenney's call for competition amongst the "fly boys" to equal or surpass Eddie Rickenbacker's score of twenty-six kills resonated especially with McGuire, who turned out to be a skilled aviator, but no matter how hard he tried, he was always chasing Bong. The competition called for by Kenney had some undesirable side effects. On one occasion, according to John Bruning, in his article in *Air & Space Magazine* titled "A Dare Turned Deadly," Bong broke formation to go after a Japanese bomber without saying anything. That is a no-no in a fighter pilot world where teamwork and the integrity of formations was a key to success and survival. McGuire, after Bong's departure for the United States, was grounded by General Kenney—McGuire at that point had thirty-eight kills, two short of Bong's score. McGuire ignored the restriction, and with the help of his squadron mates, went out to even the score with Bong, maybe even surpass him. Not something that General Kenney was looking for.

Writes Bruning: "On January 7, 1945, McGuire and his volunteers rose just before dawn; four P-38s awaited, each with a pair of 150 gallon tanks slung under the wings between the fuselage and the engine nacelles." This configuration provided McGuire and his flight with maximum range to search for Japanese aircraft, which had not shown that much of themselves over the past weeks after suffering severe losses. "A half hour after take off," writes Bruning, "they ran into bad weather. Weaver's [one of the three pilots flying with McGuire] voice broke through the silence, 'Zero! Twelve o'clock low. Coming straight at us.' It wasn't a Zero, but a late model Hayabusa [Also known as an Oscar, or Ki-43] flown by Sergeant Akira Sugimoto, an extremely experienced, high time Ki-43 pilot who was returning to Fabrica Airdrome after conducting a search for a reported American naval convoy. . . . This was McGuire's show, the whole point was to get him kills." The Oscar came head on below them, then got on the tail of one of the P-38s. McGuire, still carrying his underwing fuel tanks, which should have been jettisoned before getting into a dogfight, went into a very tight turn to intercept the Ki-43. "His P-38 snap-rolled," writes Bruning, "The nose dropped, McGuire ended up inverted for a split second, then his fighter plunged straight into the ground and exploded."

The P-38 was not a forgiving airplane when yanked into a very tight turn with "bags" on, as we in our modern air force refer to external fuel tanks, heading for the deck. I suspect that once Mc-Guire entered that steep dive he most likely entered an accelerated stall, exacerbated by the weight of the 150-gallon fuel tanks, and lost control. Something similar happened to Robin Olds flying a P-38 over France, seeing below him a P-51 in trouble with an Me 109 on its tail. Robin "rolled inverted and pulled the nose almost straight down," he writes in his memoir *Fighter Pilot*. He promptly got into a classic Mach Tuck, losing control and just barely recovering before striking the ground. "It was compressibility," he writes, "that dreaded phenomenon we had been warned about. Few pilots had ever re-covered. None ever bailed out. There'd been smoking holes out in the Mojave Desert as mute testimony." McGuire was too low to have found himself in a Mach Tuck situation like Robin Olds; however, had he been at a higher altitude, that is exactly what would have happened. And his airplane was not ready for a fighter engagement, one of the drawbacks of the multiple-switchology associated with the P-38. Just a simple snap-roll, that he got himself into, caused by an accelerated stall at low altitude will kill you as well.

Thomas Buchanan McGuire was an aggressive pilot, as was Bong. A major, like Bong, at the time of his death he was the operations officer of the 475th Fighter Group. Just two weeks earlier, on December 25 and 26, he had downed seven Japanese aircraft over Luzon, Philippines. For this action Major McGuire was awarded the Medal of Honor. Reads his citation, "The President of the United States of America, in the name of Congress, takes pride in presenting the Medal of Honor (Posthumously) to Major (Air Corps) Thomas Bu-chanan McGuire, Jr., United States Army Air Forces, for conspicu-ous gallantry and intrepidity while serving with the 475th Fighter Group, Fifth Air Force, in action over Luzon, Philippine Islands, 25 and 26 December 1944. Voluntarily, Major McGuire led a squad-ron of 15 P-38s as top cover for heavy bombers striking Mabalacat Airdrome, where his formation was attacked by 20 aggressive Japa-nese fighters. In the ensuing action he repeatedly flew to the aid of embattled comrades, driving off enemy assaults with himself under attack and at times outnumbered three to one. And even after his guns jammed, continuing the fight by forcing a hostile plane into his wingman's line of fire. Before he started back to his base he had shot down three Zeros. The next day he again volunteered to lead escort fighters on a mission to strongly defended Clark Field. During the resultant engagement he again exposed himself to attacks so that he might rescue a crippled bomber. In rapid succession he shot down one aircraft, parried the attack of four enemy fighters, one of which he shot down, single-handedly, engaged three more Japanese, destroying one, and then shot down still another, his 38th victory in aerial combat. On 7 January 1945, while leading a voluntary fighter sweep over Los Negros Island, he risked an extremely hazardous maneuver at low altitude in an attempt to save a fellow flyer from attack, crashed, and was reported missing in action. With gallant initiative, deep and unselfish concern for the safety of others, and heroic determination to destroy the enemy at all costs, Major McGuire set an inspiring example in keeping with the highest traditions of the military service." In addition to the Medal of Honor Major McGuire was awarded the Distinguished Service Cross, three Silver Stars, multiple Distinguished Flying Crosses and Air Medals and the Purple Heart. McGuire Air Force Base in New Jersey is named after him, and a P-38 Lightning, named *Pudgy (v)*, is on static display at the air base.

Bong remained the American top ace with forty victories, McGuire with thirty-eight remained number two. Over in Europe Gabby Gabreski was the high scorer with twenty-eight victories flying the P-47 Thunderbolt. And Robin Olds, another P-38 flyer, came home with a tally of thirteen, adding four more in a war yet to come—Vietnam. Clarence Emil "Bud" Anderson, flying his P-51 Mustang named *Old Crow*, racked up sixteen victories, just one short of Hub Zemke's seventeen, flying the P-47 and the P-38. When all was said and done, the P-38 claimed more kills in the Pacific than any other Army Air Corps aircraft.

The P-38 record speaks for itself. After its introduction on 27 December 1942 over Buna-Gona, shooting down eleven Japanese aircraft, P-38s joined P-40s and P-39s shooting down twenty-four

The Vought F4U-1D Corsair shown here is displayed at the National Air and Space Museum Udvar Hazy Center in Chantilly, Virginia. The airplane is painted in the colors and markings of the Corsair *Sun Setter*, a Marine close air support fighter assigned to Marine Fighter Squadron VMF-113 in July 1944. By V-J Day, September 2, 1945, Corsair pilots had amassed an 11:1 kill ratio against enemy aircraft. (Author)

enemy aircraft over Wau. Escorting bombers on August 18, 1943, seventy-four P-38s joined in the attack on Wewak, destroying 200 Japanese aircraft on several airfields. Again escorting bombers on October 12, 1943, 106 P-38s shot down twenty-six Japanese aircraft and destroyed nearly 100 on the ground without suffering a loss. And on November 2, 1943, eighty P-38s and the same number of B-25s attacked Simpson Harbor, Rabaul, shooting down sixty-eight enemy aircraft for the loss of ten B-25s and ten P-38s.

The US Navy and Marine Corps did their part as well to make the Rising Sun a rarity in the skies over the Pacific. Gregory "Pappy" Boyington, the legendary commander of Marine Fighter Squadron 214, better known as the "Black Sheep Squadron" flying a Vought F4U Corsair downed twenty-eight Japanese aircraft and became the top-scoring Marine, was an ace in a day and was awarded the Medal of Honor. His squadron alone in 1943 and 1944 shot down ninety-seven enemy aircraft, and a substantial number of those kills could be accredited to Pappy. David McCampbell, with thirty-four victories, became the top-scoring US Navy ace, and also joined the select group of flyers who became aces in one day. Donald N. Aldrich and Marion E. Carl, both flying the F4U Corsair came home with twenty and eighteen victories respectively. And Kenneth A. Walsh, another Marine with twenty-one victories, was the first to achieve ace status in the F4U Corsair, and like Pappy Boyington was awarded the Medal of Honor.

TAMING THE P-38 LIGHTNING

Why the sound barrier will never be broken.

—HAROLD WATSON

In response to an Army Air Corps request in February 1937 to industry for the design of a twin-engine high-altitude interceptor, the Lockheed Corporation, looking for a new source of revenue, decided to jump into that briar patch and make a proposal. Lockheed had never built fighters before and this one was to reach 20,000 feet in six minutes or less at a speed of no less than 360 miles per hour. A challenge indeed for a company new in the fighter business. Luck would have it that in 1933 Lockheed had hired a young aeronautical engineer fresh out of the University of Michigan at Ann Arbor—Clarence, better known as Kelly, Johnson. Kelly cut his teeth so to speak on the Lockheed Electra twin-engine transport, then jumped into the P-38 project with both feet. After all was said and done, in 1938, only a year after Lockheed submitted its proposal to the Army Air Corps, out rolled the XP-38 twin-engine, twin-boom interceptor. It wasn't a tail dragger like most fighters of the day and eventually would sport an intimidating armament consisting of a 20mm gun in its nose, as well as four 50 caliber machine guns. With the start of World War II in September 1939, top-of-the-line fighter aircraft suddenly were in great demand. The P-38s began to roll off the production line in Burbank, California, and aircrew training for all types of aircraft was accelerated. The first P-38 fighter group arrived in England in 1942.

Both in training and operationally, the P-38 turned out to be a challenge for its young pilots. At high altitudes as a bomber escort its heating system failed to function properly. Its instrumentation layout was challenging, and tail flutter at high angles of attack was joined by severe compressibility issues as the aircraft approached

Mach .68 and above. Pilots experienced total loss of control over their aircraft, the controls locked due to the differential airflow over and under the wings, digging holes in the desert, as Robin Olds referred to it in his book *Fighter Pilot*. There were many other issues with the P-38 in Europe, and as one P-38 pilot I interviewed summarized his experience, "I found the airplane to be a high performance beast and if you didn't pay attention it would kill you quicker than the Germans could."

General Jimmy Doolittle, once he assumed command of the 8th Air Force, got rid of the P-38 as quickly as he could and instead went for the P-51 and P-47, sending his P-38s to a grateful General George C. Kenney over in the Pacific. It seemed that Kelly Johnson had built the perfect airplane for the war in the Pacific. Single-engine fighters, in a world where most of it is covered by water, if you lost an engine, for whatever reason, your fate was pretty much sealed. Come the P-38 with two engines—if one was lost, you still had another to get you home. And here, in a warmer climate, the airplane excelled, achieving more victories than any other Air Corps fighter aircraft operating in the Pacific—P-39, P-40, P-47 and P-51. Our highest scoring ace with forty victories, Richard Bong, flew the P-38.

Pilot judgment regarding the P-38 is all over the place, from "The worst airplane I ever flew, a real killer," to "The best there was." It all depended on where and when you got to fly the Lightning. The compressibility problem with the P-38 was never satisfactorily re-solved, according to Robin Olds. Late in 1943 modified dive flaps were installed in P-38Js to address the issue, but with limited success. Robin Olds survived what was called a Mach Tuck situation in a high speed dive from which he barely recovered once he managed to slow the aircraft and got into denser air. Too close for comfort.

As a result of various engine and compressibility-related issues the P-38 was an ever-evolving aircraft, from the P-38E, the first combat-certified model, first flown in the Aleutians, to the P-38L which sported new engines and rocket pylons. A total of 9,535 aircraft of all models were built; a modest number when compared to the 15,579 P-47s and 14,490 P-51s that were cranked out by multiple factories.

While Lockheed and Kelly Johnson were struggling to deal with the compressibility issue, the solution was being worked out, of all places, in Germany. Back in the '30s, when Lieutenant Colonel "Tooey" Spaatz commanded a B-17 bomber group at Langley Field, Virginia, one of his young pilots was named Harold "Hal" Watson. Spaatz took great interest in getting to know the young men who flew his aircraft, and since the Army Air Corps at this time was indeed a very small organization, he took an interest in their assignments as he rose in seniority. In 1939 Watson was assigned to the Power Plant Laboratory at Wright Field. Here at the laboratory Watson would meet up with people he would be closely working with in future years— Second Lieutenant Bernard "Bernie" Schriever, a German immigrant, future four-star general, and father of the American ICBM program; and Captain Donald L. Putt, another future general who with Watson would be involved in the exploitation of foreign technology in the war that was looming on the horizon. Both of them, Watson and Putt, would rise to general officer ranks. It was a small officer corps indeed where everyone knew each other. Said Colonel Ken Chilstrom, the former chief of Fighter Test at Wright Field: "These people all grew up together. As time went by and the Air Corps grew they all got promoted, and they promoted the people they grew up with."

Watson's speciality in pilot training had been bombardment, the reason for his assignment to Langley Field in 1937. So Hal was surprised in September 1940 when he was selected to go to the University of Michigan to obtain a master's degree in aeronautical engineering—same place, same degree as Kelly Johnson's. His master's thesis? Why man would never be able to fly faster than the speed of sound. Ruth Watson, Hal's wife, recalled for me that in later years her husband had a good time telling this story at social events. Aircraft production ramped up steeply in 1941 and engines were a critical choke point. So Watson, after graduation from the University of Michigan, ended up at the Wright-Aero Factory in Cincinnati, Ohio, assuring the uninterrupted flow of aircraft engines. What bothered Watson most was that his pilot training classmates, like Hub Zemke and Phil Cochran, were gaining rapid promotion to Colonel and earning medals galore while he was laboring as a mere major with little recognition in an aircraft engine factory. Watson was a competitive guy and wanted to be an active part of the war, not shepherding aero engines in a factory.

Watson's onetime commander at Langley Field, then a mere lieutenant colonel, was running the air war in Europe as a lieutenant general. There had to be a way for him to get an assignment to Europe. Still at the Wright-Aero factory in September 1944, Watson learned that he had been selected to full colonel—and unbelievably, here came a telegram assigning him to Headquarters, United States Strategic Air Forces [Rear] in London, England. How did that happen? Well, General Spaatz had an excellent memory and he needed a guy like Watson. After all, he was the one who sent Watson to Ann Arbor, and that's why Watson ended up at the Wright-Aero factory in Cincinnati. After Watson got his feet on the ground in London, he was transferred to Paris where General Spaatz had his headquarters adjacent to his boss's headquarters, General Eisenhower. Several days after Watson got there he was invited for lunch with General Spaatz. Also present was Brigadier General George C. McDonald, the USSTAF director of intelligence, as well as Spaatz's two deputies, Major General Knerr, administration, and Major General Anderson, operations. "Over lunch General Spaatz stressed his keen interest in German V-weapons, the Me 262, the Arado 234, the Me 163 and other unusual aircraft," Watson later wrote. He clearly understood that the general wanted a number of those aircraft in flying condition sent back to Wright Field for evaluation at the earliest opportunity.

After a short stint as maintenance officer for the 1st Tactical Air Force (Provisional), in early 1945 Watson was assigned to the Exploitation Division at Headquarters USSTAF in Paris. His job was to find the aircraft Spaatz had mentioned to him during their luncheon in 1944. The task had been given the code name Operation Lusty, and Watson had all the necessary passes to allow him to go wherever he wanted to go to get the job done.

Watson collected a slew of the German advanced aircraft General Spaatz had tasked him to collect. Before sending them home on a British aircraft carrier, Watson had his pilots fly them into Melun airport near Paris, and he did a flyby of Me 262s for his general. The hardware was indeed important; however, even more important was a find by one of his fellow colonels assigned to the Exploitation Division—Colonel Donald Putt.

Eisenhower and 6th Army Group passes issued to Colonel Watson. Passes were in English, French, and German and granted him and his team access wherever he chose to go. (Ruth Watson)

Donald Putt was a Wright Field product like Watson and nearly had lost his life on Halloween day in 1935 testing the earliest model of the B-17 bomber—the X-299. In those days it was the practice to insert V-shaped wooden blocks in an aircraft's control surfaces to keep them from being blown around by the wind when parked outside of a hangar. For the X-299 Boeing had come up with internal locks. All the copilot or flight engineer had to do is step on a floor lever to engage or disengage the locks.

This was before checklists, which in my air force career were mandatory procedures to be followed verbatim on takeoff, landing, and so on. As their airplane, on this fateful day for Putt, picked up speed the nose kept coming up. Pete Hill, the test pilot in the left seat, pushed forward on the control column. Nothing happened. The airplane kept climbing until it was vertical at midfield, then did

A YB-17 bomber at Wright Field on June 4, 1937, very similar to the X-299 Putt was a copilot on, which crashed in late October 1935. (Author)

a wing-over and crashed with full fuel tanks. Pete Hill was killed in the crash. The accompanying Boeing test pilot, Les Tower, died nine days later from severe burns. Putt miraculously survived. No one had unlocked the external controls before take-off. That event lead to the implementation of checklists. Putt, like Watson, got an aeronautical engineering degree, but at Cal Tech, and before joining Spaatz's staff he was involved in a jet bomber design and selection project at Wright Field for the B-45, B-46, B-47, and B-48. Only a limited number of straight-wing B-45 bombers would be built—but over 2,000 B-47 bombers were built, forming the backbone of LeMay's Strategic Air Command, SAC.

On April 13, 1945, the Luftfahrtforschungsanstalt (LFA) Hermann Goering, was captured by Patton's troops. Colonel Putt, heading an Air Intelligence Technical team, arrived at Voelkenrode within a day of its capture. The research center was just outside the city of Braunschweig, and expertly camouflaged. No one knew of the existence of this place. The LFA consisted of six independent institutes, equipped with the finest instruments and test equipment imaginable. Even the names of the institutes relayed the importance of what they were doing: Aerodynamics Institute; Gas Dynamics Institute (Supersonic); Statics Institute; Engines Institute; Special Engine Institute; and Weapons Institute. Putt rounded up the German scientists who had scattered and gone into hiding, and marveled at the sophistication of their laboratory equipment. It was obvious to Putt that Voelkenrode was unique. It was home to seven wind tunnels of varying sizes and speeds, allowing the study of the effects of swept-back wings on aircraft.

Professor Dr. Busemann of the LFA had already devised successful wind tunnel techniques allowing him to study the behavior of swept-wing aircraft models in the critical transitional region between Mach .8 and Mach 1.2. As an aeronautical engineer, Putt immediately recognized that these findings were explosive stuff, probably the very thing needed for the jet bomber design evaluation he had been involved in before coming to Europe. Dr. Theodor W. Zobel, Putt learned, had worked out a means of making airflow visible by the way of interferometry, using mirrors and optics. Putt immediately had that equipment packed up and sent to Wright Field on a B-24 and B-17 bomber converted into transports. Braunschweig was in the future British Zone of Occupation, and Putt made sure the test equipment was flown to the United States before the Brits took possession. Colonel Donald Putt decided that Dr. Theodore von Karman, General Arnold's scientific advisor, had to see this place before the British took over.

Putt first met Dr. von Karman in 1938 when he was studying for his master's degree at Cal Tech. They maintained a personal and professional relationship over the years until von Karman's death in 1963. Von Karman was all too glad to come out and visit the LFA. He was Hungarian, but had spent a number of years at the University of Aachen, and as a result had lots of German friends in the scientific community. He had known Busemann before the war. Putt arranged a meeting between Busemann and von Karman. Also present at the meeting was the chief design engineer of the Boeing Company, George Schairer. During the meeting von Karman asked Busemann, "Why the swept back wings?" Busemann explained in simple layman's terms that "by sweeping back the wings you fooled the air into thinking that it was not going as fast as it really was, or not so fast as the airplane itself was moving through the atmosphere, and therefore you delayed the onset of compressibility drag. When you get close to the speed of sound, drag just takes off and goes up like that, moving his hand up vertically, but by sweeping the wing back and fooling the molecules of air, they don't think they are going as fast, and you delay the great rise in the drag curve."

Busemann and von Karman continued to talk. George Schairer sat quietly, listening. Immediately after the meeting Schairer wired his team at Boeing to stop all work on the design that was to become the B-47 until he got home. As a result of the Busemann–von Karman meeting, the secret of how to overcome compressibility was solved and the B-47 had swept-back wings, among many other innovative features. The B-47 bomber took the US Air Force into the jet age, and became the design baseline for the KC-135 aerial refueling tanker, which led to the 707 airliner and subsequent Boeing Company commercial aircraft designs. The B-47 put Boeing on the road to become one of the world's premier military and commercial aircraft companies. The only person missing at that key meeting in April 1945, in my opinion, was Kelly Johnson; however, he soon learned of the revelations of that meeting. North American's F-86 underwent the same conversion the B-47 did at Boeing, from straight wing fighter to swept-back wings. Thirty-five degree wing sweep became the standard. Busemann of course came to the United States as part of Project Paperclip and went to work at NACA's Langley Research Center. Nearly ten years later, Richard T. Whitcomb, a coworker of Dr. Busemann's at the Langley Research Center, developed the Area Rule, which minimized transonic drag. Dr. Busemann also held a professorship at the University of Colorado in Boulder (my alma mater) from 1963 onward. I graduated from Boulder in 1960, but I remember our Air Force ROTC lounge often being used by air force pilots prepping to become future astronauts. It was Busemann who developed the concept of using ceramic tiles as thermal protection on the space shuttle.

An interesting episode occurred at Voelkenrode which was to put General Arnold into a slight bind with his British colleagues. Colonel Putt, once he had a chance to acquaint himself with Voelkenrode and its scientists, immediately realized that he had discovered a

Dr. Adolf Busemann, whose wind tunnel tests proved the validity of the swept wing to pass through the sound barrier, holding a model of the F-86 and pointing to the 35 degree wing sweep of the aircraft. The North American F-86 Sabre Jet never broke through the sound barrier in level flight. Jackie Cochran, flying an F-86, did however break the sound barrier in the aircraft, but in a downward trajectory. The follow-on aircraft to the F-86, the F-100 Super Sabre, with a 45 degree wing sweep, was capable of supersonic speed in level flight. (Author)

scientific gold mine. The problem was that the gold mine was in the British Zone of Occupation, who were getting ready to exercise their rights. Putt decided to do some "midnight requisition" and move as much of the prized scientific equipment and documentation out of this place before the Brits arrived. In an interview he stated, "I had a little airline of my own, one B-24 and one B-17. As soon as everyone had gone to bed and the lights were out, we'd spring into action. There was an airfield just across town, and with trucks we hauled this stuff over there, and quickly loaded it on my B-17 and B-24. By the time people woke up the next morning, they were at Lakenheath or in Ireland refueling to get to Wright Field. So I had these two airplanes shuttling back and forth. This went on for some time until the British caught on. At the Potsdam Conference, July 17 to August 2, 1945, the British threw this up to General Arnold. Of course, I'm sure he must have pleaded ignorance."

This is not the end of the story. That October, Colonel Putt was visiting the Northrop Company. "I arrived in the morning, and Jack Northrop said to me, 'Gee, General Arnold is coming in this morning also.' I said, 'Well, that will be interesting.' I didn't know about the Potsdam incident at the time. We were already out on the factory floor looking at something, when General Arnold arrived. Jack Northrop introduced me and said, 'You know Colonel Putt?' General Arnold replied, 'Oh, yes, I know him alright,' and then he told them about Potsdam. The British had complained bitterly to him about Colonel Donald Putt appropriating all 'their stuff' and flying it out of Voelkenrode in the dark of night." Even in war one has to keep a sense of humor.

So ends the mystery of *Mach tuck* that had cost so many lives in the quest to break through the sound barrier, once considered unbreakable by many, including Hal Watson. Colonel Donald Putt retired with the rank of lieutenant general; Colonel Watson, who brought back the German jets, retired in the rank of major general after establishing the Air Technical Intelligence Center at Wright Patterson Air Force Base to assure that the United States would never fall behind technologically as we did prior to World War II. When I served at the center it was known as the Foreign Technology Division; its current name is the National Air and Space Intelligence Center (NASIC), and keeping with tradition, bound to change its name soon again.

ODDS AND ENDS

You know there is a saying that sunshine follows rain,
And sure enough you'll realize that joy will follow pain.
Let courage be your password, make fortitude your guide;
And then instead of grousing, just remember those who died.
—AUTHOR UNKNOWN

There are aspects in the Lightning's life-cycle that I did not include in earlier chapters but which I think should be mentioned. So I call this last chapter "Odds and Ends," a collection of well-known and not-so-well-known facts about the remarkable P-38 Lightning.

THE GERMAN P-38

Plenty of P-38s were lost over Europe and North Africa, and at times the aircraft, left on its own once the pilot bailed out, didn't always self-destruct, but made a reasonable belly landing without suffering much damage—just like the B-26 that Barney Dobbs bailed out of during the Korean war, which landed nearly undamaged, confusing his Russian interrogator who wondered what kind of a trick the Americans had up their sleeve to be able to land an aircraft undamaged once the crew bailed out. However, the Germans got ahold of several P-38s; it allowed them to test the aircraft, and one P-38 apparently was flown operationally by the Italians. The Luftwaffe actually had a wing, Kampfgeschwader 200, one of its squadrons exclusively flew captured Allied aircraft. The wing was commanded by the famed German Ju 88 pilot Oberst Werner Baumbach. Baumbach was best known for his daring and successful attacks on shipping on the Murmansk run. He commanded the Geschwader from October 1944 until the end of hostilities. KG 200 flew captured B-17and B-24

An American P-38 with German markings, most likely at Rechlin or Marienfelde, the German flight test centers.

bombers and an assortment of Allied fighters and transports. It flew special operations missions and tested modified aircraft to execute those missions. The Junkers 290 transport Colonel Watson flew back to the United States was a KG 200 aircraft, and Hauptman/ Captain Heinz Braun, its German pilot, greatly assisted Watson in the acquisition of German aircraft. The problem with many of the captured aircraft for KG 200 was that they were of American or British origin, and German anti-aircraft crews didn't take the time to look what was painted on their wings or fuselage—and fired first at the well-known shapes of American and British bombers, transports, and fighters—asking questions later.

THE MAID OF HARLECH

This is the story of an American fighter plane, a P-38F, the earliest version of the P-38 deployed to the United Kingdom and subsequently flown in North Africa. There are several renditions of this story on the internet and I recount here from the most detailed version. "On July 31, 2007, a resident of the county of Gwynedd, Wales, found a curious object on the beach of Harlech. What looked like the wing of an old plane protruded from the sand. He photographed his find and reported it to the British Ministry of Defense. Dissatisfied

A depiction of the Fork-Tailed Devil—*Gabelschwanz Teufel*—on the nose of a P-38 at Oshkosh in 2016. (A. Kambic)

with the ministry's response, the villager sent the information to a local newspaper which published the photo of the wing sticking out of the sand. A local historian, Matt Rimmer, instantly recognized it as the wing belonging to a Lockheed P-38F Lightning. How did that plane get there?" Mr. Rimmer researched the matter and found that on September 27, 1942, Second Lieutenant Robert F. Elliott of the 14th Fighter Group, took off on a tow-target mission. The switchology in this version of the P-38 was complex and Elliott apparently forgot to manually switch from one set of fuel tanks to another. His engines quit because of fuel starvation. Heading back to his base he looked for a possible landing site when he saw Harlech Beach, and managed to put down his aircraft just short of the beach—in the water. Elliot survived the landing.

The 14th Fighter Group, along with the 1st Fighter Group, were the first P-38 units to arrive in England. They had made the first Atlantic crossing on a ferry route laid out by Colonel Elliott Roosevelt, the President's son, who commanded a photo reconnaissance group of F-4 (P-38E photo version) and de Havilland F-8 Mosquitos. The development of drop tanks for the P-38F gave the aircraft a ferry range of over 2,000 miles. This made it possible for the Lightnings to fly from Bradley Field, Connecticut, to Goose Bay, Labrador, to Blui West One in Greenland, then on to Reykjavik, Iceland, and finally to Prestwick, Scotland. This was the same route taken by Jim Setchell in

The Maid of Harlech. A reminder of and testimonial of America's commitment to freedom.

1943 to fly his Mosquito to Prestwick and then on to North Africa. By August of 1942 four squadrons of the 1st and 14th Groups had made it to the UK and were assigned to the 8th AF Fighter Command. The remaining two squadrons, the 27th of the 1st FG and the 50th of the 14th FG, remained temporarily behind in Iceland to fly defensive patrols along with P-40s. It was on August 14, 1942, that a P-38F flown by 2nd Lieutenant Elza Shahan of the 27th Fighter Squadron, 14th FG, downed a German FW 200 Condor, designed by the famed German aircraft designer Kurt Tank. The Condor, a four-engine aircraft, flew high-altitude weather reconnaissance missions up near Iceland and it just picked a bad time to be in the area. This was the first kill for a P-38 in Europe in World War II, and it was the first kill in the ETO for the Army Air Forces.

Both the 14th and 1st Fighter Groups transferred to the 12th Air Force to support operations in North Africa. In the air battles over North Africa, the Mediterranean, and Italy the Lightnings had mixed success. According to the 14th Group history they were "forced to fight at lower altitudes of 15,000 feet. The twin-engines restricted maneuverability to some extent and the Lightning had a wheel control instead of the conventional stick, which may also have restricted maneuverability. Nevertheless, the Lightning had a sensational zoom climb and could rarely be matched. It wreaked great havoc among Rommel's air transport, earning for itself the German nickname—*Gabelschwanz Teufel*—"Fork-Tailed Devil."

Lieutenant Elliot was one of the early arrivals at RAF Atcham in Wales. He transferred with the 14th FG to North Africa, where he died in combat. His P-38F is still visible at Harlech Beach at low tide.

GLACIER GIRL

Glacier Girl was a P-38F assigned to the 94th Fighter Squadron of the 1st FG which, along with the three squadrons of the 1st and the three squadrons of the 14th FG, transferred early in 1942 to England. *Glacier Girl's* route was the same as that described for *The Maid of Harlech*. The fighter squadrons usually had B-17 or B-24 bombers leading the way because of the bomber's better navigation equipment. After taking off from Blui West in Greenland heading for Reykjavik, Iceland, they ran into terrible weather conditions forcing them to turn around and try to make it back to their takeoff base. That didn't happen for all of them, and six of the P-38s and their two B-17 lead ships were forced to seek safety on the Greenland ice sheet. The air crews were all rescued, but their ships stayed behind.

Glacier Girl after landing on the ice in Greenland. In 1992 the aircraft was dug out of the ice, 200 feet thick. The aircraft was restored to flying condition in Middlesboro, Kentucky, and ten years after its resurrection flew its first flight in October 2002. The pictures show *Glacier Girl* after it was dug out of the ice and on its first flight. (Al Stettner)

P-38 AS A MEDICAL EVACUATION AIRCRAFT

The Droop Snoot, a P-38 modified to carry a navigator/bombardier in the nose section forward of and below the pilot was used to identify targets and lead strikes into the target area. General Eisenhower accepted a brief ride in one of these modified P-38s. Robin Olds's experience with the Droop Snoot didn't work out so well. But fertile minds came up with other uses for the P-38, other than shooting down Japanese aircraft. Medical evacuation pods were hung where the external fuel tanks usually were carried, and a wounded passenger could be accommodated in a pod and rushed to a hospital equipped to handle serious injuries. It had to be a challenging ride for whoever rode in the pod—wounded or for other reasons. Three pictures shown here illustrate the concept.

Medical evacuation pods mounted on a P-38 fighter at Lingayen airfield in the Philippines and another showing the F-5, the reconnaissance version of the P-38, with pods attached. (US Air Force)

Patient being loaded into a P-38 medical evacuation pod, 7th Air Force, Caroline Islands, Pacific, September 1945. (US Air Force)

P-38 AIRCRAFT MODELS

The XP-38 was the first aircraft built, crashing on a cross-country flight when coming in for a landing at Mitchell Field, Long Island, when its carburetors iced up. The aircraft was piloted by Lockheed test pilot Benjamin S. Kelsey, who was also heavily involved in the design and development of both the P-38 and the P-39. The XP model was a proof-of-concept model followed by 13 YP-38 evaluation/test aircraft. The XP model was the only aircraft with a pressurized cockpit; if included in the production versions of the aircraft this would have made the Lightning a much more accommodable aircraft for its pilots. Modifications continued to be made to the P-38, adding self-sealing fuel tanks, P-38D; leading to the P-38E model of which 210 were produced, and which was the airframe used for the F-4 reconnaissance version of the P-38. Inboard underwing racks were added to carry drop tanks or 2,000 pounds of bombs becoming the P-38F—the first combat-certified version of the aircraft.

Over 500 F-models were built, equipping the first three fighter groups deploying to Europe and later to North Africa, the 1st, 14th, and 82nd. Its ability to carry drop tanks significantly increased the

A P-38F Lightning being rearmed for a combat mission. (Author)

range of the aircraft. The aircraft continued to suffer significant issues, however, while employed as a bomber escort with the 8th Air Force. The F-model also was configured as a reconnaissance version, F-5, the most widely used of all reconnaissance aircraft in Europe and very successful at that. Improvements continued to be made on an ever evolving P-38, leading to varying cockpit configurations, making it a challenging aircraft to fly for young pilots with limited training. The final model, the P-38L, sporting new and improved Allison engines and other modifications, was the most prolific model, with a production run of nearly 4,000 aircraft, including 113 aircraft built by the Vultee Corporation. All other P-38s were built by Lockheed in their plant at Burbank, California. The L-model also was around 3,500 pounds heavier than its predecessors. The total number of P-38s built, of all versions, was 9,535.

A total of seventy-five P-38Ls—with a 1,600 horse power engine versus 1,425 in earlier models—were configured as night fighters, carrying a radar pod beneath the pilot station and an operator in a slightly elevated position behind the pilot. The night fighter version of course was painted black, not easily discernable if picked up by search lights, and used only in the Pacific. A friend of mine, Dr. Joseph Gutierrez, lived as a youngster in the Philippines and personally was forced to witness some of the cruelty the Japanese occupiers used to discipline unruly, in their eyes, children, including beheadings. Recalls Dr. Gutierrez, "Toward the end of World War II, as General MacArthur was taking back the Philippines, I was a young boy living on the outskirts of Manila. I just loved to watch those P-38 planes as they engaged Japanese planes. There was a Japanese air base close to where I lived. At night a black night fighter version of the P-38 would fly over to raid the airfield. It was exciting to get up on the roof and watch some of the action. I recall one night when a dogfight occurred so close to our roof that shell casings, and clips that held the machine gun rounds together, fell on our roof while I was watching the dogfight. Wow!" The P-38 was the principal Air Corps aircraft used in the liberation of the Philippines. The fields used by the P-38s were of such a primitive nature that the P-51 Mustang was unable to use them.

INTERVIEWS

Oh, I wanted wings till I got those goddamn things.
And now I don't want 'em anymore.
Oh, they taught me how to fly and they sent me here to die.
I've had a belly full of war.
You can save those Zeros for your goddamn heroes.
Distinguished Flying Crosses do not compensate for losses.
Oh, I wanted wings till I got those goddamn things.
And now I don't want 'em anymore.

—SQUADRON SONG, 9TH FIGHTER SQUADRON, 49TH

FIGHTER GROUP

Anspach, Robert. Personal background including WWII flying the P-47 and participation in Operation Lusty. Orlando, Florida, October 2001.

Ashton, Pete. Background on his father Jim and his participation in development of the P-38. Mail/email July/August 2023.

Chilstrom, Kenneth O. Personal background including WWII flying the A-36 Apache and service in Fighter Test at Wright Field. Fairfax, Virginia, multiple occasions up to December 2022.

Dobbs, Byron A. Personal background including participation in WWII/Korea flying the P-38/F-5 and B-26. Riverside, California, January 1999.

Gutierrez, Joseph. Personal background as a child in Japanese occupied Manila. Washington, DC, multiple times 2000 to 2023.

Herzmann, Hans. World War II experience. Remagen, Germany. 2001.

Hoover, Robert A. Personal background including participation in WWII and test flying at Wright Field. Fairfax Station, Virginia (by phone/email), July 2013.

McIntosh, Frederick. Personal background and participation in WWII flying the P-38 and P-47 and participation in Operation Lusty. Leesburg, Virginia, January 2003.

Putt, Donald L. Interview of Lieutenant General Donald L. Putt by Dr. James C. Hasdorf. Atherton, California, 1–3 April 1974 (Source: AFHSO)

Setchell, James E. Interview conducted with his son about his father's service in WWII flying the Mosquito/P-38/F-4/5. Dayton, Ohio, August 2014.

Slane, Robert M. Interview on his experience as an 8th Air Force B-17 pilot. 2009.

Tucker, Albert S. Jr. Personal background and participation in WWII flying the P-38 and postwar service. Warrenton, Virginia, March 2013.

Watson, Ruth. Background on Harold E. Watson, Palm Beach Gardens, Florida, November 2001.

Wenzel, Lloyd. Personal background and participation in WWII flying P-38 and participation in Projects Overcast and Paperclip. Tequesta, Florida, November 2001.

BIBLIOGRAPHY

I FLEW

When the last checklist is run and the bag drag is over
I will reminisce of the days I once knew,
I will not remember the 3 AM alerts
But only that I flew!
I will remember the sights my mortal eyes have seen
Colored by multitudes of hues,
Those beautiful lights on cold winter nights
Seen only by those who flew.
God was extremely good to me,
And let me touch his face,
He saw my crew threw war and peace
And blessed us with his grace.
So when I stand at Saint Peter's Gate
And tell him that I am new
I know he'll smile and welcome me,
Because he knew
I FLEW

—BRAD BAKER

Ambrose, Stephen E. *The Wild Blue: The Men and Boys Who Flew the B-24s over Germany*. New York: Simon & Schuster, 2001.

Army Air Forces Statistical Digest, World War II, Tables 35, 159–60. HQ Army Air Forces, Washington, DC, 1945, maxwell.af.mil

Baxter, James P. *Scientists Against Time*. Cambridge, MA: MIT Press, 1946.

Berg, A. Scott. *Lindbergh*, New York: G. P. Putnam's Sons, 1998.

Blum, Allen H. *War Diary of a Lieutenant Colonel, 1943–1944*. Unpublished manuscript in possession of the author.

Bodie, Warren M. *The Lockheed P-38 Lightning: "It Goes like Hell."* Hiawassee, GA: Widewing Publications, 1991.

Brown, Eric "Winkle." *Wings on My Sleeve*. London: Orion Publishing Group, 2006.

Bruning, John R. "A Dare Turned Deadly." *Smithsonian Air & Space Magazine*, July 2020.

Bruning, John R. *Race of Aces: WWII's Elite Airmen and the Epic Battle to Become the Masters of the Sky*. New York: Hachette Books, 2021.

Butcher, Harry C. *My Three Years with Eisenhower*. New York: Simon and Schuster, 1946.

Chilstrom, Kenneth O. *Test Flying at Old Wright Field*. Omaha, NE: Westchester House, 1993.

Crossfield, A. Scott, with Clay Blair Jr. *Always Another Dawn*. North Stratford, NH: Ayer Company, 1999.

Crouch, Tom D. *Wings: A History of Aviation from Kites to the Space Age*. Washington, DC: Smithsonian National Air and Space Museum, 2003.

Davis, Albert H., Russell J. Coffin, and Robert B. Woodward. *The 56th Fighter Group in World War II*. Washington, DC: Infantry Journal Press, 1948.

Doolittle, James H., and Caroll V. Glines. *I Could Never Be So Lucky Again: An Autobiography by General James H. "Jimmy" Doolittle*. New York: Bantam Books, 1991.

Dugan, James, and Carroll Stewart. *Ploesti: The Great Ground-Air Battle of 1 August 1943*. New York: Random House, 1998.

Ethel, Jeffrey L., and Rikyu Watanabe. *P-38 Lightning*. New York: Crown, 1983.

Ferrell, Robert H., ed. *The Twentieth Century: An Almanac*. New York: World Almanac Publications, 1985.

Freeman, Roger A. *Mighty 8th War Diary*. London: Jane's, 1981.

Hall, R. Cargill. *Lightning Over Bougainville*. Washington, DC: Smithsonian Institution Press, 1991.

Haulman, Daniel L. *One Hundred Years of Flight: USAF Chronology of Significant Air and Space Events 1903–2002*. Maxwell AFB, AL: Air University Press, 2003.

Hansell, Haywood S. *The Air Plan That Defeated Hitler*. Maxwell AFB, AL: Air University Press, 1973.

Hoover, Robert A. *Forever Flying*. New York: Pocket Books, 1996.

Infield, Glenn B. *Disaster at Bari*. New York: Macmillan, 1971.

Kempel, Robert W. *The Race for Mach One—Who Was the Winner?* Beirut, Lebanon: HPM Publications, 2010.

Kirkland, Richard C. *Tales of a War Pilot*. Washington: Smithsonian Institution Press, 1999.

Lopez, Donald S. *Fighter Pilot's Heaven: Flight Testing the Early Jets*. Washington, DC: Smithsonian Books, 1995.

Makos, Adam. *A Higher Call*. New York: Penguin Group, 2012.

Neilands, Robin. *The Bomber War: The Allied Air Offensive Against Nazi Germany*. New York: Barnes & Noble, 2001.

Olds, Robin. *Fighter Pilot: The Memoirs of Legendary Ace Robin Olds*. New York: St. Martin's Press, 2010.

Reporting World War II, Part One/Part Two American Journalism 1938–1944/1944–1946. New York: Library of America, 1995.

Rich, Ben R., and Leo Janos. *Skunk Works*, Boston: Little, Brown, 1994.

Samuel, Wolfgang W. E. *I Always Wanted to Fly—America's Cold War Airmen*. Jackson: University Press of Mississippi, 2001.

Samuel, Wolfgang W. E. *American Raiders: The Race to Capture the Luftwaffe's Secrets.* Jackson: University Press of Mississippi, 2004.

Samuel, Wolfgang W. E. *In Defense of Freedom: Stories of Courage and Sacrifice of World War II Army Air Forces Flyers.* Jackson: University Press of Mississippi, 2015.

Setchell, James F. *Diary of WWII Operations in ETO—1943–1944;* letters and notes.

Smith, Richard J., and Eddie J. Creek. *Arado 234 Blitz.* Sturbridge, MA: Monogram Aviation Publications, 1992.

Stahl, Peter W. *KG 200: The True Story.* London: Jane's, 1981.

Stanaway, John, and Bob Rocker. *The Eight Ballers: Eyes of the Fifth Air Force.* Atglen, PA: Schiffer Military History, 1999.

Splendid Vision, Unswerving Purpose: Developing Air Power for the United States Air Force during the First Century of Powered Flight. History Office, Air Force Materiel Command, US Air Force, Wright-Patterson AFB, Ohio, 2002.

Toliver, Raymond F. *Fighter General: The Life of Adolf Galland.* Zephyr Cove, NV: AmPress, 1990.

Thompson, Rachel Yarnel. *Marshall: A Statesman Shaped in the Crucible of War.* Leesburg, VA: George C. Marshall International Center.

United States Air Force Combat Victory Credits. Washington, DC: Office of Air Force History, US Air Force, 1974.

The United States Army Air Forces in World War II. Washington, DC: AAF, War Department, 1945.

The United States Strategic Bombing Survey, Air Campaigns of the Pacific War, Washington, DC: Military Analysis Division, July 1947.

The United States Strategic Bombing Survey, Statistical Appendix to Over-All Report (European War). Washington, DC: Department of War, February 1947.

The United States Strategic Bombing Survey, The Fifth Air Force in the War Against Japan. Washington, DC: Military Analysis Division, June 1947.

Yeager, Chuck, and Leo Janos. *Yeager: An Autobiography.* New York: Bantam Books, 1985.

Zemke, Hubert. *Zemke's Stalag.* Washington, DC: Smithsonian Institution, 1991.

Zemke, Hubert. *Zemke's Wolf Pack.* New York: Orion Books, 1988.

COMBAT UNITS AND AIRCRAFT INDEX

GENERAL INDEX

ABOUT THE AUTHOR

Courtesy Wolfgang W. E. Samuel

Wolfgang W. E. Samuel, Colonel, US Air Force (Ret.), was born in Germany in 1935 and immigrated to the United States in 1951 at age sixteen with an eighth-grade education and no English-language skills. Upon graduation from the University of Colorado, he was commissioned 2nd lieutenant in the US Air Force, then flew over one hundred strategic reconnaissance missions against the Soviet Union during the Cold War. His first book *German Boy: A Refugee's Story* garnered favorable reviews from the *New York Times* and numerous other outlets. He is author of eight books published by the University Press of Mississippi.